Leadership and Management in Integrated Services

Acknowledgements

We would like to thank our fellow authors for their thoughtful contributions to the book, together with all those colleagues and students who have helped to shape our views of leadership and management. On a more personal level we would also like to thank our respective husbands, Sam and Alan, for their constant love, support and encouragement.

Creating Integrated Services – titles in the series

Children as Victims	ISBN 978 1 84445 136 4
Effective Communication and Engagement with Children and Young People, their Families and Carers	ISBN 978 1 84445 265 1
Leadership and Management in Integrated Services	ISBN 978 1 84445 204 0

To order other titles from Learning Matters, please contact our distributors:
BEBC Distribution, Albion Close, Parkstone, Poole, BH12 3LL. Telephone: 0845 230 9000, email: learningmatters@bebc.co.uk

You can find more information on our titles and other learning resources at **www.learningmatters.co.uk**

Leadership and Management in Integrated Services

Edited by

JUDY MCKIMM

and

KAY PHILLIPS

Series Editors: Jonathan Parker and Greta Bradley

LearningMatters

First published in 2009 by Learning Matters Ltd

British Library Cataloguing in Publication Data
A CIP record for this book is available from the British Library

ISBN 978 1 84445 2 040

Cover design by Code 5 Design Associates Ltd
Text design by Code 5 Design Associates Ltd
Project Management by Swales & Willis Ltd, Exeter, Devon
Typeset by Swales & Willis Ltd, Exeter, Devon

Learning Matters Ltd
33 Southernhay East
Exeter EX1 1NX
Tel: 01392 215560
E-mail: info@learningmatters.co.uk
www.learningmatters.co.uk

Contents

About the authors

Paul Close is a senior lecturer in educational leadership at Sheffield Hallam University. He runs a postgraduate course on multi-agency team development as part of an MA in integrated working and has wide experience of facilitating learning sets for Health, Education, and Social Care professionals on integrated working issues; notably on the Valuing People Project and in children's services. He is also a former tutor for the National Professional Qualification for Integrated Centre Leadership (NPQICL) and current evaluator of the Multi-Agency Team Development programme for the National College of School Leadership. Paul holds Masters' degrees in both Educational Leadership and Organisation Development.

Trish Hafford-Letchfield is a senior lecturer at Middlesex University where she teaches on a number of pre and post-qualifying programmes in mental health and social work. Trish has extensive experience in managing adult social care services and is currently Chair of her local Age Concern. She has been involved in leadership and management development both in Higher Education and in the field and is particularly involved in widening participation in learning. Her current research interests lie in promoting the lifelong learning of older people using social care services. In her spare time, Trish is a keen amateur musician.

Sam Held is a Senior Lecturer at the University of Auckland and also works as an independent education and training consultant. Sam has a background in the public and voluntary sectors and is experienced in working both within and across health, social care and community development boundaries, developing partnerships and introducing complex systemic change. Posts included Patient Involvement Co-ordinator for the Scottish South-East Cancer Network and Implementation Manager (Supporting People), East Lothian Council. Sam has wide experience of teaching and training in Further and Adult Education settings as well as more recently in higher and health professionals' education. He has facilitated masters' level programmes, workshops and in-house training events for staff in social care, academics and health workers on various topics including: leadership development; change management; user involvement; commissioning; strategic planning; managing staff and volunteers and project implementation. He is a qualified counsellor, is in advanced training as a transactional analysis psychotherapist and is actively involved in the Anglican Church.

Judy McKimm currently works at the University of Auckland is Visiting Professor of Healthcare Education and Leadership at the University of Bedfordshire and Honorary Professor at Swansea University. She trained as an orthopaedic and general nurse, and has worked in further, adult, higher and medical education for over twenty years. Whilst at Imperial College School of Medicine, she co-ordinated the development and implementation of a new six-year MBBS/BSc programme. She has developed, implemented and evaluated a number of successful postgraduate faculty development programmes for medical and healthcare educators and advanced practitioners. Judy also worked for the Higher Education Academy, developing the new professional standards framework and reviewing the national accreditation scheme for teachers in higher education; she managed a national leadership development project for health and social work educators, funded by FTDL and in 2007, was network co-ordinator for a national interprofessional project (the ICS-HE project) which brought together stakeholders, academics and practitioners to share expertise and develop HE responses to the Integrated Children's Service agenda.

Judy regularly speaks at national and international conferences, researches and publishes on medical and healthcare education and leadership and is working on a large scale research project investigating into the effectiveness of teaching, learning and assessment of law in social work and medicine. Since 1987, she has worked on international health reform, capacity building, quality assurance, professional licensing and education/training projects in many transition and former Soviet Union countries and most recently in South Australia, New Zealand and Samoa.

Bernard Moss is Professor of Social Work Education and Spirituality and the Director of the Centre for Spirituality and Health at Staffordshire University. His teaching excellence was recognised by the Higher Education Academy in 2004 with the awarding of a National Teaching Fellowship, and also in 2008 when he was made a Senior Fellow of the Academy. Through his writing and his conference presentations he is keen to explore the secular as well as the religious aspects of contemporary spirituality to a wide range of people-work. www.bernardmoss.org.uk

Kay Phillips is Head of Continuing Professional Development in the Faculty of Health and Wellbeing at Sheffield Hallam University. She works with external provider organisations and commissioning partners to support organisational development and service improvement. Kay joined Sheffield Hallam University in 1998, having previously worked as a secondary school teacher, a further education lecturer and an NHS training and development adviser. Before taking on her current role she was responsible for managing the University's Centre for Professional and Organisation Development. Her academic interests centre on leadership and management development for those working in the health and social care sectors.

Kay is committed to interprofessional learning and has been responsible for developing a number of programmes that have brought together professionals from across the health and social care sectors. These include the interprofessional MSc in Health and Social Care Leadership and the MSc in Advanced Professional Development. She has been a Mentor on the NPQICL programme for children's centres leaders and recently worked with the British Association for Adoption and Fostering to develop a collaborative programme in Safeguarding and Caring for Children and Young People. In 2007 Kay was a member of the research team commissioned by the Children's Workforce Network to explore mobility within the children and young people's workforce.

Michael Preston-Shoot is Professor of Social Work and Dean of the Faculty of Health and Social Sciences at the University of Bedfordshire, England. He is Chair of the Joint University Council Social Work Education, which represents the perspectives of United Kingdom social work education in higher education institutions. He was Editor of Social Work Education: The International Journal between 1993 and 2006 and was Managing Editor of the European Journal of Social Work between 2003 and 2007. He is one of the Founding Editors of the journal Ethics and Social Welfare. He was awarded a National Teaching Fellowship by the Higher Education Academy in 2005. His research and writing has concentrated on the interface between law and social work practice, on which in 2005 he co-authored a systematic review on teaching, learning and assessment of law in social work education for the Social Care Institute for Excellence (SCIE). He has subsequently co-authored a resource guide and ten e-learning objects on the subject of law and social work, also published by SCIE. He has also undertaken research and published in the areas of social work education, group work, the involvement of service users in social work education and research, and on the needs and service outcomes for young people in public care and older people requiring care in the community.

Introduction

Judy McKimm and Kay Phillips

This book is primarily addressed to undergraduate and postgraduate students of social work, nursing and midwifery, allied health professions, medicine, dentistry and social administration/policy. It may also be relevant to trainee teachers and lecturers involved in teaching leadership and management to health and social care students. The book is designed to be most relevant to students in later stages of an undergraduate degree as well as to students studying at postgraduate levels and practitioners working in integrated care settings. The book aims to familiarise the reader with current models of leadership in the context of integrated practice. It challenges the notions that people are born (or promoted) to leadership, and supports skills acquisition through a range of case studies and activities designed to promote reflective practice and encourage practitioners to challenge orthodoxies.

Leadership and management in integrated service settings

Government drivers promote integrated health, social care and public services for children and adults, yet the field is immensely complex, with the involvement of multiple agencies, professionals and other stakeholders. The book aims to help students, new and experienced practitioners make sense of this rapidly changing scene. It provides an overview and introduction to core leadership and management principles, the key management structures and organisations that comprise integrated services and considers some of the differences and dilemmas arising from the range of professions and organisations involved in delivering integrated services.

The current government agenda for modernising and transforming personal, social and health services emphasises the need for integrated services, with alignment of previously siloed provision: siloed in terms of professions, of professional and non-professional education and training and in terms of provision by voluntary, independent, private and statutory organisations and agencies.

Current models of leadership and management focus on collaborative and partnership working, models that are philosophically aligned with the development and delivery of integrated services with the client/service user/patient at the heart of the provision. However, in practice, many factors interact to slow the pace of change and stifle the confident and competent leadership that is so vital if integrated practice is to become the norm rather than a 'gold standard' aspiration.

Contemporary leadership models reflect the emergence of the concept of leadership at all levels and the urgent need for collaborative leaders and managers, who are equipped to work across traditional boundaries, build new coalitions and challenge the causes of inertia. These 'new' leaders are typically emotionally intelligent, flexible, visionary and value-led, yet their traditional positional power in their organisation may well not reflect their positive impact on teams, colleagues and service delivery. This book provides an overview of contemporary leadership theory, set within the context of integrated services, collaborative practice and partnership working, identifying key challenges and some solutions for today's public sector practitioners.

Book structure

Chapter 1 The emergence of leadership theory: From the twentieth to the twenty-first century

The first chapter introduces some of the key ideas and thinkers who have been influential in leadership research and practice. It looks at leadership in its contemporary contexts, taking a chronological and historical perspective on leadership development: from trait theory through transformational leadership (currently popular in the National Health Service (NHS)), to servant leadership within public sector organisations, to the network forms of knowledge and collaborative leadership that are often associated with integrated service leadership. Leadership is considered in the light of organisational development as well as personal and professional qualities and skills. This chapter explores how contemporary leadership theory offers insight into managing and leading integrated services, focusing on situational leadership, collaborative and partnership working, leaders as 'connectors' and distributed leadership. The chapter also looks at the interplay between management and leadership and the concept of 'followership'.

Chapter 2 Repeating history? Observations on the development of law and policy for integrated practice

This chapter discusses the political context and emergence of integrated practice in UK public services, identifies how legal rules relating to policy drivers and government strategies have evolved. The chapter also considers the underlying rationale, key initiatives and the current and future challenges in providing integrated services. The chapter offers brief discussions of some of the core issues involved in partnership working, collaborative practice and multi-professional working, looking at examples from a range of sectors and pro-fessional perspectives.

Chapter 3 Management and leadership: From strategy to service delivery

In this chapter we introduce the concepts and theoretical frameworks around strategic management and leadership in the context of integrated services and practice and partner-ship working. The concept of leading strategically is essential in the context of integrated working to ensure management structures and processes are aligned.

The concept of translating and implementing strategy in terms of multiple stakeholder organisations is explored. The chapter also introduces some strategic management and planning tools and techniques, using illustrations from different sectors as examples, considering participation, commissioning, decision-making and the impact of policy initiatives on the power dynamics in organisations.

Chapter 4 Leading in complex environments

Contemporary public sector organisations are complex and often 'messy'. This chapter provides an introduction and theoretical underpinning to organisational theory and complexity theory, linking this to a discussion of the advantages and disadvantages of different management strategies and leadership skills and approaches. The theoretical principles of complex adaptive systems are explained in the context of organisational responses and management structures and systems. Change and complexity in the leadership environment create a demand for different leadership and management approaches; these are explored in the chapter.

Chapter 5 From transition to transformation: Leading the management of change

This chapter focuses on a key management and leadership skill: the need for leaders at all levels to be able to manage and cope with change. The role of the manager and leader in transforming organisations that can effectively embed change when 'change is the only constant' is central to the concept of integrated practice. Integrated services are constantly in a state of flux and this chapter introduces some core theories and concepts around managing and leading change, providing examples to illustrate key concepts, ideas and theories drawn from professional and service contexts. The chapter also considers issues of professional and organisational culture in integrated services.

Chapter 6 Ethics, vision and values: The challenge of spirituality

In this chapter you will explore theories and concepts that will help you to understand and contextualise the ethical and value base(s) that underpin integrated practice. Core ethical standpoints are discussed in the context of a range of service environments. The chapter discusses some of the tensions and dilemmas facing those involved in leading and delivering services, particularly services based on consumerism and a market economy. The chapter also suggests how an understanding of spirituality and Spiritual Intelligence (SQ) provides a framework and signposting for those working with people in integrated services.

Chapter 7 Emotional intelligence, emotion and collaborative leadership

This chapter takes one of the core concepts in current leadership and management approaches in the public sector: that of emotional intelligence (EI). The theory is described and explored with activities and examples provided at individual, team and organisational level of emotionally intelligent leadership. The chapter considers the relevance of emotion and EI in the workplace, specifically in integrated and collaborative working and explores the relationship between EI and emotion. The chapter also considers the way in which different professions have developed systems and structures to support the 'emotional labour' of practitioners.

Chapter 8 Professional roles and workforce development

In this chapter we consider issues concerned with defining, developing and maintaining an effective workforce for integrated services. You will explore how different professional groups and bodies interact and define themselves as they participate in the management and leadership of integrated services, considering further issues around vision, values, power and the potential impact that operating within different models of care might have on service delivery. We review opportunities and challenges for leadership and professional development for integrated services and consider theories of 'communities of practice' and 'activity theory' in the context of workforce interactions and professionalisation.

Chapter 9 Leadership in practice: Difficulties and dilemmas

In this chapter we pull together some of the key themes from the book to consider a range of difficulties and dilemmas relating to the development and delivery of integrated services. The chapter is organised around three different contexts, which relate to varying levels at which individuals operate: the policy context – considering the challenges associated with the implementation of complex change and how policies define and shape service agendas; the organisational context – reviewing the impact of systems and the importance of collaboration within and between organisations; and the personal context – focusing on some of the personal and interpersonal issues that people face when working in integrated services. The chapter also offers some strategies and solutions to address these difficulties drawn from the practical experience of practitioners in different service contexts.

Learning features

Each chapter follows a similar format with a chapter overview, then the core text followed by a summary and further reading. References are summarised at the end of the book. Each chapter also includes a number of activities and case studies to help you apply the learning in context. These range from applying a theory to a practice setting or scenario to carrying out an analysis of something in your own setting. Activities can be carried out by yourself or with others, these are designed to raise awareness, consolidate your understanding of theories and ideas and enable you to practice using the models and approaches.

Chapter 1

The emergence of leadership theory: From the twentieth to the twenty-first century

Judy McKimm and Sam Held

Introduction

Our most common image of leaders and leadership is that of the 'hero leader', who can overcome every crisis through extraordinary actions, awe inspiring charisma, excellent communications and a certainty of belief in what is right. This image is not sufficient for the everyday work of developing our public services into the seamless, multi-agency, citizen-centred processes which we are all striving for

(van Zwanenberg, 2003, p1)

An understanding of leadership theory and how it has evolved, particularly over the last twenty years, will help you to appreciate and analyse some of the leadership successes and failures of recent years. The concept of 'leadership' has been defined in many ways. Through a chronological consideration of how leaders and leadership came under scrutiny and what explanations were put forward to explain the success or failure of leaders, we can see how prevailing ideas and trends have influenced what we expect of leaders as well as how we can better prepare leaders of the future.

Current models of leadership and management focus on collaborative and partnership working, models that are philosophically aligned with the development and delivery of integrated services with the client/service user/patient at the heart of the provision.

Chapter overview

In this chapter some of the key ideas and thinkers who have been influential in leadership research and practice will be introduced. Leadership will be explored in its contemporary health and social care contexts, taking a chronological and historical perspective on leadership development: from trait theory through transformational leadership (currently popular in the NHS) to the network forms of knowledge and collaborative leadership that are often associated with integrated service leadership. Activities will help you to apply the theories and concepts to your own experience and professional development.

Models of leadership

Leadership models and theories draw from different subject disciplines, including management theory, psychology and sociology. Each of the models helps us to understand more about what leadership is, what leadership means to leaders themselves and to their 'followers' and the impact of what leaders do on organisations. It is important to remember that although throughout history, there have been many tales of individual leaders, the notion of 'leadership' is socially constructed. Therefore the prevailing theories and models of leadership tend to reflect events of the time, our expectations of leaders and public reactions and 'mood'.

In broad terms there has been a relatively recent shift from the way in which, prior to the 1980s, leadership was seen very much as a subset of management, often concerned with leading teams or groups, through the rise (and fall?) of the 'hero' or transformational leader, to current thinking which emphasises the 'thoughtful', 'value led' leader, highlighting the role of followers, the notion of 'leadership at all levels' and bringing to the fore ideas concerning 'collaborative leadership' and 'learning leadership'. As Bryman (1996, p277) notes: *each of these stages signals a change of emphasis rather than the demise of the previous approaches.* Contemporary leadership theory attempts to take into consideration how leadership operates within complex and changing situations, at organisational level as well as within teams and interpersonal relationships. Some theory also considers the intrapersonal aspects, drawing on psychology and psychotherapy to explain how leaders think, behave and feel.

In the following sections, we will explore some of the dominant theories of leadership

Leadership and management

Many writers have found it useful to distinguish between management and leadership. Although there is some overlap, particularly with strategic management and leadership, differentiating between the two helps to explain some of the assumptions made about and expectations of, people working in complex integrated care settings. However, like any model, the distinction can sometimes lead to erroneous assumptions and a partial picture.

ACTIVITY 1.1

Thinking about an organisation where you have worked or studied, can you list some of the key differences between leadership and management?

What do you think are the key tasks of a leader and of a manager?

Does it help you to think about sport? For example, what are the differences between a football manager and a team captain?

Bennis and Nanus note that *managers are people who do things right and leaders are people who do the right thing* (1985, p221). Managers are often seen as performing functions in organisations such as managing finance, estates or human resources. Their management function is usually linked to a formal title within a department established to carry out specific activities within a hierarchical structure. Management is concerned with planning, organising, co-ordinating, commanding or controlling the activities of staff (Fayol, 1949).

Leaders are often seen as different from managers in that they seek to guide and influence others into pursuing particular objectives or visions of the future and to motivate them into wanting to follow. Yukl (2002, p7) suggests that *leadership is the process of influencing others to understand and agree about what needs to be done and how it can be done effectively, and the process of facilitating individual and collective efforts to accomplish the shared objectives.* In this model, the link between management and leadership is through the articulation and implementation of shared organisational goals or objectives.

Northouse summarises the differences between leadership and management as follows:

Table 1.1 Management and Leadership

Management 'Produces order and consistency'	Leadership 'Produces change and movement'
Planning/Budgeting	*Establishing Direction*
• Establish agendas	• Create a vision
• Set timetables	• Clarify big picture
• Allocate resources	• Set strategies
Organizing/Staffing	*Aligning People*
• Provide structure	• Communicate goals
• Make job placements	• Seek commitment
• Establish rules and procedures	• Build teams and coalitions
Controlling/Problem Solving	*Motivating and Inspiring*
• Develop incentives	• Inspire and energize
• Generate creative solutions	• Empower subordinates
• Take corrective action	• Satisfy unmet needs

Source: Northouse, 2004, p9

Kotter's (2001) work aligns with this approach suggesting that leadership sets a direction, develops vision for the future and promotes change and direction, whereas management is more concerned with providing order and consistency in organisations through planning. Covey *et al.* put a slightly different slant on this suggesting that whereas management works within certain paradigms, leadership creates new ones. Leaders are seen as leading people and seizing opportunities, not managing resources and 'things' or focusing on problems (Covey, *et al.*, 1994). But does this mean that some people are 'natural' leaders or managers and that leadership and management cannot be learned?

The management literature typically used to see leadership as a subset of management, focusing on leading teams and managing organisations. Recent thinking suggests that effective leadership demonstrates understanding of management principles and practice, and vice versa.

Transactional leadership

Blagg and Young (2001) quote David Thomas of the Harvard Business School that *increasingly, the people who are the most effective are those who essentially are both managers and leaders.* Contemporary leadership theory would suggest that in practice it is often the same person who operates in both capacities and that people at all levels in the organisation have the potential to perform and display leadership. This can be further explained by looking at management as a form of leadership: transactional leadership, which Kotter contrasts with 'transformational leadership' as in Table 1.2.

Table 1.2 Transactional and transformational leadership

	Transactional leadership (management)	Transformational leadership
Creating the agenda	Planning and budgeting: Developing a detailed plan of how to get the results	Establishing direction: Developing a vision that describes a future state along with a strategy for getting there
Development of human resources	Organising and staffing: Which individual best fits each job and what part of the plan fits each individual	Aligning people: A major communication challenge, getting people to understand and believe the vision
Execution	Controlling and problem solving: Monitoring results, identifying deviations from the plan and solving the problems	Motivating and inspiring: Satisfying basic human needs for achievement, belonging, recognition, self-esteem and a sense of control
Outcomes	Produces a sense of predictability and order	Produces changes, often to a dramatic degree

Source: Kotter, 1990

The key message around management and leadership is that successful organisations and teams need both sets of skills and roles and one is not superior to the other. As Glatter points out: *methods are as important as knowledge, understanding and value orientation . . . Erecting this kind of dichotomy between something 'pure' called 'leadership' and something 'dirty' called 'management', or between values and purposes on the one hand and methods and skills on the other would be disastrous* (1997, p189). This is useful to bear in mind when conflicts arise around managing and leading change, particularly when services are being redesigned or reorganised which leads to movement of staff both within and between organisations. This can be felt particularly acutely when staff are working in newly integrated services which contain a legacy of different management systems, values and leadership styles coupled with potentially competing and conflicting professional roles and responsibilities. These issues are further explored in Chapters 5, 6 and 9.

The idea of transactional leadership is now seen as synonymous with 'management' or managerial leadership (Bush and Glover, 2002). This takes place within a hierarchical structure in which the leaders have positional power or authority over those beneath them but are usually accountable to internal and external bodies such as boards, committees or councils. The leader's relationships with others are primarily defined through the nature of the transactions occurring between different levels of the organisation. This model draws from sociological theory including Weber's concepts of bureaucracy, authority and control (Weber, 1947).

Leaders and followers

Before we go on to look at some of the theories that aim to explain different aspects of leadership, it is useful to consider one of the other underpinning assumptions around leadership: the notion of 'followership'. Grint (1999) argues that there would be no leaders without followers and that the relationship between leaders and followers requires a sense of community.

The traditional, earlier models of leadership (particularly the ideas around the 'hero' or 'charismatic' leader) emphasise the implicit understanding that where someone leads, then others follow.

ACTIVITY **1.2**

How does the notion of 'followership' fit with your experience and understanding of how integrated care teams work in practice?

List some of the issues around different professional groups being viewed as 'leaders' with an implicit assumption that other professional groups are then seen as 'followers'

This notion has been challenged by many writers. Alimo-Metcalfe (1998) suggests that the word 'followers' implies that people passively receive the process of leadership. This does not sit easily with the idea of professionals working together as equals, bringing different perspectives, knowledge and skills to the care pathway for patients or clients. The reality is often much more subtle and 'moment to moment' than on the one hand, some people always leading and others passively following, or a situation in which professionals and others negotiate tasks and roles within an equal power relationship. As Kouzes and Posner (2002) note, *leadership is a relationship between those who aspire to lead and those who choose to follow* (our emphasis). Possibly conceptualising 'followers' in this way enables us to take account of individual and group agency within complex and rapidly changing public services and therefore helps our understanding of how leadership roles and activities can shift in response to events and context.

The failure of the traditional concept of 'leaders and followers' to make sense, as applied to contemporary public sector services, has led to the development and predominance of the idea of transformational leadership. This model has been adapted to apply to the culture of British organisations such as the NHS by writers such as Alimo-Metcalfe and Alban-Metcalfe who describe the model as *not based on heroism but enabling others to lead themselves . . . not about being an extraordinary person but being an ordinary and humble one – or at least very open, accessible and transparent* (2005, p32). We will consider transformational leadership further in the sections below: for now, keep in mind that some of the problems and issues arising within interprofessional teams may relate to differing expectations and assumptions around leadership and followers.

Personality traits and personal qualities

The early work on leadership was largely grounded in psychology and focussed on generating understanding of how leaders worked in practice, and in particular how their style and behaviours impacted on groups.

Writers such as Bernard (1926) looked at leadership in terms of *personality traits*, physical abilities or personal qualities. This approach was based on the assumption that leaders were born rather than made and this gave rise to the pervasive idea of the 'great man' who, as Grint (1999) notes, as long as they have the appropriate personality traits will be *a leader under any circumstances.*

---

*ACTIVITY **1.3***

Identify someone who you think is a 'great leader'. This can be someone you know from work, education or from any other walk of life.

List the qualities that make him or her 'great'.

What do you notice about these qualities?

Do you think that the leader you have identified is 'born' or 'made' and which of the qualities could be learned or developed?

Elements of these models pervade all cultures, largely being drawn from historical, religious, military and mythological sources which emphasise the idea of charismatic, 'hero' leaders through story telling and legend. Various attempts have been made to define the attributes and qualities common to leaders that differentiate them from followers, but no single set has yet emerged. Despite the problems in identifying 'core' traits, certain (possibly unfashionable) qualities of the 'hero leader', such as bravery, tenacity, intelligence and honour can be argued to be as relevant and necessary today as they ever were. In Activity 1.3 you may well have thought of someone charismatic and many writers have developed lists of 'leadership qualities' (McKimm, 2004; Bose, 2003; Edwards and Townsend, 1965, or Argyris, 1964), which probably have much in common with your own list. When we apply these ideas to contemporary public sector organisations or businesses however, they do not explain the whole story. For example, there any many examples in politics or business where leaders fail to make the transition from one context to another or who are excellent in a crisis but cannot manage a stable organisation in the longer term. Drucker, in his study of successful executives suggests that *there is no 'effective personality' . . .all they have in common is the ability to get the right things done* (1967, p18). He goes on to list five elements of competency which he believes anyone can learn to be more effective in:

1 the management of time;

2 a focus on results;

3 an ability to build on strengths – their own and that of superiors, colleagues, subordinates and the overall situation;

4 a concentration on a few major areas where superior performance will produce outstanding results;

5 making effective decisions – taking the right steps in the right sequence.

(Cited in Gilbert, 2005, p44)

In the post-war years, *style theories* of leadership emerged which focused on the behaviours of leaders, their dominant styles and the resulting impact on groups. Blake and Mouton's (1964) identification of 'task-focused' and/or 'people-focused' leaders suggests that both of these leadership behaviours are required by a successful leader, however one type of behaviour will be preferred over the other according to context and circumstances. This perspective on leadership suggests that situations determine leader behaviour, as opposed to trait theory's assertion that leader behaviour determines situations. Attention to both task and people is necessary, particularly in complex or rapidly changing environments.

Goleman (2000), in his study of 3,871 executives, examined the relationship between leadership style, financial performance and organisational climate. He identified six leadership

Table 1.3 Six styles of leadership

Leadership style	Key feature	Message	Impact on climate and, in turn, performance
Coercive	Leader demands compliance	*'Do what I tell you'*	Negative impact – people resent and resist
Authoritative	Leader mobilises people towards a vision	*'Come with me'*	Positive impact
Affiliative	Leader creates harmony and builds emotional bonds	*'People come first'*	Positive impact
Democratic	Leader forges consensus through participation	*'What do you think?'*	Positive impact
Pacesetting	Leader sets high standards for performance	*'Do as I do, now'*	Negative impact – people get overwhelmed and burn out
Coaching	Leader develops people for the future	*'Try this'*	Positive impact

Source: Adapted from Fullan 2004

styles and their impact on performance and climate. Fullan (2004 p43–44) added to this by identifying messages that each of the six styles might use as related to school leadership.

Fullan points out that leaders need to employ different styles and approaches at different times, particularly when change or innovations are being introduced or in crisis situations. If the ship is sinking, you need a coercive leader not a coaching leader. Conversely, when organisational change is occurring, people need support and guidance to help them overcome the natural 'implementation dips' through coaching and affiliative leadership styles. Such leaders recognise that anxiety, lack of skills and resistance are natural responses to change and will listen and through the process of change with people. *The affiliative leader pays attention to people, focuses on building emotional bonds, builds relationships and heals rifts. The coaching leader helps people to develop and invest in their capacity building* (Fullan, 2004, p51).

ACTIVITY **1.4**

Taking each of the leadership styles listed above, identify a situation in which you, or someone you have worked with, has used each of the styles.

What was the 'message' they used? The forms of words, tones of voice, gestures, metaphors or stories?

What was the impact on you and others around you?

New paradigm models

In the early 1980s, the limitations of contemporary leadership thinking, notably in terms of explaining the relative inability of public sector hierarchies to cope with the pace of change, led to the evolution of a new leadership paradigm. McKimm and Swanwick (2006, p11) cite the emergence of transformational, charismatic and visionary leaders who *define organisational reality through the articulation of a clear vision and its supporting values.* 'New paradigm' leaders were seen as the managers of meaning rather than the architects of new processes, able to influence followers and thereby organisations *by inspiring them, or pulling them to a vision of some future state* (Alimo-Metcalfe, 1998, p7). Though it is feasible that the new paradigm leaders may have been simultaneously transformational, charismatic and visionary, it was transformational leadership which came to the fore and became almost synonymous with the development of leadership initiatives across the public sector. Charismatic leadership, meanwhile, was increasingly considered to be something of a mixed blessing as it was soon observed that charismatic leaders frequently became slower to adapt and change than their followers.

Transformational leadership

The leader who looks around and sees only followers will surely fail as a transforming leader

(Bate, 2000)

Transformational leadership (latterly evolving into the concept of *distributed leadership*) is a dominant paradigm in contemporary British public sector organisations. Transformational leadership (Bass & Avolio, 1994) is suggested to be the ability of a leader to facilitate the transformation of followers and organisations in such a way as to meet the desired outcomes.

Bass and Avolio identify the 'four I's' of transformational leadership as:

1 Idealised influence;
    developing a vision, engendering pride, respect and trust

2 Inspirational motivation;
    motivating by creating high expectations
    modelling appropriate behaviour and using symbols to focus efforts

3 Individualised consideration;
    giving personal attention to followers, giving them respect and responsibility

4 Intellectual stimulation;
    continually challenging followers with new ideas and approaches.

Transformational leadership is particularly relevant for complex and complicated environments such as healthcare where change is essentially the norm (Plsek and Greenhalgh, 2001). Leaders are seen as engaging with their followers, successfully conveying their vision of the future so that it becomes a common goal. In the process, such leaders become strong role models encouraging others to emulate them. Transformational leadership theory has been seen as particularly relevant to large statutory organisations, especially those in the throes of major restructuring and reform. One example is the NHS Leadership Centre which developed the NHS Leadership Qualities Framework (2006) around this approach.

There are fifteen qualities within The Framework covering a range of personal, cognitive, and social qualities. They are arranged in three clusters – Personal Qualities, Setting Direction and Delivering the Service (NHS Leadership Qualities Framework 2006, p4). A diagram of the LQF can be found in Chapter 7 (Figure 7.1).

1 Personal qualities
    • self belief
    • self awareness
    • self management
    • drive for improvement
    • personal integrity.

2 Setting Direction
    • seizing the future
    • intellectual flexibility
    • broad scanning
    • political astuteness
    • drive for results

3 Delivering the Service
- leading change through people
- holding to account
- empowering others
- effective and strategic influencing
- collaborative working.

ACTIVITY 1.5

Look at the NHS Leadership Qualities Framework document at www.nhsleadership qualities.nhs.uk/portals/0/the_framework.pdf

What do you think are the key leadership principles and assumptions underlying the framework and programme?

Compare this with other professional or organisational leadership frameworks such as:

Social Work Scotland Delivery through leadership www.socialworkscotland.org.uk

Social Care Institute for Excellence (SCIE) Leading the way in social care – Social care leadership development programme 2007–8 www.scie.org.uk

National College for Schools Leadership (NCSL) Leadership development framework www.ncsl.org.uk

(You may wish to find other leadership frameworks relating to your own profession or interest by Google searching on 'professional leadership frameworks'.)

What are the main similarities and differences between them?

Some commentators suggest that in the transformational context a 'hero' leader may be seen to emerge, personifying the notion of charismatic leadership (Fisher and Koch, 1996) Transformational leaders need to engender trust and ensure that they show moral, value-led leadership which resonates with their followers. Latterly the concept of the 'hero' leader has come to be regarded as both unhealthy and ultimately unsustainable (at least in the context of the statutory services). Furthermore, in the context of integrated working, the task of the transformational leader may be seen as exhorting the individual/organisational members to a shared commitment and increased capacity to achieve a unified, collective goal. The reality of the situation may be very different and constituent organisations and individuals will sign up to a broad shared vision, whilst pursuing a range of political and/or subjective goals, which may not be wildly different from the agreed goal but nonetheless subtly reduce the real impact of the desired transformation. This possibility, coupled with the complexity of modern-day public sector organisations with their 'managed chaos' has helped to shift the focus of leadership theory towards the not–dissimilar concepts of *distributed* leadership and *situational* or *contingent* leadership.

These approaches embrace the concepts of fluid team-centred leadership, empowering at all levels, distributing responsibility and developing successful networks within and across the culture and structure of the organisation, for the ultimate benefit of all. These highly pluralistic approaches to leadership move away from one of the fundamental tenets of transformational leadership, the notion of unified vision and goals, in favour of *subjective* models of leadership.

Subjective models of leadership

According to Bush (2003, p113):

> *Subjective models of leadership assume that organisations are the creations of the people within them. Participants are thought to interpret situations in different ways and these individual perceptions are derived from their background and values. Organisations have different meanings for each of their members and exist only in the experience of those members.*

Bush also claims (2003, pp127–8) that post-modern leadership aligns closely with his concept of a subjective model. Citing Keough and Tobin's (2001, p2) proposal that *current postmodern culture celebrates the multiplicity of subjective truths as defined by experience and revels in the loss of absolute authority*, Bush proposes that leaders should respect the diverse and individual perspectives of stakeholders. His view clearly questions the validity of reliance on the hierarchy because the concept has little meaning in such a fluid context.

Post-modern leadership

Sackney and Mitchell (2001) stress the importance of acknowledging that power to engage with change and evolve is located throughout the organisation and enacted by all its members. They claim that post-modern leaders should *shift the focus from vision to voice, paying attention to the cultural and symbolic structure of meaning as constructed by people and groups within the organisation* (ibid. pp13–14). Post-modern leadership is not defined by a series of techniques or specific skills and qualities; rather it is the drawing together of a number of key features identified by Keough and Tobin (ibid. p.11) as:

- language does not reflect reality;

- reality does not exist; there are multiple realities;

- any situation is open to multiple interpretations;

- situations must be understood at local level with particular attention to diversity.

It is possibly most helpful to see post-modern leadership as a generic term which takes in a number of particular approaches and which attempts to work within the bounds of complexity, fluidity and change, as a constant state. The ideas enshrined in post-modern leadership can be helpful when we are thinking of rapidly changing and shifting services, or when taking into account complex systems involving multiple stakeholders. One example is that of the Integrated Children's Service (ICS) agenda which involves a wide range of professionals, non-professionals, children and families and statutory, voluntary and not-for-profit organisations at local, regional and national levels. This has resulted in some of the dominant 'voices' in the agenda being managed through networks, collaborations and partnerships such as the Children's Workforce Development Confederation (CWDC) and the Children's Workforce Network (CWN). Though mandated by government, these organisations work in a very different, cross-sectoral way from traditional government departments and bureaucracies.

However, many public sector services and systems are hierarchically structured and managed, and this is important in terms of accountability. We explore these issues further in Chapters 4 and 9.

Situational leadership

The ability of a leader to evaluate the immediate context in which she or he is operating and adopt an appropriate leadership style is the key characteristic of *contingency theories*. Contingency theory proposes that there is no single best way for managers to lead. Situations will determine the required leadership. The solution to a leadership challenge is contingent on the factors that create the context. Similarly *situational* leadership suggests that the prevailing situation dictates the optimum style needed to achieve the goal or goals. As we saw above, Goleman (2000) refers to a range of styles – coercive, authoritative, affiliative, democratic, pace setting and coaching as being appropriate at different times and in different situations. Goleman also asserts that leaders who are 'fluent' in at least four of these styles are the most likely to succeed. Each style has its strengths and weaknesses, but the strength of the overall 'situational' style is its inherently adaptive nature.

ACTIVITY 1.6

Thinking once more about the leadership styles Goleman identifies above (and which you thought about in Activity 1.4), consider the scenarios below. Which of the leadership styles might be appropriate in work-based situations involving integrated professional teams working together?

Scenario 1

A young man aged 15 is in long term foster care. The foster mother telephones the key worker to say that they have been away for a long weekend and have come home to find the house a mess and the young man collapsed, apparently drunk, on the living room floor. She demands that 'they have had enough, something has to be done immediately or they are calling the police'.

You are the key worker. What are the next steps and what leadership styles are most appropriate.

Scenario 2

You are a team leader, looking after a large mixed team of professionals involved in integrated children's services. You begin to realise that the team is not functioning properly, there are cliques forming and you hear rumours that two of your best workers are thinking of resigning.

What might you do, and what leadership styles would be most relevant.

Complex adaptive leadership

Healthcare and related systems are complex and often anachronistic when viewed from the outside. Rouse (2000) applied complexity theory to a healthcare system with implications for leadership styles across the whole range of similar systems but with particular relevance to integrated working.

Characteristics of complex adaptive systems

- *They are non-linear, dynamic and are not inherently disposed to equilibrium.*
- *System behaviours may appear to be random or chaotic.*
- *They are made up of independent agents whose behaviour stems from physical, psychological, or social rules rather than the dynamics of the system.*
- *Because agents' needs or desires are not homogeneous, their goals and behaviours are likely to conflict. In response to these conflicts, agents tend to adapt to each other's behaviours.*
- *Agents are intelligent. As they experiment and gain experience, they learn and change their behaviours accordingly. Thus overall system behaviour inevitably changes over time.*
- *Adaptation and learning tend to result in self-organisation. Behaviour patterns emerge rather than being designed into the system. Emergent behaviours may range from valuable innovations to unfortunate accidents.*
- *There is no single locus of control. System behaviours are often unpredictable and uncontrollable, and no one is 'in charge'. Consequently, the behaviours can usually be more easily influenced than controlled.*

(Rouse, 2000)

People, acting within teams, networks and communities, form the basis of culture: Complex cultures are the product of their unpredictable interactions.

In complex adaptive leadership the key commodity is connectivity – the capacity to connect with stakeholders and the desire to connect them with one another. A connected leader helps create meaning, without which teams are rarely creative. Leaders should find out what is meaningful to their colleagues by discovering the individual and corporate 'stories'. This perspective on leadership is far removed from order and predictability. Pascale, *et al.* (2000) summarised this as *surfing the edge of chaos*.

They apply four key principles from complexity science to healthcare organisations.

1   When a living system is in a state of equilibrium, it is less responsive to change: equilibrium is close to inertia.

2   Faced with threat, living things move to the edge of chaos. This increases levels of experimentation and mutation, from which creative solutions can emerge.

3   When this occurs, living systems self-organise and new forms or patterns emerge.

4   Living things cannot be *directed* along a linear path – unforeseen consequences are inevitable. The challenge is to disturb or disrupt the movement to provoke the desired outcome.

You will read more about complexity theory in Chapter 4.

Collaborative leadership

Leaders need to be transformational but also to embrace uncertainty and emergent realities, allow for autonomy and creativity, and position themselves as part of interactive networks (Plsek and Greenhalgh, 2001; Mennin and Richter, 2003). How to be a transformational leader in the post-modern environment has led most recently to theories of value-led, thoughtful and *collaborative leadership*. Collaborative leadership focuses on a commitment to partnership working for the good of the service users, emphasising qualities and behaviours such as being able to assess the environment; demonstrate clarity of values; see commonalities and common interests and make connections; share vision and build and mobilise people and resources; build, promote and sustain trust; share power and influence; develop people and reflect on oneself. *Collaborative leaders are personally mature. They have a solid enough sense of self that they do not fear loss of control* (Turning Point Program 2003).

---

*ACTIVITY **1.7***

Search the internet for examples of collaborative leadership in integrated services.

What are some of the key features of collaborative leadership?

How do you think it differs (if at all) from partnership working and networking?

Leadership theory and changing perspectives on the nature of organisations

Leadership theory tends to be viewed as an historic process in which new thinking is embraced and old discarded as no longer fit for purpose. This is not the case in reality, as there are numerous approaches to leadership, and many more applications and contexts for which a given approach may be particularly appropriate.

In looking to the future, Storey and Mangham conclude that *models of leadership cannot be understood in isolation from wider tendencies, theories and patterns in social organisation* (2004, p343). It is perhaps useful, then, to consider leadership development as it maps onto the progress of organisational understanding.

Figure 1.1 Leadership in the context of organisational theory

The organisation as a complex machine

- Trait theory and Great Man theory – a good leader makes the machine run more smoothly and productively.
- Behavioural and style theory – leaders can make the machine run even better if they play to their strengths: people or task focused.

The organisation as a complex organic structure

- Transformational leadership – the leader builds the capacity of the organisation to achieve its goals through communicating the vision and management of meaning.
- Transactional leadership – goals are achieved through a continuum of political transactions between leader and followers in which achievement of the shared vision is the ultimate 'win/win' outcome.

The organisation as a loose agglomeration of complex organisms – complexity and chaos approaches

- Contingency theories – the leader draws on a toolkit of styles appropriate to situation and the followers at a given point.
- Distributed leadership – leadership at many levels is developed through widespread participation in the process of leadership.
- Complex adaptive leadership – the leader constantly monitors and interprets the random and chaotic activities within organisations and 'captures' the beneficial elements of the resultant behavioural adaptations that are an inevitable product. The key leadership quality is the ability to create connectivity within and across systems.

The complex adaptive leader's skill set could be seen as a fluid amalgam of inherent traits (e.g. the ability to 'surf the edge of chaos' and make sense of it) and learnable competencies such as 'connectivity mapping'. This questions the essentially linear way in which the development of leadership theory is normally expressed and the implication that each development somehow renders the previous one obsolete, perhaps also suggesting that some individuals are more 'natural' leaders than others.

This seems to reveal that there is still an underlying question about whether leadership is innate and simply awaiting the appropriate environment in which to flourish, or whether it is something which, like project planning or risk assessment, can be taught then applied. Recent work on the future of leadership development, particularly in the public sector, has focused on those least tangible but possibly most essential elements of good leadership, identified as integrity, authenticity, trust and values. There is some irony then that the theoretical underpinnings of a leadership approach which embodies these qualities were first recorded thousands of years ago, yet are the subject of much debate today.

Moral, thoughtful and value-led leadership: The servant leader

Beverly Alimo-Metcalfe and John Alban-Metcalfe can claim with some justification to have changed the way our health and social care sectors are led through their work advancing transformational leadership. It must been seen as significant then that in a more recent paper (2005) they pose the question *time for a new direction?* They propose an understanding of leadership that goes beyond transformational models, recognising the significance of Greenleaf's concept of 'servant leadership'.

Greenleaf is considered by some commentators to have defined the concept of 'servant leadership': *it begins with the natural feeling that one wants to serve, to serve first. Then conscious choice brings one to aspire to lead. . .* (1977, p13). The concept of servant leadership is, however, ancient and first seen in written form in the Tao Te Ching (circa 600 BC). In western history the concept is closely linked with the Judeo-Christian tradition and is explicitly included in the teaching of Jesus to the Disciples in the Gospel of St Mark (10: 44): *whoever wants to become great among you must be your servant, and whoever wants to be first must be slave of all.* Indeed, the very idea of 'public service' incorporates fundamental concepts around the altruistic nature of the care provided and professionals who work in public services (such as health and social care professionals and teachers) are 'duty bound' to work within ethical frameworks and values that centralise the patient, client or learner, rather than being focussed on the people delivering the service.

Kouzes and Posner (1989, p233), working on their premise that *leadership is in the eye of the follower,* looked to followers to elicit the key characteristics in a leader that would persuade them to be led. They distilled their findings into four qualities: integrity, competence, the ability to create a vision and the ability to create a climate of inspiration. They went on to draw up a list of five fundamental actions which informants said built the credibility of their leaders:

1 know your constituents;

2 stand up for your beliefs;

3 speak with passion;

4 lead by example;

5 conquer yourself.

Peter Gilbert (2005), in his examination of the human, moral and spiritual aspects of leadership suggests that leadership *throughout the centuries* seems to be about integrity, authenticity, trust, values, ability to provide direction and inspiration and the ability to deliver. These, or very similar essential qualities are identified by a number of leadership theorists, including Covey (1992) who lists integrity and trustworthiness at the personal and interpersonal level as the foundation of everything else. Greenleaf (ibid. 1977) suggests that servant leaders have three core skills: that of listening deeply, the ability to build creative consciousness and an approach which honours the paradox. These issues and that of spiritual and emotional intelligence are explored further in chapters 5 and 7.

ACTIVITY *1.8*

It has been suggested that many of today's leaders in public sector services 'lead from behind', supporting organisations, teams and individuals without necessarily being in a position of power or status.

What implications do you think this approach might have in mixed professional teams?

How do you think other issues might impact on leadership approaches and styles, such as gender, age, race or ethnicity?

The application of these fundamental qualities is essential to the exercise of leadership in the education, health and social care sectors. Professionals and other workers working in integrated services are highly skilled individuals who tend to have strong altruistic values concerning issues such as patient, client or student care, social justice and equity. Consequently leadership styles must be congruent with these characteristics if they are to be successful.

Both transformational and distributed leadership models refer explicitly to value-led, moral leadership, and they appear to be widely viewed as the most effective style of leadership in many public sector environments. This may however be dependant upon the degree of decentralisation and 'self-management' afforded to individual institutions (Bush, 2003). Greater degrees of centralised control (which may be said to reflect the current political climate) are likely to considerably reduce the scope for true transformational leadership (with the individual qualities this demands) which may in turn lead to a situation in which many individuals 'do' leadership, as distinct from 'being' leaders.

CASE STUDY

School leadership

Below is an example of how the above concepts, which reflect the shifting understanding of leadership, are enshrined in the UK Schools Leadership ten propositions.

School leadership must:

- *be purposeful, inclusive and values driven;*

- *embrace the distinctive and inclusive context of the school;*

- *promote an active view of learning;*

- *be instructionally focused;*

- *be a function that is distributed throughout the school community;*

- *build capacity by developing the school as a learning community;*

- *be futures oriented and strategically driven;*

- *be developed through experiential and innovative methodologies;*

- *be served by a support and policy context that is coherent and implementation driven;*

- *be supported by a National College that leads the discourse around leadership for learning.*

(Source: Hopkins, National College of Schools Leadership, 2001)

The transformational and distributed models of leadership seem to have been effective models for delivering leadership in the context of health, social care and education, especially given the ever-changing environment and organisations amidst a multitude of competing agendas. The success of these (or any other) approaches, however, must ultimately be underpinned by the personal qualities of integrity, trust, values and the ability to inspire. In the current climate of increased emphasis on the development of leadership *skills* the transcendental *qualities* of leadership cannot and should not be overlooked. The emergence of these qualities in leaders may ultimately be identified by their followers, but it will be the achievements of their institutions which provide the evidence.

Raise your 'leadership antennae' and apply some of the models and theories you have read about in this chapter to your everyday observations.

Observe leadership approaches of those that you meet at work, see in the media or in other contexts to see what styles they adopt and how this impacts on those around them.

C H A P T E R   S U M M A R Y

Instead of focusing leadership development almost exclusively on training individuals to be leaders, we may learn to develop leadership by improving everyone's ability to participate in the process of leadership

(Drath and Palus, 1994, p6)

This approach takes as its first principles that the organisation and its culture and values not only permits but also promotes active participation in leadership and organisational development by people and teams at all levels. Perhaps its second principle should be that participating in the process of leadership may not necessarily equate with conventional concepts of being a leader. We have discussed the concept of servant leadership, with its inextricable link with values and integrity, and the servant leader may also be unlike the accepted stereotype of a leader. In the context of integrated services with its inherent paradoxes of shared values and competing agendas, once again the conventional leader figure is the exception rather than the rule. Instead the connector-leader, who can live with ambiguity and follow unpredictable threads of complexity on the edge of chaos, comes to the fore. Perhaps we are moving ever closer to the opportune moment to move the locus of leadership study in the public sector into the foreground of the bigger organisational picture, and identify how and why leadership can shape not just the way organisations function, but the way they think, and react to their wider environment. To do this will require re-examining the constant and enduring qualities of leadership which have survived intact for a far greater period than the study of leadership has existed.

As you will learn throughout this book, translating the rhetoric to reality on the ground to implement integrated practice, is not easy or simple, particularly taking into account the 'messy' and complex interactions between various public sector organisations and professionals.

FURTHER READING

Gilbert, P (2005) *Leadership: Being effective and remaining human*. Lyme Regis: Russell House Publishing.

Northouse, PG (2001) *Leadership: Theory and practice*. Thousand Oaks, CA: Sage.

Chapter 2

Repeating history? Observations on the development of law and policy for integrated practice

Michael Preston-Shoot

Introduction

The modernisation policy for health and social services (Department of Health (DH), 1998a) is based on an assessment that services had been of insufficient quality, inflexible, reflective of institutional rather than individual needs, and unresponsive. Policy goals, therefore, have included breaking down barriers between services and improving inter-agency co-operation. The policy has explicitly challenged service fragmentation and professional hierarchies, and promoted new ways of working. In keeping with this policy direction is the recognition that service users' needs do not present themselves in neatly compartmentalised boxes and that to meet effectively the demands of education, health, housing and social care practice requires reliance on a range of knowledge and skills not routinely the preserve of just one professional grouping. The welfare of children in need or requiring protection, and of adults requiring care or services, if ever the responsibility of just one agency, must now be seen through a multi-agency and interprofessional prism.

The history of inter-agency and interprofessional working together suggests that practice which effectively crosses organisational and professional boundaries is not easily achieved. Some understanding is required, therefore, of what makes the achievement of inter-professional collaboration so challenging and what facilitates effective realisation of integrated practice.

Chapter overview

This chapter will:

- survey how the legal rules, particularly in England, relating to policy drivers surrounding inter-agency co-operation and integrated practice have evolved;

- critically examine the degree to which the legal rules have brought about in practice the shifts required by policy;

- explore the emerging complexity and highlight the limitations of the legal rules alone in achieving change;

- discuss the areas on which leadership and management must focus at national and local levels if the experience of service provision is to be transformed.

Structure of the legal rules

Legal rules begin with primary legislation (Acts of Parliament). The duties and powers contained therein are amplified in secondary legislation (Regulations or Statutory Instruments). This too may be expressed in either directive or permissive language. Government departments may then issue guidance to outline further how these duties and powers should be implemented. When issued as policy guidance, under Section 7 Local Authority Social Services Act 1970, it must be followed. By contrast, practice guidance can be departed from, but only with good reason as it outlines how professionals should ordinarily act. Courts are sometimes required to interpret the meaning of these legal rules as well as to arbitrate in disputes between public bodies or between them and individuals.

It is not unusual, however, for authorities to practise according to their own procedures. These procedures may not necessarily be a lawful interpretation of the requirements of the legal rules (Braye, *et al.*, 2007). Accordingly, it is good practice to audit agency approaches against the legal rules to ensure that the organisation is practising lawfully.

ACTIVITY 2.1

Audit agency procedures

Take the procedure manual used by the agency. From your research, identify the relevant legal mandates given to the agency. Identify the key requirements, expressed as powers and duties, in the Acts and Regulations. Identify also how guidance expects these mandates to be implemented. Then map these requirements against the agency's approach and evaluate the degree to which law in practice, in this organisation, is a reasonable interpretation of the law in theory.

CASE STUDY

Who knows the legal rules?

A local authority commissions a series of seminars to enable practitioners and managers to update their knowledge of the legal rules and to consider the implications for practice, in the context of service modernisation which includes the emphasis on personalisation, choice and control, individual budgets and social work practices. It proves very difficult to secure attendance by managers. Practitioners and students express considerable concern and anxiety, in the wake of publicity about child protection failures, regarding how they should respond when their managers overturn their needs assessments and recommendations in respect of safeguarding children and vulnerable adults, or when the arrangements for their supervision and management of their workloads break down. They are also concerned about how they should respond when other professionals dispute their interpretation of the legal rules, for instance when they request information. Whilst aware of their obligations as a consequence of being registered with the General Social Care Council, and knowledgeable about the Public Interest Disclosure Act 1998, they are hesitant to report concerns outside of line management structures within the authority, or of blowing the whistle to relevant independent regulatory or inspection organisations. They are aware of how whistle blowers have been treated within the public sector. Discussion in part focuses on the viruses that can affect how cases are approached – workloads, images of service users and of other professionals, resource constraints, and an unwillingness to question previous decisions. Knowledge of the law in theory, for which the seminars have been commissioned, meets the law in action. Practising at this interface appears very challenging in the context of this particular organisation.

Law in theory: The legal rules for working together

Some pieces of legislation exhort or command authorities to work together, but without changing the organisational structures through which they should do so. Thus, the National Health Service Act 2006 imposes one duty on health authorities to co-operate with each other and another (section 82, formerly section 22, NHS Act 1977) on health organisations and local authorities to co-operate to secure and advance people's health and welfare.

In community care, the National Assistance Act 1948 (section 26) allows local authorities to delegate to voluntary bodies the provision of residential accommodation, entirely if they so wish (*R v Wandsworth LBC, ex parte Beckwith* (1996)). The Carers (Equal Opportunities) Act 2004 provides for co-operation between authorities and other bodies in relation to the planning and provision of services relevant to carers. A more forceful approach is adopted in the Community Care (Delayed Discharges, etc.) Act 2003. Here, local authorities can be fined for delays in moving people, when they can be discharged safely, out of hospital into residential care or back home with support from community care provision. Once notified by an NHS body of the likely need for community care services, and given a discharge date, the local authority will initially have two days to put together a discharge plan. This applies to people in receipt of acute medical care but not to those in mental health care, maternity care, palliative care, intermediate care, or care for recuperation or rehabilitation (DH, 2003).

Section 47(3), NHS and Community Care Act 1990, allows the local authority to request assistance and services from health and/or housing authorities when undertaking an assessment to establish the need for community care provision. However, the Act is silent on how these public bodies should respond. Integrating assessments has been moved forward with the National Service Framework for Older People (DH, 2001a). Care should be person-centred, which is to be achieved through a single assessment process. Policy guidance has followed (DH, 2002), which aims to ensure that older people receive appropriate and effective responses to their health and social care needs. The process seeks to avoid duplication of assessments by medical, nursing and social work practitioners. Housing and other services should also be involved in a co-ordinated response to promoting people's well-being and independence.

In work with children and their families, the Disabled Persons Act 1986 (sections 5 and 6) and the Education Act 1996 require an inter-agency approach to services for young people with disabilities, for instance when approaching transition from children's to adult services. Local education authorities (section 322(1), Education Act 1996) may request help from health and local authorities in relation to young people with special educational needs. Schools must also co-operate with child abuse investigations and promote and safeguard children's well-being (section 175, Education Act 2002). Teamwork is crucial for the protection and well-being of children (Department for Education and Skills (DfES), 2006) and fundamental to the implementation of duties in the Children Act 1989 in respect of young people leaving care (section 24), children in need (section 17), day care (section 18) and children requiring protection (section 47). Sections 27, 28, 30 and 47 provide duties and powers involving co-operation between Social Services Departments, education, housing, health and independent authorities. Social services may seek assistance. When they do, other agencies must comply as long as the request does not unduly prejudice the discharge of their functions (section 27) or is not unreasonable in the circumstances of the case to assist (section 47).

The corporate responsibility for children in need and children requiring protection is further emphasised in policy guidance (DH, 2000a; DfES, 2006). A range of professionals and agencies are identified as having a role in children's well-being and development, their knowledge is seen as essential to decision-making, and an inter-agency collaborative model is promoted to ensure an effective service response for children and families about whom there is concern. The roles and responsibilities of different bodies are described, with staff required to understand the perspectives and language of other agencies. Senior manage-ment commitment, inter-agency training, and protocols are seen as the means by which working collaboratively will be valued, tasks and responsibilities appreciated, communication improved and intervention integrated at strategic and individual case levels. The corporate responsibility for identifying early the needs of children and young people, and for co-ordinating provision, is taken a stage further by the Common Assessment Framework (CWDC, 2007), which aims to reduce the number of assessments that families experience. A similar corporate responsibility for the handling and sharing of case information concerning children in need within local authorities and across agencies is constructed by the Integrated Children's System (DfES, 2005a).

In criminal justice, the Crime and Disorder Act 1998 makes local authorities responsible for youth justice provision through youth offending teams (section 39). The police, probation services, health and education authorities must co-operate. The Criminal Justice Act 2003 (section 325) imposes a duty to co-operate on responsible authorities, such as police, probation and prison services, together with agencies such as housing authorities, education authorities, councils with social service responsibilities and youth offending teams. The aim is to clarify roles and responsibilities, and to encourage joint working. It is designed to reinforce the Multi-Agency Public Protection Arrangements (Criminal Justice and Court Services Act 2000) whereby police and probation services, drawing on the support of other agencies, must have joint arrangements for assessing and managing violent, sexual and other dangerous offenders. Local agencies will need to have protocols or memoranda to define how they will co-operate.

Other legislation also addresses components of inter-agency practice. The Data Protection Act 1998 enables agencies to share information to prevent abuse and neglect. To assist with data sharing, local authorities must have information protocols with partner organisations in respect of safeguarding and promoting the welfare both of children and vulnerable adults (DH, 2000b; 2000c). The Children Act 2004 establishes databases on all children to support professionals in working together and sharing information in order to identify difficulties and provide appropriate support. Working together is also strongly highlighted in the preparation, production and implementation of youth justice plans (section 40, Crime and Disorder Act 1998), strategies for reducing crime and disorder (section 6, Crime and Disorder Act 1998), children and young people's plans (section 17, Children Act 2004), community plans to improve the economic, social and environmental well-being of an area (section 4, Local Government Act 2000), and joint health and social care strategic needs assessments (Local Government and Public Involvement in Health Act 2007, sections 106 and 116).However, more recently a different legislative tack has been adopted, especially in England. Powers and duties to work together have been accompanied by the creation of new organisational configurations. This reflects a policy shift from working together to integration (DfES, 2005b). These shifts are discussed further in terms of management and complexity in Chapters 3 and 4.

The Health Act 1999 (now consolidated into the NHS Act 2006) gives statutory backing to partnerships between health and local authorities. It allows the transfer of money between the National Health Service and local government and permits new partnership and funding arrangements to make it easier for health and social services to work together. Partners may create lead commissioning arrangements, delegating to one agency responsibility for commissioning all services for a service user group, transferring funds and transferring or seconding staff to facilitate this (section 75, NHS Act 2006). Partners may create integrated provision, allowing different professions to work together within one management, budgetary and administrative structure. Arrangements must follow consultation with all stakeholders and must be shown to be likely to improve services. Arrangements can cover all health-related local authority functions, including social services, education and housing.

The Health and Social Care Act 2001 continues the attempt to dismantle barriers between health and social care. It permits local and health authorities to merge their powers into

Care Trusts, responsible for commissioning services. Where services are failing, the Secretary of State may direct local partners to enter into partnership arrangements.

The Children Act 2004 similarly facilitates the creation of Children's Trusts by allowing pooled financial and staffing resources in order to promote co-operation (section 10(6)). Local authorities must promote co-operation between partner agencies and other bodies, which are listed in section 10(4), to improve the well-being of young people. Partner agencies must co-operate in these arrangements, and other relevant bodies, such as voluntary agencies, are expected to do so and ensure that their functions are discharged having regard to the need to safeguard and promote the welfare of children. Policy guidance has been issued (DfES, 2005b) on inter-agency co-operation, which outlines the essential features of a children's trust. These include a child-centred outcome-led vision, integrated front-line delivery rather than pre-existing professional boundaries or existing agencies, and integrated processes for assessment, planning, commissioning and information sharing. Local Safeguarding Children Boards are established (section 13). Children's services authorities, together with named partner agencies including the police, NHS and youth offending teams, must ensure the effectiveness of safeguarding and promoting the welfare of children. Their role is elaborated in policy guidance (DfES, 2006) and includes planning and commissioning, enhancing awareness, constructing policies and investigating serious case failures.

The theme of integration and new organisation and practice configurations is continued by the Childcare Act 2006. This requires early childhood services (early education provision, health services, social services and employment services) to be provided in an integrated manner (section 3) that facilitates access to services. The NHS and Jobcentre Plus must work in partnership with the local authority to deliver these early childhood services in an accessible and integrated way. Section 4 creates a duty to work together to deliver integrated early childhood services to improve outcomes for children and to reduce inequalities in achievement. There is a power to share resources and pool budgets to deliver fully integrated front line services. The Act also introduces a new legal framework for integrated regulation and inspection of education and childcare services.

These Acts attempt to break down the barriers which have unhelpfully fragmented and often frustrated the meeting of people's needs. However, barriers to improved co-ordination and collaboration remain, reflected in occupational cultures, lack of clarity about roles, disputes over responsibility occasioned by different rules on charging for services, and difficulties implementing single assessment processes (Hudson and Henwood, 2002; Lymbery, 2006). We explore these issues further in Chapters 4, 5, 6, 8 and 9.

ACTIVITY **2.2**

Monitoring organisational change

What evidence of working together do you see in your agency setting? How are agencies in your experience working together and moving towards integration? How have the legal rules on working together and on service integration impacted on your work? What outcomes for service users and carers do you see as a result of new organisational configurations and ways of working?

CASE STUDY

The extent of organisational change

In one local authority the flexibilities and signposts introduced by the legal rules have resulted in the division of the former Social Services Department. Mental health social work and social care practitioners and managers have been transferred into a Mental Health Trust, to work alongside community psychiatric nurses and other health care staff. Child care social work now sits within an emerging Children's Trust, alongside early years and education colleagues. Adult social care staff now work alongside housing and leisure services. Each separate organisation is now fully engaged in developing policies, procedures and practices which will integrate previously separate professional groups. Focus is on the development of protocols for joint working at strategic and operational levels, and exploring what integration means in terms of culture change, leadership, and new ways of working. At the same time, bridging posts have been created that link staff formerly working in the Social Services Department. Continuing professional staff development is included here alongside staff whose responsibility it is to enable service users to manage particular transitions, for example leaving care.

Law in practice: continuity or change?

Case law periodically tells a different story. Continuing care has been a particularly fertile ground for conflict between health and social care authorities (*R* (Grogan) *v Bexley NHS Care Trust and South East London Strategic Health Authority and Secretary of State for Health* (2006)). This is partly because NHS services are free at the point of delivery whereas local authorities may, and in some cases must, charge for community care services. The guidance (DH, 2001b) is also difficult to interpret when requiring health authorities to agree with local council's joint continuing health and social care eligibility, and setting out their respective responsibilities for meeting these needs. In *St Helens Borough Council v Manchester Primary Care Trust (PCT)* (2008), the local authority took the extreme step of bringing judicial review proceedings against the NHS. The PCT had refused to accept a recommendation from a multidisciplinary assessment. The court was critical of inter-agency litigation surrounding decision-making and funding.

In *R v Northavon District Council, ex parte Smith* (1994), the House of Lords ruled that, where need exists that cannot or will not be met by other agencies, in this case housing, social services must provide appropriate services. In *R (M) v Hammersmith and Fulham LBC (2008)*, the House of Lords gave detailed guidance on how housing and children's services should work together to ensure that the housing needs of homeless 16 and 17 year olds are met. Both bodies have accommodation obligations (Housing Act 1996, Homelessness Act 2002, Children Act 1989) and the borderline is unclear, with the result that resource considerations can infect decision-making. Housing authorities should take the lead and, where necessary, provide interim accommodation whilst the longer term position is resolved. For this purpose a framework for joint assessment should underpin working together in specific cases. In child care (*R (Stewart) v Wandsworth LBC, Hammersmith and Fulham LBC and Lambeth LBC* (2001); *R* (M) *v Barking and Dagenham LBC and Westminster City Council (interested party)* (2003)) and community care, disagreements also surface between councils with social services responsibilities about which is responsible for providing services because an individual or family is ordinarily resident there. Courts have had to remind authorities that the welfare of children should not become subservient to arguments about resources and that local authorities must co-operate in preparing a care plan when, during care proceedings, parents and children move (*Hackney LBC v C* (1996)). In *Hertfordshire CC v FM* (2007), mental health and children's services were reminded to work together to ensure the safety of the children of a mentally distressed father. The Court had been critical of their failure to work together effectively.

The Ombudsman too has been critical of working together. For example, a joint health and local government ombudsman report (2008) into the transfer of learning disability services in Buckinghamshire found maladministration because insufficient scrutiny was given to the quality of the services being transferred (*03/A/04618 against Buckinghamshire CC and HS-2608 against Oxfordshire and Buckinghamshire Mental Health Partnership Trust*). The report details poor integration of human rights considerations at all decision-making levels, with the receiving authority not fully aware of the quality of the service being taken on, which was poor. There was a failure to clarify responsibility between the local authority and the NHS Trust. Communication between them had been poor and the vulnerable adult at the centre of the case did not have his needs regularly assessed. Nor was he provided with an individual care plan.

In mental health, inquiries (Sheppard, 1996; Stanley and Manthorpe, 2004) have pointed to the absence of partnership working ; agreed methods of multi-disciplinary assessments and of discharge planning, and poor linkages between departments within councils with social services responsibilities and between them and other public authorities, such as housing. They have highlighted the need for regular reviews of multi-agency working and for strategies for joint commissioning and planning future provision, and for liaison and communication on individual cases. They criticise highly compartmentalised views of services, since limiting professional responsibility to certain tasks results in poor information sharing and collaboration, and thereby reduces the effectiveness of other professionals' contributions.

Nonetheless, mental health research continues to uncover difficulties. Real differences remain between health and social care approaches to eligibility, determination, assessment and priorities in respect of community care for people with mental distress (Cestari, *et al.*, 2006). Some health staff appear not to see social care needs as a priority and have not had training to assess such needs. Rather than an integration of mental health and social care assessment practices, separation is maintained structurally because the Care Programme Approach has not been merged with Fair Access to Care Services and care management.

There is evidence of improved integrated planning between health and social care in respect of services for older people. However, arrangements for seamless working between agencies are variable, with uncertain progress in forging partnerships with independent providers, and sometimes poor management of change and leadership in transforming strategic direction into achievable plans and good outcomes (Bainbridge and Ricketts, 2003). Wistow (2005) also reports better co-ordination across health, education and housing, and a shift from good relationships to strategic partnerships. However, he suggests that new powers of budget flexibility are under-utilised and argues that the major policy focus on the interface between social care and the NHS has resulted in the relative neglect of problematic relationships with other public services. This warning is timely as, for example, meeting the needs of disabled people can fall between housing and social services departments, with the absence of an integrated approach resulting in serious neglect of their right to private and family life and the award of damages against the local authority (*R* (Bernard) *v Enfield LBC* (2002)). Chapter 3 discusses some of the implications for management failures in integrated services.

Implementation of the single assessment process (DH, 2002) for older people, which should merge disparate approaches to assessment, has encountered problems with professional boundaries, resources and absence of agreed assessment documentation (Clarkson and Challis, 2004). Perceptions of the purpose and content of assessments differed; with some practitioners reluctant to accept other professionals' assessments (see also Chapter 8). Where, however, a lead person co-ordinated the assessment and information was pooled, older people benefited.

There are several points where adult and children's services within councils with social services responsibilities should connect. Adult and children's services should work together to provide a seamless service for carers. There should also be a multi-agency strategy, covering information provision, monitoring implementation of the Carers (Equal Opportunities) Act 2004, and training. However, carers still struggle and assessment practices are still highly variable (Robinson and Williams, 2002). Disabled parents also report high levels of unmet need. This appears partly due to a lack of co-ordination between child and adult services, confusion about the entitlement of disabled parents to services through community care legislation to support them in their parenting role, and stereotypical assumptions about disabled people as parents, leading to unnecessary removal of children from their care (Goodinge, 2000). Finally, working together for young people leaving care is patchy (Harris and Broad, 2005).

Change within the policy and organisational context for children's services is being driven by inquiry findings where poor leadership, role confusions and suspicions, and difficult relationships are highlighted. Among long-standing systemic problems remain uncertainty about the legal rules, for instance on the lawfulness of sharing information about welfare concerns (Bichard, 2004), inadequate information exchange between agencies, complicated by divergent notions of confidentiality, poor structures for communication between agencies, and reluctance by social workers to question information received from other professionals (Sinclair and Bullock, 2002; Laming, 2003; Reder and Duncan, 2004).

The Children Act 2004 and subsequent guidance is, therefore, an attempt to replace traditional organisational and professional boundaries with a more integrated inter-professional approach focused on specific outcomes for children and families. Research by Morris (2005) concludes that collaborative services remain under-developed and that directing resources explicitly at promoting working together still encounters barriers in the development of front-line collaborative practice. Thus, the degree to which joined-up working is offering early intervention and preventing poor outcomes for children and families remains an emerging, if tentatively positive picture. There is positive evidence of culture and role change but also increased workloads and problems with developing a language for integrated practice (see Chapters 5, 6 and 8). Having a clear and shared high profile vision is a key feature in confidently integrated authorities but more work is needed on accountability arrangements and engaging professionals at all levels and in all locations. Managers face the challenge of being responsible for a range of different professional groups but improved relationships positively impact on referral practice and co-ordinated responses to presenting problems (Lord, *et al.*, 2008).

Initial evaluations (Bell, *et al.*, 2007) of the Integrated Children's System (DfES, 2005a) have found that practitioners welcome the principle of agencies sharing information, and that the policy has promoted inter-agency work and improved assessment and recording practice. However, the picture is not uniform across all local authorities. Implementation has been impeded by doubts about the compatibility between the Integrated Children's System and the Common Assessment Framework, and by inter-agency disputes surrounding the acceptability of documentation, records and assessments. Management direction, staff involvement, a culture of learning, and a strong focus on change management appear key to effective implementation of the system. Chapter 5 explores change in more depth.

Thus, whilst a co-ordinated approach to working with children and families is required, collaborative working arrangements have been undermined by, and remain vulnerable to divergent ideologies or priorities, separate training, blurred roles and responsibilities, financial constraints, competitiveness and different views on approaches to cases. This suggests again that law and guidance are insufficient to achieve role clarity and relationships which foster professional understanding and use of expertise. This message is reinforced in critical evaluations of inquiry reports (Reder and Duncan, 2003, 2004; Sinclair and Corden, 2005), which document the need to understand and monitor relational processes in interprofessional contacts if polarisation, exaggeration of hierarchy, isolation, and closed systems are to be avoided.

Law in-between: Translating theory into practice

The space in-between the formulation and the practice of the legal rules is where managers translate the powers and duties given to their organisations into agency procedures (Jenness and Grattet, 2005) and practitioners work through the issues that arise from operationalising the legal rules as expressed through agency policies. Such translation will be affected by the degree to which central government and local communities can exert meaningful influence, and the agency is aligned with the proposed policy. In other words, the effectiveness of central government policy on working together and integration will depend on the perviousness of local authorities and their partners to community demand, especially from actual and potential service users, and to the reach of policy-makers, for instance through statutory inspection. Thereafter, the degree of alignment between managers and practitioners will also affect the outcomes of the policy on integrated practice. These issues are explored in Chapters 3, 4, 5 and 9.

Achieving integrated practice is also affected by the degree to which there is policy conflict and policy ambiguity (Matland, 1995). Thus, it is easy to be uncritical of partnership working (Glasby and Dickinson, 2008), to assume that it is automatically a good thing, without being clear about what outcomes are sought and what forms of partnership are therefore needed. There has been a tendency both to focus on potentially positive outcomes without considering potential drawbacks, and also to see partnership as an end in itself rather than a means to an end (Wistow, 2005).

One example of policy ambiguity is the meaning of integration and seamless provision. Wistow (2005) interrogates such meaning by suggesting that, in fact, what is important is how service users and carers experience provision. He suggests that services need strong seams in order to ensure that provision is joined together and fits individual need. Disabled parents, learning disabled young people making the transition to adulthood, and disabled adults reaching older age are cases in point since their needs cross legislative provision and service divisions.

One example of policy conflict is the misalignment of some policy agendas across health, education, and social care services. Young offenders and unaccompanied asylum-seeking minors are regarded in social policy and legislative terms quite differently from other children in need. In adult services, social care and the NHS operate under separate legal mandates, which configure differently the relationship between needs and resources, and between universal and means-tested services. The commitment to personalisation features more strongly in social care, through direct payments and individual budgets, than in health care. Wistow (2005) refers here to institutional barriers, such as the non-alignment of performance measures for health and social care bodies. Chapters 3, 4 and 9 explore this further.

Matland (1995) also argues that successful policy implementation depends on the degree to which top-down and bottom-up approaches are appropriately applied or combined. Implementation has been variable partly because faith has been placed in modifications to the legal rules and in organisational, procedural and bureaucratic solutions (Reder and Duncan, 2004; Sinclair and Corden, 2005), essentially top-down approaches to change management. However, the intractability of the problem of working together, and the degree of change required, suggest this approach alone will prove insufficient. Reder and Duncan (2003, 2004) in particular argue persuasively that agency mergers are no guarantee of better information sharing, and that reorganisations may emphasise rather than reduce interprofessional conflicts. Procedural changes on information sharing overlook the psychology of communication and the influence of contextual factors, such as workloads and resources. They stress the importance of front-line staff having positive working conditions if working across professional and agency boundaries is to improve, directing attention therefore to bottom-up approaches and to contextual factors. Similarly, Harlow (2004) notes that prescriptive guidance does not necessarily result in clear and well-functioning systems. Effective organisational systems must also encourage thoughtfulness about cases and oneself as a professional, and manage the experience of the dynamics of professional networks and engagement with individuals and families. A social policy approach to working together must also, therefore, appreciate and respond to the emotional and relational aspects of collaboration (see Chapters 6 and 7).

Implementation has also been variable because a framework has been created for structural reorganisation but the process of implementation evolves locally (Hudson and Henwood, 2002). Here there may be nervousness that pooled budgets means a loss of financial control, or poor commissioning capabilities (Wistow, 2005). Equally, the focus has been on integration at senior directorate levels, clarifying leadership and accountability, and bringing together planning mechanisms and budget cycles, without necessarily integrating all other levels or, indeed, front-line services (Lymbery, 2007). Moreover, although policy emphasises whole systems change, it then focuses upon processes such as planning and delivery (Children's Workforce Development Council (CWDC), 2007) rather than additionally on education and training for a common set of values, knowledge and skills. This allows long-standing blockages and divisions to resurface.

- Professional – different values and roles, different attitudes towards territorial dominance, different models of assessment and intervention, and the influence of stereotypes. Professional groups have a tendency to create their own boundaries regardless of organisational structure (Harlow, 2004) and trust and convergence of interest cannot be assumed (Reder and Duncan, 2003; Lymbery, 2007). See also Chapter 8.

- Attitudes – 'new image' projects grafted onto 'older style', long established professional practice cultures. Practitioners and managers may be preoccupied with changes in their own organisations, and suspicious of the cost shunting implications of change, frustrating closer collaboration (Hiscock and Pearson, 1999).

- Status and legitimacy – differences in whether accountability is to elected or appointed representatives, and different degrees of power, autonomy and professional status (Lymbery, 2007).

- Accountability – inspection, performance management frameworks and audit focus organisations inwards rather than towards shared responsibility for cross-sector partnerships (Harlow, 2004).

To move forward, partnership working is required at three levels (DH, 1998b). The first is strategic planning – planning jointly for the medium term and sharing information about how agencies intend to use their resources towards the achievement of common goals. Joint investment plans and the children and young people's plan are examples. The second level is service commissioning – developing a common understanding of community and population needs and the type of provision likely to be most effective. Integrated organisations can develop new approaches to joint commissioning. The third level is service provision – ensuring that service users receive a coherent, integrated and relevant care package based on a single or common assessment. At each of these levels, several components are crucial if effective working together or integration are to be achieved. Chapters 3 and 4 explore the concepts of partnership and collaboration in more depth.

Leadership

New ways of working require robust and continued leadership commitment. Senior and middle management must champion and support culture and practice change (Cleaver, *et al.*, 2004; Wistow, 2005; CWDC, 2007; Lord, *et al.*, 2008; McKimm, *et al.*, 2008). This is more likely to be successful when attention is paid to governance and decision-making structures, especially for managing cross-professional disputes, to developing clarity of purpose in service user outcome terms, and to constructing a vision that addresses the challenge from the perspectives of those involved. Successful prior relationships are not essential when establishing agreed policies, procedures and planning mechanisms at strategic and service commissioning levels, and co-ordinated assessment and care planning at the service provision level (Brandon, *et al.*, 2006; National Institute for Health and Clinical Excellence (NICE), 2006).

Language

Practitioners from different traditions use different terms to describe the needs of children and families. For example, prevention may be understood by different professionals in different ways (Morris, 2005). Professionals also hold different systems of meaning (Reder and Duncan, 2003). Achieving a common language and agreeing a conceptual framework is therefore important. Practitioners also gain a better understanding of their respective roles and responsibilities when they are involved in a process of agreeing a common language and developing a conceptual framework. This includes making explicit and discussing the relevance for integrated practice of implicit knowledge (Frost, *et al.*, 2005). Involvement also ensures understanding of what has been decided upon (Cleaver, *et al.*, 2004; Lord, *et al.*, 2008; McKimm, *et al.*, 2008). Chapters 6, 7 and 8 explore further how language operates in practice settings.

Training

Exhortation to work together must be accompanied, but often is not (Frost, *et al.*, 2005), by multi-agency/multi-professional training to prepare staff and to embed change (Laming, 2003; Cleaver, *et al.*, 2004; Brandon, *et al.*, 2006).

Professional education is still predominantly separate at qualifying and post-qualifying levels (Glasby and Dickinson, 2008), with ineffective joint training and stretched resources for continuing professional development generally; one explanation for the persistence of divergence between health and social care (Hiscock and Pearson, 1999; McKimm, *et al.*, 2008). Regulators have their own requirements which make the development of interprofessional approaches a challenge. Universities similarly are noted for boundaries between disciplines and departments (McKimm, *et al.*, 2008), unaligned with the pace and complexity of change in policy for integrated practice. Indeed, the professions involved in children's services are not proceeding at a uniform pace in relation to interprofessional education (Taylor, *et al.*, 2008). A review of benchmarks reinforces this observation. For example, the benchmark for medicine (Quality Assurance Agency (QAA), 2002) requires doctors to be able to work with other health care professionals, to give appropriate input to multi-disciplinary teams, and to promote effective interprofessional partnerships. There is little mention of liaison with social care systems. By contrast, the shift from working together towards integration is captured fully in the social work benchmark statement (QAA, 2008). Contemporary social work increasingly takes place in an inter-agency context, with practitioners and managers working collaboratively with others towards inter-disciplinary and cross-professional objectives. Social workers must be skilled in consulting actively and acting co-operatively with others, negotiating across differences such as organisational and professional boundaries, developing effective partnerships but also challenging others when necessary. Chapter 8 considers issues concerned with leadership and management development within the context of workforce reconfiguration.

The value of interprofessional education is widely assumed. Participants welcome the opportunity to reappraise their own value base and to learn new knowledge and skills together. However, research findings are equivocal about the impact of training together on interprofessional interaction, stereotyping, and changes in practice (Pollard, *et al.*, 2004; Carpenter, *et al.*, 2006; Taylor, *et al.*, 2008). Learning for integrated practice is inadequately conceptualised and theorised in a context of logistical challenges when developing such learning, namely its resource intensive nature, the development time required and the uni-disciplinary structures that have to be negotiated (Taylor, *et al.*, 2008).

Values

For health and social care (QAA, 2004) and for the children's workforce (General Teaching Council (GTC), *et al.*, 2007), joint values statements have been produced. These emphasise the importance of effective relationships, of commitment to improving interprofessional practice, and of sharing expertise for shared goals. Uni-professional statements, such as that for teachers (GTC, 2006) and social workers (General Social Care Council (GSCC), 2002), similarly emphasise team working, respect for the roles and expertise of colleagues, and sharing knowledge. Policy regards common aims and vision as fundamental to integration (CWDC, 2007). However, different professional values and belief systems continue to impact on collaborative working. For example, they emerge with the advent of Approved Mental Health Professionals (Mental Health Act 2007) expressed as concern that occupational therapists and psychiatric nurses will approach assessment of the need for compulsory admission to hospital from a medical rather than social model perspective. They frequently alight on different approaches to confidentiality (Frost, *et al.*, 2005). They emerge too in evidence that practitioners are not accepting assessments from other professionals, in respect of older people (Clarkson and Challis, 2004) and children (Brandon, *et al.*, 2006), despite policies on common frameworks, therefore duplicating assessments because of divergent perceptions of their purpose and content. Wistow (2005) reports concern that integration will result in a return to the medical model, and a takeover by health of social care and by education of child care. Chapters 6 and 7 consider the place of values, ethics and emotion in integrated services.

ACTIVITY **2.3**

The practice of working together

What issues, dilemmas and challenges do the statutory changes and the legal rules on working together raise for you in your work? How are the same legal rules viewed by different professions with whom you work? What barriers remain and what changes are observable?

Looking forward

Diverse organisational configurations are emerging, for instance linking adult social care not just with housing but also with leisure and culture services to promote community living and participation. Already some partnerships between health and social care authorities are unravelling. No set model for Children's Trusts is emerging either. Collaborative working can be delivered at least in three ways. First, through multi-agency panels, where cases and strategic roles are shared but workers remain located in their own agency. Secondly, through multi-agency teams delivering services, using secondments or direct recruitment, but with supervision by the seconding agency. Thirdly, through an integrated service, where funding, management and practice are co-located. Equally, there is some evidence that the fragmentation of social work and social care, in councils with social services responsibilities, is being rethought. Some authorities are employing a senior manager to take responsibility for both adult and children's services. Having integrated children's services, the next challenge arises, namely how to respond to the new boundary with adult services. It remains a paradox that the drive towards integration also inevitably involves fragmentation and newly drawn boundaries. A commitment to integration, accompanied by knowledge and skills for crossing boundaries will always be a core requirement for professional practice.

C H A P T E R   S U M M A R Y

Working together remains a key theme in social policy for health and social care. More recently, in England particularly, integrated provision has been promoted as the way to achieve improved outcomes in adult and children's services. However, a legal and procedural approach to systems change continues to address inadequately the importance of context. The challenges of different orientations to values, resource competition and constraint, professional stereotyping and its connection to power and status, and concerns about isolation when working in multi-disciplinary teams have long been prominent. Policy makers and managers will need to focus here too if the integrated agenda is to achieve the aspirations expressed for it in the legal rules. They will need to demonstrate strong leadership to realise the vision of partnership working across workforces, sectors and professions.

FURTHER READING

Balloch, S and Taylor, M (eds) (2001) *Partnership working: Policy and practice.* Bristol: The Policy Press.

Braye, S and Preston-Shoot, M (2009) *Practising social work law,* 3rd edn. Basingstoke: Palgrave Macmillan.

Weinstein, J, Whittington, C and Leiba, T (eds) (2003) *Collaboration in social work practice.* London: Jessica Kingsley Publishers.

Chapter 3

Management and leadership: From strategy to service delivery

Trish Hafford-Letchfield

Introduction

In the previous chapter we identified substantial challenges emerging from current UK government legislation and policy. These aim to reinvigorate the engagement of local authorities with health, education and relevant organisations in the social care sector; all necessary to oversee the wellbeing agenda for whole populations. The government's agenda and policy framework provides important levers to ensure that all the stakeholders involved, engage or re-engage with these agendas in the need to find joined-up solutions to complex health, social care and community problems. They also inform the strategic direction by which health, social care, housing, education and other aspects of welfare and community wellbeing are brought together across a diverse population in order to create and maintain sustainable communities. These outcomes are not achievable without significant investment in the development of effective cross-cutting partnerships supported by attention to strategic leadership and management. The translation of policy towards implementation by *strategising* is necessary in order to achieve tangible outcomes from service delivery. This involves moving beyond, and keeping pace with, any rhetoric in order to assess the limitations of more dominant or managerialist assumptions about how such changes can be realistically achieved, or how practice realities might flout rhetorical ambition in policy (Callaghan and Wistow, 2008). Fulop, *et al.* (2002) distinguish between stated drivers for change i.e. those set out in formal consultation documents as *espoused theory* with those privately held by stakeholders, the *theories in use*, or unstated drivers. Lack of insight into these tensions can throw us off course but greater appreciation will enable us to be more dynamic in the way we approach change and engage successfully with the reality of those potentially affected.

Chapter overview

This chapter keeps an eye on the bigger picture by paying attention to the significance of the strategic planning process and some of the management tools available to implement partnership working. We will be referring throughout to broader concepts underpinning leadership, linking with the more detailed discussion of the evolution of leadership theory and its manifestations in Chapter 1. This chapter will specifically:

- consider the environment when developing strategy in the context of partnership and integrated working and identify management tools available to help plan or manage implementation;

- look at theories relating to different types of partnerships and implications for organisational structures and cultures;

- explore some of the specific issues and challenges in developing integrated working in relation to participation, commissioning, decision-making and the impact of policy initiatives on power dynamics at an organisational level.

The importance of leadership

Achieving outcomes that promote health and well-being increasingly require a multi-disciplinary and preventative approach which emphasises the need to look at individuals as a whole in relation to their environment. This calls for a broadly integrated and multi-disciplinary approach to the prevention of social problems as well as to principles of 'cure' or care at the local level. Partners and associated provision of services need to achieve a level of teamwork by encouraging flexibility and collaboration within and across the organisations involved. Organisations whose cultures support teamwork, flexibility in decisions-making, with an open flow of communication and a shared vision, are said to be better able to deliver more positive outcomes (Payne, 2000). The effective combination of managerial analysis and interpersonal skills in public sector leadership are an essential aspect of service delivery (Rogers and Reynolds, 2002). Leadership is not the sole prerogative of those at the upper end of organisational hierarchies, nor held only by those with management roles and responsibilities. Potential for achieving change also lies in the development of leadership capabilities within the whole organisation, in which the structure or culture leans towards creating more empowered teams and encourages the distribution of responsibility by forging networks between the various stakeholders involved (Johnson, *et al.*, 1993, DH, 2008b, Skills for Care and CWDC, 2008). We will see later on that this can be facilitated by organisational structures as well as hindered by them.

> *Good leaders aim high – they listen to people's aspirations and support them to achieve. Leaders have a vision to do more than simply keeping their service ticking over; they tackle the challenges that others judge to be too difficult. They question the status quo and do not accept conventional wisdom. They recognise that they have the power to change people's expectations – to turn potential problems into opportunities – to do something about the processes that get in the way of good services for people – and to put people who use services at the centre of everything they do. They create organisations that talk and collaborate with each other and they tackle the 'little things' as well as the big transformational and organisational changes. Effective leaders do not say 'that's not my job'. They do not make excuses.*
>
> (Denise Platt, 2007)

Combining principles of strategic leadership with a critically reflective and evidenced-based approach should increase potential for developing a systematic and appropriate analysis to implement service integration. This is commonly known as *leading strategically*. Leading strategically takes account of the differing needs of stakeholders (particularly service users and employees) and seeks to maximise their involvement (Beresford, 2006). It means giving attention not only to the overarching collaborative aspects of leadership and management in the context of delivering integrated services and practice but also capacity for developing leadership at many other levels. Leadership thus becomes an interpretive device in translating and implementing strategy within multiple stakeholder organisations. In summary, the process of leading strategically involves assessing the environment and creating clarity in order to develop vision; mobilising resources and building trust when working with different stakeholders. It is vital to share power and influence in the business planning process and most importantly to develop people and their potential. We will now turn to look at these individual elements.

Developing strategy

Strategy occupies a privileged position within management theory and practice and is presented as the embodiment of rational thinking that incorporates logic, planning, monitoring technique and leadership (Alvesson and Wilmott, 1996). Acting strategically involves using a set of rational techniques for managing complex business in a changing environment. Processual views (Mintzberg, 1994) tend to adopt modernist accounts which are functional in nature and take for granted the legitimacy of what management seeks to do and the conditions under which any 'knowledge' is determined and enacted (Grandy and Mills, 2004). In essence, strategic management is fundamentally about setting the underpinning aims of an organisation or enterprise, choosing the most appropriate goals towards those aims and fulfilling both over time.

ACTIVITY **3.1**

What do you understand to be the strategic aims of your organisation? Try to articulate these both in terms of outcomes for service users or the community you serve and expectations from specific government legislation or policy statements. What are the implications of these for partnership working at a strategic level and identify the key other stakeholders involved?

Example of a strategic aim for Sure Start

Here we are going to look at an example of a *strategic aim* within Sure Start. We can start by identifying one of its very broad aims, for example one which talks about working with parents-to-be and parents and children to promote the physical, intellectual and social development of babies and young children. We might next consider the underpinning *relevant policy* such as Every Child Matters, (2004) and the Children's Plan (2007) Then we would move on to focus on one of the specific objectives within the above. One *objective* would be to improve the health of children by directly supporting their parents in caring for their children to promote health development before and after birth. To make this realistic and tangible, we may then set a *target* which states what we might achieve within a certain time period and can be measured and evaluated, for example, to achieve by x date. In the Sure Start area this could be a 20% reduction in mothers who smoke in pregnancy. Finally, we could go on to state a number of *delivery targets* which gives us more detailed information about what we are actually going to do in more practical terms as well as what we want to achieve. For instance, this could be the intention to provide smoking cessation programmes for x people within the Sure Start area; the provision of support and information about the effects of smoking on babies and young children included in all local health clinics and playgroups and a 20 per cent reduction in children in the Sure Start area aged 0–3 admitted to hospital with respiratory infection. The above example would clearly identify which stakeholders need to be involved such as primary care staff, voluntary groups, those involved in health promotion, expert patient groups, and of course, parents and carers.

Strategic management is often contrasted with operational management, which is short term and detailed both in content and process (Cole, 1997). Operational management takes place in the context of immediate or near-future events with a sense of predictability closely aligned to the immediate business concerned. In the real world these are not exclusive, as these two aspects of management are inevitably linked. However, you may realise that existing traditional theory around organisational behaviour often provides one-dimensional views and is unhelpful in analysing the dynamics of relationships which develop over time such as those within partnership working. Within public services the complexity and power differentials at play have to take account of the effects of local strategic partnerships in their wider context. For example, those charged with the development of community and neighborhood renewal strategies addressing major issues such as child poverty, health inequalities and crime. Whilst national policy contexts for service provision remain the same regardless of locale, the history of partnership working and service aspirations within any given area will be unique, with implications for strategic choices (Freeman and Peck, 2007). As partnerships themselves draw organisations into increasingly complex relationships, there are also a range of legal, financial and governance concerns which need to be considered locally and in operational terms.

Environmental analysis

Within the current policy and practice environment, government strategies seek to achieve fairly long term objectives with 10–15 year plans to develop a multi-agency approach and in many cases fully integrated environments. Thinking through the implications of policy and translating these into action however is devolved to the local level. These have to relate to the longer term future of the whole sector and outcomes for service users in response to Local Area Needs Assessment and conducted in conditions of considerable unpredictability.

> *Huge cultural, transformational and transactional change is required in all parts of the system . . . for services across the whole of local government and the wider public sector. The scale and purpose of this ambition should not be underestimated. . . .*

Local priority setting will be focused on meeting local needs and playing a leading role in shaping strong and cohesive local communities . . .

(DH, 2008a, pp1–6)

As indicated above, strategy is perceived as a mediating force between the organisation and its environment, the internal and external context. Familiarity with the operational or practice domain is crucial as is addressing these within the social, cultural and political environment to make the most of any rational model and to assist thinking and planning (Johnson and Scholes, 1993) This is where management tools and techniques of environmental analysis can be useful. Strategic leadership may involve two different techniques of environmental appraisal in order to assess the context for implementing change and providing a starting point for involving others.

SWOT analysis

Determining an organisation's strategic direction involves assessing the external environmental forces acting upon it. When planning for any change, either major, such as influencing the future direction of services, or on a smaller scale, such as reviewing a system or specific work practice, you can create a storyboard or more structured approach to analysing the different forces involved and the conditions within which any change is being considered. This encourages momentum (Martin, 2003). The SWOT approach is one such method which asks you to consider the relative *Strengths* and *Weaknesses* of your scenario and then to involve key individuals in identifying and exploring any *Opportunities* and *Threats* in proposed new conditions. We will be returning to this tool again in Chapter 4 but will introduce you to it here.

ACTIVITY 3.2

In the previous activity you noted current drivers for change when considering the strategic aims within your own particular organisation or associated with your professional discipline. You also identified what might be required to increase partnership or integrated working. You are now asked to give attention to any specific roles and responsibilities that you hold personally in finding ways to responding to these. Use this focus to consider the questions asked in the SWOT analysis below and use the four factors to analyse and record your current position. Try and answer the questions posed from the perspective of your own context.

Analysis using SWOT is the first step in strategic formulation which involves evaluating the issues identified and making strategic choices that enable the organisation to meet its goals and how these align with other stakeholders. This will inevitably involve political choices and processes. SWOT tends to emphasise the strategic importance of exploiting internal strengths and neutralising internal weaknesses outside of these. A PESTL analysis on the other hand offers additional dimensions when undertaking environmental analysis.

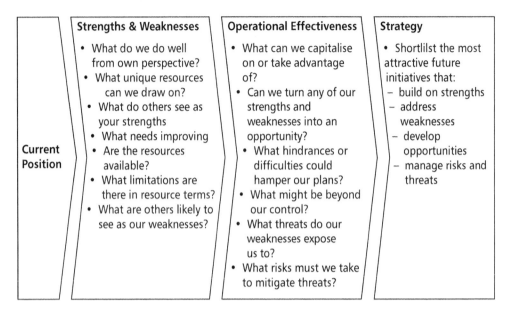

Figure 3.1 SWOT analysis

PESTL analysis

Chapter 2 referred to the political, economic, legal and social contexts driving integration. Increasingly technological developments are impacting too, as well as environmental and sustainability factors. Changing demands from stakeholders and service users' and carers' expectations of social care services are further significant drivers regarding the types of services commissioned and provided (Beresford and Croft, 2001). All have to be appraised if the range of organisations involved is to respond effectively to these forces. Detailed analysis of these help managers not only to understand the complexities and interrelationships to be taken into account in predicting future trends affecting their organisations, but also to provide awareness of the key factors affecting the success or otherwise of the organisations they manage. Relationships between organisations and their environment are not just two-way but are virtually symbiotic, taking into account the mixed economy of care and ideological shifts towards public participation and the redistribution of power to service users. Consideration of these factors lends themselves to a more complex environmental analytic tool commonly known as a PESTL analysis (Political, Economic, Social, Technological and Legal). Farnham (2005) recommends that data gathered within these areas can be used for environmental analysis in two ways. Firstly as a 'macro' (outside-in) approach where organisations engage in scanning, monitoring, forecasting and assessing to identify and examine plausible alternative future environments that might confront them. The driving force is to ensure organisations understand the dynamics of change within each environment, before deriving organisational specific implications. The second approach, Farnham terms 'micro' (inside-out) where the organisation is a starting point to examine its products, markets, technologies and so on. Given these contexts, one might asked questions about which elements of the external environment should the organisation scan, monitor, forecast and assess? Your role as a strategic, middle or first line manager or senior practitioner might determine which approach is preferable.

To illustrate this further, one might consider public policies towards older people and the rising importance of ageing as a policy issue and the emergent interest in 'ageing well', 'active ageing' and 'quality of life'. Activity around developing services to meet older people's needs have led to sustaining activity beyond employment through retirement and the promotion of healthy ageing and community participation targeted at the fourth age. *Both have win-win potentials for older people and society in terms of social inclusion, well-being, and quality of life and in reducing pressures on public spending on pensions, health and social care* (Walker, 2005, p164). Simultaneously, focusing on how an established service response might deliver in a way that meets an older person's own aspirations and goals may involve reviewing contractual relationships and making links to educational or leisure services to support the quest for greater independence and choice of those already using services.

ACTIVITY **3.3**

To help you undertake a PESTL analysis, some indicative examples thought to be commonly found in interprofessional environments under each relevant factor are given below. Try to build on these examples and analyse your own service.

The political environment

Government decisions affect the way care and support services are configured and managed and frequent changes in legislation (including the EU), policy changes and regulations affect a range of issues. For example, the rights and demands of service users and their representatives have led to political changes such as increased involvement and participation and the need to adapt to these.

It may also be that the future shape of provision is driven as much by the entrepreneurial ambitions of providers as by the strategic planning of commissioners. Given the significant degree of integration at the local level, political and managerial responses of local government may also be a key influence in many localities.

What can you say about your political environment?

Economic forces

These are of vital concern as the overall economic climate determines 'business' opportunities and because an expanding economy stimulates demands for goods, services, investment and labour. Within care, long-term and short-term trends need to be addressed proactively for example much attention has been given to the long term care needs of older people (Wanless, 2007) and to equality issues such as the life chances of disabled people from different communities (Begum, 2006). The sorts of issues you might want to appraise are; the availability of resources such as finance, capital assets, workforce; messages from research and development studies around prevention; costs of services using benchmarking or Best Value techniques; stakeholder and partnership opportunities for pooling costs.

What economic forces are affecting your service?

Social Factors

These include demographic and local performance information. Monitoring access to services by giving attention to diversity, mobility, income and geographic distribution levels will aid your analysis and thinking about these. Utilising critical based research and evaluation studies will also aid analysis. Patterns of service use and monitoring of unmet needs based on your current service information can be used to inform your commissioning and contracting activities and service development plans.

What social Factors influence the provision of your service?

Technology

Technological change is one of the most visible and pervasive forms of change. The impact of new technologies in care enters every aspect of an organisations' management and delivery of services as well as having an impact on the way we live and work (Weiner and Petronella, 2007). Awareness of technological developments is essential for most organisations and impacts on the performance and quality of services and types of support provided. Examples might include those developments used to enable us to collect data from a large number of inter-disciplinary sources such as information processing systems as well as those impacting directly on service users such as for self assessment, and administration of care (such as telecare and clinical interventions).

What technological factors impact on your environment?

Legal factors

As well as the duties and powers derived from legislation and guidance, other areas affected by legislation include; the type of services developed and produced; the funding and resourcing of care, for example through merging with partners or as a result of the Health Act 1999; workforce development; workplace design; for example health and safety; accounting and budgeting practices.

What legal factors are affecting your service?

The use of analytic tools such as SWOT and PESTL assist managers and their stakeholders to question and examine areas in a more systematic way. Some critics argue however that they simplify reality, distort by simplification or a 'one size fits all' approach and are more likely to obscure than illuminate (Grandy and Mills, 2004). In the face of these criticisms, it is even more important that you combine such tools with critical reflection using evidence based information wherever possible or combine these with other methods. We will be revisiting the application of these tools again in Chapter 4 when we start to look at the practical implications for partnership working and the concept of complex adaptive systems theory.

Further and alternative tools for analysis

Appreciative Inquiry

Material generated from environmental analysis can be used to inform the business planning process. Other interprofessional techniques to kick start the process include *appreciative inquiry*, a form of action research that attempts to create new theories, ideas or images that assist in the development of a system (Cooperrider and Whitney, 2003). This method promotes co-operative searching for the best in people and their organisations through the practice of asking questions that strengthen a system's capacity to heighten positive potential. Appreciative inquiry is also based on the principles of equality, where everybody involved is asked to speak about their vision for the service or changes they wish to make as opposed to traditional approaches to change where current problems are identified, emphasised and amplified. As an alternative, appreciative inquiry looks positively for what already works and is appropriate for managing tensions that can arise from new structures within integrated environments. The tangible result of the inquiry process is a series of statements that describe where the team/organisation/service wants to be, based on the pinnacle moments of where they have been already. It presupposes that because the statements are grounded in real experience and history, people know how to repeat their success.

CASE STUDY

Using appreciative inquiry to promote inclusion in special educational needs

A project called Growing Talent for inclusion has grown out of a Local Authority Support Service which assists schools to meet the needs of pupils with a range of additional educational needs. Faced with a large number of individual referrals, many relating to the emotional, social and behavioural needs of pupils, it was considered that an eco-systemic approach was required and that a priority was to support pupils and teachers in developing more effective and satisfying interpersonal relationships in the classroom.

Growing Talent for Inclusion uses appreciative inquiry to investigate a management change process which has been used within large organisations and communities but less commonly at classroom level. It is a type of action research which is solution not problem focused and therefore lends itself well to a research focus of improving classroom dynamics. The process was able to guide the identification, acknowledgment and amplification of skills pertinent to improving social dynamics within the classroom in a more collaborative and participative way. An evaluation of this approach was found to improve working relationships in four different primary and secondary classrooms in three schools. Seventy-six pupils and four teachers have been involved in the project since its inception in 2002 with classes in a further three primary schools using the approach during the academic year 2005–2006. Findings from the project show an increase in the number of pupils with whom other pupils are happy to work, a reduction in the number of pupils identified as socially excluded at the beginning of the project and enhanced capacity of the group in terms of the talents identified for growth. Feedback from staff and students also suggests that the process of noticing and acknowledging strengths has contributed to improvements in working relationships.

(Doveston and Keenaghan, 2006)

Delphi Technique

Alternatively, the *Delphi Technique* brings together a number of experts from different disciplines or levels within strategy formulation to analyse specific aspects of the current and future environments or problems. This technique enables multi-disciplinary contribution to each other's understanding of the issues and opportunities to refine opinions as a result of structured interactions with one another. The Delphi technique involves the following steps.

- Each expert is asked to make an initial prediction.

- Predictions are tabulated and clarified by a neutral person.

- The output is then fed back to the experts who are asked to make a second round of predictions based on the information provided to them.

This process of making predictions and receiving feedback can go on for several rounds and provides opportunities to involve users and carers and frontline staff as experts and participants.

In conclusion, the above section highlights that, in order to develop partnership and integration of services, clear understanding of the relationship between strategic and operational planning within the sector is required. Strategic planning involves defining mission, goals, policies, structures and funding. These in turn drive the direction and priorities of the service through the formulation of detailed operational plans which specify targets, budgets and resources towards specific outcomes. Designing clear governance arrangements and quality assurance systems then feed back into the strategy regarding how well implementation is going. Some of these processes are demonstrated in Figure 3.2.

Within these overlapping areas, space to share concerns should encourage and support any emerging leadership. Leadership provides the bridge between key decisions about strategy and actual implementation through operational units of the business. Leadership involves seeking clarity, establishing good communication by asserting its role in articulating or facilitating change.

Public sector organisations devote serious time and resources to developing a strategy and business plan to help build and sustain partnership work as determined by government policy priorities. Those same organisations often fail to devote sufficient attention to the leadership component of their plans and the organisational and human capabilities needed. An effective leadership strategy encompasses active consideration of organisational values and culture as well as structure. It pays attention to the role of systems in facilitating organisational development which includes activities for improving the effectiveness of individuals and teams. These might range from workforce development initiatives such as inter-disciplinary training, coaching, mentoring and team building, and seconding staff to undertake developmental assignments as illustrated in the case study below. We have referred to a notion of strategy being *deliberate* in an environment where strategy should also be allowed to *emerge* by creating more fluidity. This is important in the context of evidence based practice, the flourishing of communities of practice and user involvement.

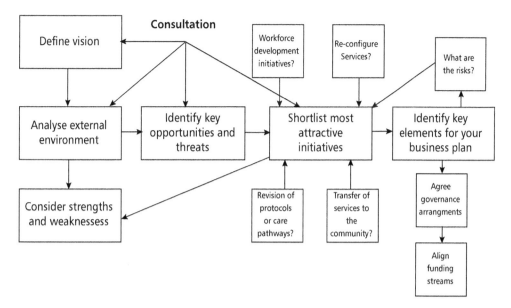

Figure 3.2 The strategic development framework

Applying a business model has limitations. Rationality and technique should not be privileged at the expense of concern with professional or service user knowledge and values, equality and diversity. There is great complexity in delivering services in a managerial and interprofessional organisational climate (Lawlor, 2007). Discourses about strategy and its implementation have to address the more problematic features of organisational life (Grandy and Mills, 2004) and take advantage of the complex network of interests and opportunities within which there is potential for leadership to emerge.

CASE STUDY

Leading change in Oldham: Implementing individual budgets (IBs) within the transformation agenda

Oldham council has been one of the earlier leaders in implementation of individual budgets. During 2005–6 Oldham undertook a programme of actions in its preparation phase. Key actions included the development of a resource allocation system; the revision of care management processes to incorporate IBs; the development of support planning; training and development and communications. Business process remodeling was undertaken to identify and agree new efficient transitional processes whilst initially maintaining existing structures.

Some of the innovative steps taken during this preparation phase were:

- *establishing a 'drop in' clinic for individuals and their families;*

- *developing a 'support planning pack' for users;*

- *a series of visits by senior management and project staff, combined with regular and substantial training and development activities;*

- *regular presentations and discussions with a range of user and carer groups;*

- *separate consultations with all service providers;*

- *alignment of social care budgets with other funding streams;*

- *seconding dedicated project staff to undertake joint work with other agencies to establish jointly developed protocols and procedures;*

- *a launch of 'community of practice' forum to share learning about best practice and problems.*

(Jackson, 2008)

What type of partnership? Theoretical models

The literature in public services is rich with references to the need to 'work together' in 'partnership' and 'collaboration'. Much of the terminology is policy driven, promoting concepts such as 'joined-up thinking' so that services can be delivered 'seamlessly' (Carnwell and Carson, 2005, p3). Having looked at developing a strategic framework, we are going to briefly look at different types of partnerships and implications for organisational structures and cultures.

Attributes of partnership given in the literature refer to trust, respect, joint working, team work, the elimination of boundaries, forming alliances and sharing identity. These have a substantive ethical content, as we shall see in Chapter 5. Carnwell and Carson (2005), Glasby and Dickenson (2008) differentiate types of partnership by the type of commitment undertaken. These include:

- Project partnership, which is time limited around a specific project and ends when funding ceases. An example might include an initiative to design an electronic patient information pathway that brings together national cancer resources that can be accessed by people working and using cancer improvement services, see www.cancerimprovement.gov.uk

- Problem-orientated partnerships formed to resolve specific public issues such as crime or substance misuse and which involve a strategic multi-agency approach to addressing the issues for as long as they are a problem.

- Ideological partnerships arising in response to an issue or viewpoint and which may evolve into more overt political partnerships as the ideological context widens. An example may be a focus group established to advise planners and commissioners about service gaps and priorities in the area of domestic violence. Current domestic violence strategies originated from campaigning women's groups and the voluntary sector but have since developed into strong and dynamic multi-agency partnership under a community safety umbrella with a wide remit across services.

- Forced partnership where legal provisions and duties are devised to send out powerful symbolic messages about the importance attributed by policy makers to partnership. Mandated collaboration can be seen in hospital discharge arrangements (e.g. The Community Care (Delayed Discharges Act, 2003) where strong financial incentives compel joint working.

Integration takes partnerships one step further where an organisation acts as a hub for the community by bringing together a range of services, usually under one roof, whose practitioners then work in a multi-agency way to deliver integrated support such as in mental health or children and families. Key features include:

- common location and common philosophy, vision and agreed principles for working with service users;

- a visible service hub in the community with a perception by users of cohesive and comprehensive services;

- a facilitative management structure;

- delivery in a familiar community setting (e.g. school or health centre);

- staff working in a coordinated way to address needs including some degree of joint training and joint working in multi-disciplinary teams;

- service level agreements setting out the precise arrangements between the different partners with pooled or single budgets.

(Source: www.cwdcouncil.org.uk/multi-agency)

ACTIVITY 3.4

Based on the above models, think about how these align with your own practice experience and are you able to identify some of the more problematic features of the partnership you are familiar with?

As you may have identified in the above activity, some definitions hint at possible negative and cynical motivations towards partnership (Glasby and Dickinson, 2008, p6). Barriers to working in partnership can arise through role boundary conflicts and tensions between agencies, unrealistic expectations and interprofessional differences of perspectives such as approaches to risk or the blurring of roles which impact on some professionals striving to maintain their own identity. The Office of Department of Prime Minister (ODPM) (2005) discusses the potential different levels of engagement as partnerships develop. They refer to defensive participation, where organisations become concerned about the perceived resource implications or fear that they 'might lose out'; opportunistic participation, where organisations might not see partnership as core to their own objectives but as a means to seize other opportunities, where they might take more than they contribute and active participation, where there is strong commitment to the partnership as a natural extension to tackling items on their own agenda (cited in Glasby and Peck, 2006, p17).

As you have seen, partnership attributes include both structure and process phenomenon and the needs of service users and carers have a central place in understanding the politics of partnership. Their voices and presence need to be recognised in any type of partnership created. Despite policy aspirations for divestment and plurality for provision, local markets for provision (vertical supply chains) will also be strongly influenced by market interests, commissioning behaviour, and their suppliers and the nature of existing relationships between providers and their future ambitions (Freeman and Peck, 2007). Mapping existing relationships in your strategic plan helps to reflect on the different relationships and their fitness for purposes.

Traditional partnerships such as adult health and social care may not be familiar with working with more remote stakeholders such as leisure or transport (Peck, *et al.,* 2002, Glasby and Peck, 2006), whereas children's services have tended to focus on a broader range of potential partners (education, social work, health, youth offending) but have less experience of formal integration and deeper ways of working. The concept of the *lead professional* (CWDC, 2007) provides one mechanism to make sure services are co-ordinated, coherent and achieving intended outcomes in the delivery of integrated frontline services. Designating lead professionals to work with operational management can help to develop close links and open channels of communication between different service managers and in setting criteria for resolving conflicts or disputes. In developing the journey towards achieving a positive culture for partnership, being open to appointing lead professionals from different disciplines such as GPs, health visitors or youth workers may serve to promote inclusivity and professional development.

Implementing partnerships – specific issues and challenges

Leading community partnerships and participation

There is an implicit assumption that partnership working adds value by bringing relevant partners together, focusing their collective skills and resources towards the issue at hand. Strategically, difficulties can arise where partnerships bring together stakeholders with diverse skills and resources, different working cultures and substantial disparity in their income and power. Bigger players within partnerships and integrated services such as NHS Care Trusts and Local Authorities (LAs) respond to the policy context in a number of ways. They may seek to develop joint structures for health and social care services in commissioning and/or provision. They will consider what criteria are important in shaping local provider markets (commissioning), appraising potential providers (procurement) and assessing the strengths and weakness associated with different types of providers (Foreman and Peck, 2007). This is what Lyons (2006) refers to as *place-shaping*. Place shaping involves:

- building and shaping local identity;

- representing the community;

- regulating harmful and disruptive behaviours;

- maintaining the cohesiveness of the community and supporting debate within it, ensuring smaller voices are heard;

- helping to resolve disagreements such as how to prioritise resources between services and areas, for example where new housing should be located;

- working to make the local economy more successful, to support the creation of new businesses and jobs;

- understanding local needs and preferences and making sure that the right services are provided to local people through a variety of arrangements including collective purchasing, commissioning from suppliers in the public, private and voluntary sectors, contracts or partnerships and direct delivery;

- working with other bodies to respond to complex challenges such as natural disasters and other emergencies.

Source: Lyons 2006, p39

Locality based services that are integrated through the direct involvement of community stakeholders are very different from those centred around professional or organisational integration. In particular, as more control is vested in the community, there is a corresponding shift in the power base to the people whose voice, knowledge and insights are fundamental to service design and provision.

CASE STUDY

Developing community knowledge for the design and management of local services

Connected Care was a government pilot involving a housing estate in Hartlepool which was experiencing immense problems arising from poor health, social and economic status and traditionally low levels of participation amongst residents. The LA, NHS commissioners, service providers, community associations, residents and elected members worked together to commission local research on how the community viewed its services. This took the form of an audit with twofold aims: firstly to develop community based knowledge for designing responsive and joined up services; secondly to build knowledge by developing the capacity of the community itself and shift the balance of power between them and professionals. The experience concluded that communities are not homogenous but characterised by subgroups with competing interests. Various tensions

---

CASE STUDY *continued*

emerged in the different timescales of the stakeholders wanting to complete the project, with the aim of supporting co-production using the expertise of the community itself. Securing the legitimacy of community involvement challenged any coherence between the theoretical basis of the initiative and its structural and organisational context. For example the tendering process divided competing community organisations who usually worked collaboratively. In terms of research skills needed to complete the audit, it was found that true community involvement implied accepting some professional control in gathering information about community needs. This challenged the validity and structural differences between the researchers and researched and raised a number of issues about participatory community research. Citizen research was valuable in producing important information about social needs within a locality consistent with the social model and in promoting the needs of the whole community rather than just the service user. There was also advantage in gaining support for the changes being developed and in giving a steer for future service design. The findings from the audit were used to later counter a possible reassertion of professional control within the service specification and implementation phase. However, the experience raised questions about the sustainability of relationships between community and professional knowledge beyond the audit stage.

(Source: Callaghan and Wistow, 2008)

The above case study draws out some of the complexities underlying the design and delivery of integrated services and the tensions involved in achieving true participation and community involvement. This complexity extends to the third sector where partnership with the NHS or LA is a significant feature of the everyday environment within which many voluntary and community sector organisations work (National Council for Voluntary Organisations (NCVO), undated). With active support from the *Department for Communities and Local Government* (2007), Third sector involvement and social enterprise provides a considerable number of potential benefits and advantages in the context of partnership. Examples are addressing current unmet needs characterised by undifferentiated public provision; enhanced (direct) user involvement in service development; and innovative approaches to service delivery (Foreman and Peck, 2007). Organisations working in partnership with these bigger players however often find themselves challenged about their accountability or legitimacy in relation to those they support or represent.

Involving providers and the third sector in partnerships

Analysis of the strengths and reasons for involving the third sector may include:

- their expertise in service delivery;

- knowledge of user and community needs;

- ability to reach those who are either excluded by, or exclude themselves from, mainstream provision delivered via traditional agencies in the sector;

- ability to work flexibly and innovatively to address complex and changing needs.

Source: National Strategic Partnership Forum, 2007

However, concerns have been raised about voluntary organisations becoming 'funding led' rather than 'needs led', raising questions as to who the intended beneficiaries of some partnership activity are and dilemmas for third sector organisations. Whilst offering opportunities to influence service provision and policy direction and achieving sources of funding for existing or new services, many of these partnerships, unlike cross-sectoral partnerships involving statutory authorities, are not formally constituted. They often have no legal status with the public sector body taking responsibility for convening and managing the partnership, especially financial accountability (NCVO, undated). Requirements for senior representatives to be able to make decisions on behalf of their organisation might not always be operationally possible for third sector smaller organisations. Mechanisms for feedback to trustees or service user groups must therefore be clear and supported by offering skills or financial support to facilitate these types of roles and responsibilities within the third sector. Separating lead and accountability aspects can help to share power and a sense of shared accountability more evenly within such partnerships (NCVO, undated). Where partners are also providers, and/or working with a potentially vulnerable client group, their reputation in that community is arguably their best asset, bringing representation or direct knowledge of users to the table. This should not be jeopardised if a partnership is not properly formed or supported (NCVO, undated).

Partnerships in the care sector have given rise to the potential for a flexible combination of networks, hierarchies and markets in the delivery of public services, without favouring an ideological preference for any of them (Glasby and Peck, 2006). Whilst these emphasise the importance of collaboration, some partnerships have become obligatory with delegated responsibilities and have brought to the fore challenges for the third sector particularly the realities of defined contractual relationships. This is an area for considerable complexity and confusion particularly where governance is concerned. In forming any partnership, there should be space for reflection on the potential conflict of interests that may arise or where the term partnership is used rhetorically rather than being genuinely reciprocal (Glasby and Peck, 2006, p8).

The speed at which localities can develop effective new ways of working in partnership has been underestimated and the time needed should be thought through carefully. Partnership overload leads to ineffective joint working. There remains a major need for capacity building – in the statutory sector as much as in the voluntary/community sector – if collaborative working is to become a reality'.

(Neighbourhood Renewal Unit, 2002, p22)

Allowing time to develop external and internal relationships is fundamental to the development of trust within partnerships which itself enables partners to discuss sensitive or confidential information that will impact on the work of the partnership as a whole.

CASE STUDY

Making partnerships work

Joint working between statutory organisations in Nottingham and a third sector organisation Base 51 (a charity supporting young people aged 12–15) targeted some of the most vulnerable and disadvantaged young people in the area. The organisation works holistically with the young person and offers many services all under-one-roof, including: a medical service, counselling service, under 18s service, support for homeless young people, young parents and unemployed young people. Base 51 has developed good working relationships with statutory and voluntary organisations. One example is the role of the centre nurse, an extended nurse prescriber employed by Nottingham PCT but based full time with the Base 51 team and jointly managed by Base 51 and the PCT. The nurse works together with the other workers in the team to actively support a group of young, homeless men with poor health, drug and alcohol dependency, to take more exercise. The nurse has been the catalyst in the formation of the Base 51 football team, enabling the young men to have the confidence to compete against others and take responsibility for themselves in working together as a team.

(Source: Department of Health, 2007a, p9)

Joint funding and commissioning

This chapter concludes with reference to joint funding and commissioning as it goes without saying that more effective use of resources has been a significant driver for partnership and is essential to the delivery of quality services. In order to shape services around the needs of the user, formal agreements to commit funding and resources towards agreed shared outcomes provide scope for innovative service design; integration; close partnership working; and the opportunity to consider redeploying and re-investing resources around prevention (DH, 2007a, p6). Local Area Agreements and legislation (Children Act, 2004, S.10, Health Act, 1999, S.31 and NHS Act 1997, S28A and 28BB) provide mechanisms for partners to create discrete pots of money and enable one partner to commission or contract on behalf of others; resulting in clear processes and decision making to deliver the vision. Pooling budgets can reduce transactional costs, overheads, bureaucracy and delays as well as generate economies of scale and deploy resources more effectively (DH, 2007a). Depending on the size, shape and nature of services required many different levels of funding and resources can be integrated at the front line through integrated teams, to a more strategic level of joint commissioning arrangements comprised of joint boards, panels and supporting teams and units. The models shown in Figures 3.3a and 3.3b demonstrate different levels of integration and methods of joint funding and commissioning.

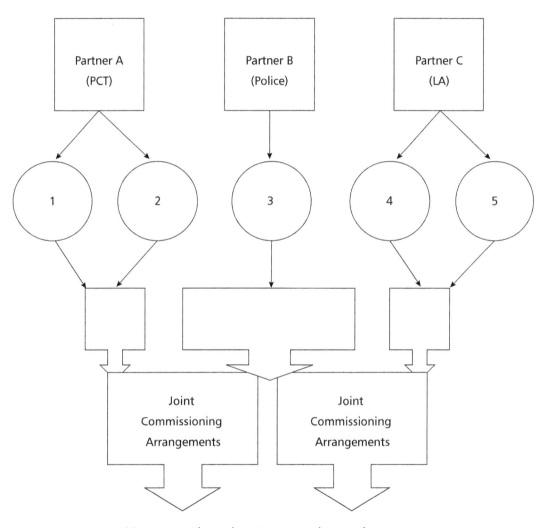

Figure 3.3a Example of an aligned budget towards agreed outcomes where partners retain their own performance monitoring and accounting mechanisms

Source: Adapted from DH, 2007, p13

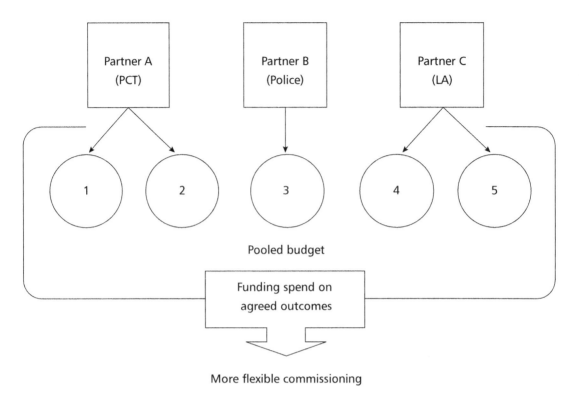

Figure 3.3b Example of a managed pooled budget

Source: Adapted from DH, 2007, p14

The provision of care becomes complicated by the pressures on agencies who must allocate scarce resources between chronic and acute needs and between health related or other forms of social care (Johnson, *et al.*, 2003). Further complications arise when the provision of care occurs across agency and organisational and professional boundaries. Pooled funding and joint commissioning offer one solution to these types of impediments and concerns over costs.

ACTIVITY 3.5

What are the incentives for joint funding in your own service area? Are there any other types of initiatives that you can think of within your area of practice that would make better use of resources other than monetary ones?

Competition over scarce resources, political differences, and internal organisational factors can create barriers to effective collaboration to meet defined outcomes. Differences in professional cultures, for example where regimes revolve around the needs of professional in providing care, can clash with the notion of empowerment and hinder the progression of person-centred care. These will not be resolved by new funding structures alone but hopefully you have identified the importance of joint training and team building and management style to develop cultures in which true collaboration can thrive.

C H A P T E R   S U M M A R Y

The rationale behind the creation of cross-sectoral partnerships and integrated services includes the need to make policy intervention and service delivery more responsive to the needs of local people. Their creation however continues to fuel an ongoing debate about the nature of leadership and democracy and participation at the local level. Substantial disparity in the size and power of organisations involved, the extent of participation and consultation, sources of funding and commissioning and contracting arrangements impinge on the success of partnership working when implementing government strategy at a local level. Management and leadership in an inter-agency partnership is a difficult and challenging task, raising questions of how managers might live up to the growing integration agenda and link effectively with government legislation and policy as well as with the aspirations of staff, users, carers and the community they serve. Local strategic partnership working is dependent on the history and geography of the area as well as the vision, skills and behaviour of key individuals. It is through shared exploration and creative thinking that partners learn to work together and need to make time for shared thinking and learning.

FURTHER READING

Department of Health (2006b) *Business Planning Sourcebook* outlines the characteristics of good strategic planning universal to all organisations. It provides key tasks and tools required with templates, frameworks and guidance notes to steer you through the process of pulling your business plan together. Available from: **www.dh.gov.uk/en/Publicationsandstatistics/Publications/PublicationsPolicyAndGuidance/DH_4130735**

Charities Evaluation Services (2006) *Using an outcomes approach in the voluntary and community sector: A briefing for funders, commissioners and policy makers on the National Outcomes Programme.*

Available from **www.ces-vol.org.uk/index.cfm?format=126**. Explains what is meant by an 'outcomes' approach and how this can benefit funders, commissioners and Voluntary Sector Organisations and the challenges involved in introducing this into the business planning process.

CWDC (2008c) *Multi-agency working*. There are a number of ways of delivering multi-agency services and this online resource is available for managers and practitioners within Children's Services in a range of settings, who are starting to work with families in new ways. Available from: **www.cwdcouncil.org.uk/projects/multiagency.htm**

Chapter 4
Leading in complex environments

Kay Phillips

Introduction

In the last two decades, a range of political initiatives for service improvement and integration have meant that many leaders and managers, for example those working in education, health, social care, economic and social regeneration and criminal justice, have needed to develop new capabilities in order to be effective in delivering change. Public, private, charitable and voluntary sector organisations are increasingly tasked with working together to meet local and regional stakeholder needs. In short, the environment has become much more complex. This chapter covers a range of themes around managing and leading in inter-agency settings, formal partnerships and networks. It aims to provide you with a better understanding of the leadership challenges that these new organisational arrangements present.

Chapter overview

Complexity stems from *what* we're required to make sense of to bring about change and deliver specified objectives and outcomes. It encompasses an understanding of *who* needs to be involved and the organisational *structures, systems and processes* that might best support our endeavours. Perhaps most importantly it also incorporates *how* leaders and managers need to work with others to make a genuine difference. This chapter addresses each of these themes as follows.

- The first section revisits some of the tools introduced in Chapter 2 for analysing and making sense of your environment. This will help you focus more specifically on national and general trends and key developments in your current service context.

- In section two, the theoretical principles of complex adaptive systems are explained and we consider how application of the theory can help organisations to respond to the need for radical change.

- Section three reviews how organisations have developed to manage complexity. The challenges of working within partnerships and networks are discussed.

- The final section considers some of the different leadership skills and behaviours which these complex environments require.

Understanding the service environment

Individual professional practitioners, teams, service managers and leaders all need to have some understanding of the environment within which they are operating in order to function effectively. For leaders and managers tasked with delivering integrated services, an understanding of the environment is crucial because one of their functions is to interpret it for colleagues, helping them to cope with change and uncertainty.

The required level of knowledge will not be the same for everyone but an understanding of our working context helps us to respond to changing levels of demand, identify areas for service improvement, meet service user expectations and position our services in l ine with political, social and economic changes. For example, if your work involves delivering services to older people these are just a few of the questions you might want to address.

- What national policy changes have taken place in the last decade? Are there any major policy developments on the horizon?

- What are the issues regarding the funding of services for older people, nationally and locally?

- What are our legal responsibilities regarding the protection of vulnerable adults? Are we fulfilling them?

- What is the current thinking on issues like dementia care and support for people in the community?

- What do we know about the demographic impact of an ageing population and is this a particular issue for our local area?

- How are services commissioned and is this likely to change? What is the potential impact of individualised budgets?

- What are our future workforce development needs? Do staff have the skills to deliver what service-users require?

- Do we know what older service users want? How do we involve them?

- Are local services 'joined up' from a service-user perspective?

- Which voluntary sector interest groups have an influence in decision-making?

- What is the extent of private sector provision? How good is it locally?

- Are there organisational barriers to integrated working?

- What are our relationships like with other public sector agencies? Who has lead responsibility?

You should be able to see from this list that an environmental analysis should encompass national, regional and local factors.

Environmental analysis tools

In Chapter 3 we identified that environmental analysis can be a huge task, especially for those working across a number of different organisational boundaries. We saw that one of the ways of undertaking an analysis is by using the PESTL model to analyse the general environment. This will enable you to consider the implications of political, economic, social, technological and legal trends for your specific service environment. The list of questions in the previous paragraph contains both national and specific issues; you might find it useful to try to differentiate them.

Analysing the general environment using PESTL requires you to review national trends and developments relevant to your sector and profession. Although a PESTL framework is essentially a checklist, it can help you towards further analysis of the most relevant and pressing factors requiring your attention. This is a starting point for making sense of your environment. It is also a good exercise to undertake as part of any business planning process. Mapping the general and specific service environments prompts the more important question: What does this mean for me and my service or organisation?

Using a SWOT analysis to identify priorities

A thorough environmental analysis can generate a large amount of information so findings may need to be condensed into a more workable form. Another simple tool which can support this process is the SWOT analysis, which you were first introduced to in Chapter 3. As you may recall, SWOT stands for Strengths, Weaknesses, Opportunities and Threats. In this chapter we are using it specifically to prompt an evaluation of the likely impact of current and future environmental factors, by comparing them to your current service. The perceived strengths and weaknesses of your service are considered in relation to the potential threats and opportunities in your external environment. A simple template can be used to summarise your SWOT findings.

ACTIVITY **4.1**

Completing a SWOT analysis

Work with at least two other people to analyse a service that you are working in/have worked in. If you are a student this might be something you could do on placement. Use the table shown. The prompt questions will assist your critical thinking.

Table 4.1 SWOT analysis template

(Internal) Strengths	(Internal) Weaknesses
What do we do well?	What could we be doing better?
Do we have the skills/people to take the service forward?	Are there system weaknesses?
Are staff receptive to change?	Do we have enough resources?

(External) Opportunities	(External) Threats
How can we capitalise on current policy developments?	Who are our competitors?
What changes can we take advantage of?	Is our service seen as a priority?
Is there new funding?	Could funding and commissioning constraints threaten the future of our service?

It can be productive to undertake the SWOT with others so that different perspectives can be discussed. What one person sees as an external threat might be viewed as an opportunity by another. The involvement of service users in the process can also add value, particularly in evaluating current service strengths and weaknesses.

If you have a service leadership or management responsibility you will need to critically reflect on the results of the SWOT analysis. The following questions may help you to focus your thoughts.

- Which of the issues that you have identified are likely to have the most impact?

- How can threats be turned to opportunities or minimised?

- How can internal weaknesses be addressed and how can you build on strengths?

- Which are the most urgent priorities?

- Which ones are you personally responsible for addressing?

- Who else needs to be involved?

- What are the potential challenges and pitfalls?

- Are there resource implications?

Most environmental analyses will indicate a need to work with other people. These might be your colleagues, service users or commissioners. They could be other professionals working in different teams, departments, organisations or even sectors. There is an increasing expectation that people will work across these boundaries, manage networks of contacts, involve the recipients of the service and collaborate to deliver integrated services. Complex adaptive systems theory can help us to navigate our way through this tangled web.

Complex adaptive systems and integrated services

The principles of complex adaptive systems theory were outlined in Chapter 1. Although the basic ideas are not difficult to grasp, it can sometimes be harder to see how they might be applied in practice. The starting point is to understand that complex adaptive systems theory is a means of making sense of our working world and of taking a more analytical approach to the management of change. Paul Plsek has written a number of articles and papers (see Plsek and Greenhalgh, 2001; Plsek, 2003) which demystify the theory. These provide a good introduction, especially for those working in the health and social care sectors, from which he draws many of his examples of the theory in practice.

The implementation of change in service delivery can be extremely slow, especially in public services. Even relatively small changes may impinge on many systems, requiring multiple adjustments to be made. A complex adaptive system is a collection of individual agents, all of whom can act in predictable or unpredictable ways. What one agent does will have an impact on others, changing the context. As an illustration, consider the impact of a decision to merge several local schools to provide integrated education to the community's children aged 3–18. The decision might be made by a small number of people but its impact will be felt across many systems.

Organisations and individuals will be affected and behaviours and patterns will change to accommodate it. Importantly, the responses will be diverse, the speed of change will vary and predicting what will happen, with any degree of accuracy, is largely impossible. On a smaller scale, think about the implications of changing the opening hours of a general practice or childcare facility. Structures and processes inside and outside of the organisation will be changed. Service users and staff will make choices as new possibilities emerge. The full impact of the change may not be known for some time.

Formal *structures and processes* are only part of the picture. Within a complex system there are *patterns* of behaviour, relationships, values, a 'history' (perhaps of conflict or blame) and traditions. Some of these are explicit but others might be hidden. Understanding these patterns is crucially important. As an analogy, imagine a family tree diagram. We can see the basic structure of the family and the factual recordings of birth, marriage, divorce and death, but the actual relationships within that family, their personalities, values and beliefs are only understood by gaining knowledge of how people interact and connect.

The theory also acknowledges that, within any complex system, there exist *simple rules and mental models*. These affect what we do and how we respond. For example, in a discussion with a service user with multiple needs, you might have a social model of care as a deep-rooted mental model; a colleague might be making a diagnosis of need based on a medical model of care. Our models and internalised rules have a significant impact on our receptiveness to new ideas and change. What is important to remember is that they are often hidden from others and surfacing them is therefore part of the change process.

Similarly, complex systems theory acknowledges the importance of *attractor patterns* in responses to innovation. When we encounter a plan for change, especially if the change is one imposed on us, we evaluate it from our personal perspective. We may be attracted to some elements, resistant to others and this can be a group response. Defending our professional identity and status is a common example of an attractor pattern. We are likely to be unreceptive to change which might erode it. Witness for example the resistance to redefinition of health professionals' roles in recent years which is explored further in Chapter 8.

Plsek draws attention to other features of complex adaptive systems. The elements can change themselves, evolving to meet new needs and to manage those parts which fail to adapt. There is an *inherent non-linearity,* and change can occur at any point in the system. The boundaries of the system are often difficult to map; individual systems impact on each other and there are layers of systems, at local, regional, national and sometimes international levels. These are referred to as *embedded, co-evolving systems.* Finally, we should acknowledge that, within and between organisations, there are both formal and shadow systems. The latter can be very powerful and they exist everywhere. Shadow systems may operate, for example, in informal social networks and special interest groups within organisations, supplementing the formal arrangements for decision-making in teams and departments. They are part of the complexity and part of a process through which agents self-organise using locally-applied rules (Plsek, 2001).

It is because we are confronted by complex problems that the adaptive system model is so attractive. We cannot deliver integrated, user-focussed services simply by fixing a broken bit of the process. Agreement has to be negotiated with others and we may have to work with high levels of ambiguity and uncertainty. Many of the 'wicked issues' will not be *solved*; instead the goal will be to achieve some progress towards reducing the problem.

Later in this chapter we'll consider the new forms of organisation that have emerged in response to the challenge to integrate. Their aim is to bring people together to share and generate knowledge and to facilitate the implementation of new approaches to service delivery. There remain, however, everyday dilemmas, contradictions and tensions to be negotiated. These include balancing collaboration and competition between service providers, meeting the needs of individuals whilst satisfying wider community interests and working with a distributed leadership model whilst maintaining transparent accountability arrangements.

There is a further, fundamental paradox. Complex adaptive systems thinking is predicated on minimum specification of the required change, leaving it to the agents to agree what will work for a particular context. In the last decade, however, a different, more mechanistic culture has dominated. All public sector service providers have had to comply with statutory requirements, tightly defined performance targets, detailed monitoring processes and prescriptive outcome measures. This has made it extremely challenging for leaders and managers to work more intuitively and creatively in line with the principles of complex adaptive systems theory.

Working in networks and partnerships to develop integrated services

At this point it is appropriate to consider the types of organisational arrangements which might best support the application of complex systems thinking. Traditional hierarchical organisations are the prevailing model in the public sector but in the last 20 years there has been a significant trend towards networks and partnerships. New roles have been created to span the boundaries within and between organisations to deliver change, service integration and improvement. These are considered further in Chapters 5, 8 and 9.

Networks

In the mid 1980s, writers like Miles and Snow (1986) began writing about a new type of organisation. Using the example of high tech industries in California they championed network forms of organising, seeing them as a radical departure from traditional, hierarchical organisations. Nohria and Eccles (1992) supported the view that network organisations were more flexible and responsive. Characterised by decentralised decision-making processes and horizontal communication channels, networks were also viewed as less bureaucratic.

At about the same time, Thompson, *et al.* (1991) compared networks, hierarchies and markets as three different forms of organising. They noted that, in the shift from hierarchical to network forms, there needed to be a change; from the use of role power to influencing; from command and control to diplomacy. Pettigrew and Fenton's work *The innovating organisation* (2000) examined case studies from different sectors to illustrate new forms of networks that were emerging. They argued that three different elements, structures, processes and boundaries, all needed to change to create the new type of organisation. They observed, however, that it was extremely difficult to simultaneously change all three core elements. As a result, organisations often exhibited 'dualities', or opposing forces that had to be balanced. So, for example, the organisation might move to more project-based working processes but retain its old hierarchical line-management structures. Networks didn't replace hierarchies; they supplemented them within the same organisation.

CASE STUDY

NHS experiments with networks in the late 1990s

The growing debate around the potential of networks to effect change coincided with the launch of the ambitious public sector reforms of the 1997 Labour government. Restructuring and improving the NHS was its first priority and networks were seen as a way of bringing together professionals from hospital, community, primary healthcare and social care. Change was required to create more 'joined up', efficient services.

Service Improvement Collaboratives and Clinical Networks were launched to encourage interprofessional service development and collaboration between organisations. But there

---

was a tension. These more flexible ways of working were very heavily performance managed and monitored, in a way that was more akin to hierarchical, bureaucratic systems (Bate, 2000). They also had to demonstrate improvement in a very short timescale. As a result, short-term improvements often disappeared when the funding ran out and people reverted to their old ways of working. Professional 'silos', clinical accountabilities and long-established working patterns were cited as barriers to change but perhaps the real problem was that there was insufficient attention paid to surfacing the tacit knowledge within the organisation that might have led to more sustainable learning (Gillies, 2000, Huxham, 2000).

Networks are intended to support a more intuitive approach to dealing with difficult problems or 'wicked issues' as they are sometimes referred to. Their function is to be creative, horizontally-connected, self-organising systems. Advantage is gained by drawing on the contribution of individuals in the network, but it is the inter-dependence *between* the members that gives the network its real potential to effect change.

ACTIVITY **4.2**

Network analysis

Choose an example of a network. It could be one that you belong to as a formal member or one with which you're familiar. Your example does not have to be work-based. A social network may be easier to analyse.

- *What is its core purpose?*

- *How is it organised? (Formal or informal, structured/loose, closed or open membership.)*

- *What/how do members contribute to it? What do they get out of it?*

- *Is it effective? What criteria would you use to make this judgment?*

Network purposes
Child and Faulkner (1998) have analysed the reasons for network creation and suggest that they can serve a variety of different purposes. These include:

- reducing uncertainty and providing support systems, enabling people to respond to change;

- providing information and releasing knowledge;

- enabling a speedy response to opportunities;

- providing greater flexibility (and perhaps reducing overheads);

- generating capacity via network members and associates;

- gaining access to resources and skills.

Whatever the underlying purpose, they are characterised by an ethos of *collective* responsibility to the overall aims of a network, as opposed to an *individual* accountability for managerial or professional performance. In the public sector, many networks created in the last decade have had the purpose of bringing about change by releasing the tacit knowledge of members. It is argued that by surfacing knowledge in this way the capacity of the network, and its ability to learn, is increased.

Why do some networks succeed and others fail?

Having identified why networks are created, can we also predict what makes them succeed or fail? Case studies of particular networks have examined the factors that appear to have an impact. These are summarised as follows.

- The purpose of the network needs to be clearly defined in order to enable it to focus. Defining the purpose may also allow members to consider the type of knowledge and learning that they are trying to generate. For example, is the purpose to transfer and spread explicit knowledge across the network or is it more concerned with tacit knowledge generation? Being clear on purpose will help the members to define how the network will function.

- Co-ordination and facilitation of the network, especially in its early phase, can be crucial. In her book *The Change Masters*, Rosabeth Moss Kanter (1983) showed how 'change agents' could mobilise networks of people to bring about development and change. Their purpose was not to seek personal power but to serve the organisation. These change agents effectively act as brokers, working to link others together. In more recent work they are sometimes referred to as boundary spanners (Bradshaw, 1999).

- For a network to survive there needs to be some perceived benefit of working together. If there is no added value, people are unlikely to engage. Cropper's (1996) work on collaborative networks in the public sector explored this notion of value. However defined, value engenders commitment and enables the network to continue, sometimes long after its initial purpose has been achieved.

- The linkages between members, their power in relation to each other and the quality of their relationships are all important. Within any network, roles, identities and meaning are constantly being interpreted and renegotiated. Resolving these uncertainties through successful interaction is an important part of network working.

- Trust and reciprocity in network relationships are desirable but notoriously difficult to achieve. Some writers take a critical perspective (Jarillo, 1988; Nohria, *et al.*, 1992), arguing that members are usually seeking to use the network for their own purposes. Others take a more optimistic view, seeing members as potential allies and being aware of their needs and goals. Ferlie and Pettigrew (1996) identified trust, reciprocity, understanding and credibility as skills and capabilities for successful networking.

- The form of a network, its membership and boundaries can all impact on its chances of survival. Some networks are managed from the centre whilst others have a radial form, connecting members directly with each other. A third form is more organic, enabling members to create multiple mini-networks. Social networking sites like Facebook would be an example of this. The form needs to be appropriate for the network's purpose for it to succeed.

Partnerships

All organisations need to learn in order to survive and public sector organisations are no exception. They operate in a crowded and complex environment. Plurality of provision means that they are far more market-driven than in the past. For example, private, voluntary/charity and public sector boundaries have become increasingly blurred in the provision of childcare, education, social care, health and prison services.

Added to this is the realisation that many of the key social and economic issues of the early twenty-first century are too challenging for a uni-professional approach. Consider, for example, childhood obesity, one of our current public health problems. Teachers, dieticians, community nurses, health visitors, social workers, doctors, midwives, school catering staff, primary care service managers, psychologists, sport and youth workers, and others, have opportunities to work with children, young people and their families. Developing an effective strategy to address the problem at a local level could involve all of these groups, together with local community and voluntary sector representatives.

It is partly because of this growing complexity that there has been a perceptible movement away from informal collaborations and networks to more formally constituted partnerships. What has emerged in the last few years has been a legal requirement to work in partnership. In many cases these are not just partnerships between organisations; increasingly they span two or more sectors. The example of children's services illustrates why formal partnership working has developed.

Partnership working in Children's Services

The Labour Government's policies on children's services initially focussed on early childhood, before extending to cover all children in pre-school, primary and secondary education. All local authorities had to develop a Children and Young People's Plan by 2006, appoint a Director of Children's Services and establish Children's Trusts by 2008. Inspection systems have been unified for all children's services and the full package of reform was set out in *Every child matters: Service change for children* and the *Children Act, 2004*. The *Ten year strategy for childcare, 2005,* specified a massive expansion of childcare services. The vision is that Children's Centres and Extended Schools will be at the core of the community, providing 'wrap around care' before and after school, integrated service delivery and holiday play-schemes. Dealing with the particular needs of older children is generating yet more policy.

The legislation and guidance provides the formal framework within which health, education and social care professionals must deliver. Multi-agency working is a given. They have to share information, assessment systems, strategic planning processes, funding and early intervention strategies. These statutory requirements also have to be supplemented at local level with plans to address the specific needs of neighbourhoods and communities. It is not a case of 'one size fits all'!

The diverse needs of different groups and populations, community engagement strategies, financial constraints, inspection requirements and the need to develop new types of workers are all issues that agencies must manage (Anning and Edwards, 2006).

Similar policy-driven models of partnership working have emerged to safeguard the interests of other vulnerable groups, such as older people and those with learning disabilities or enduring mental health problems. What they have in common is that partners are *required* to work together to deliver on political priorities; this is a statutory duty of partnership. Local Strategic Partnerships in England are the most obvious example.

This 'top down' approach is in sharp contrast to community-led partnerships of service users, carers and providers. Integrated service delivery may still be the goal but the means of achieving it are very different, as the example below illustrates.

CASE STUDY

Sheffield Children's Centre: A community partnership

The Sheffield Children's Centre is based on a co-operative model, with democratic delivery and control. Beginning as a community programme in a church hall it developed into a multi-faceted community provider, with a clear identity, employing a wide range of different types of worker. It is multicultural and multiethnic. The Centre has been described as 'a heartland of influence upon the wider community and a catalyst for change via its services and fundamental tenets of practice' (Broadhead, Meleady and Delgado, 2008, p3). Ordinary people have influenced social change based on local demands. Its work with families recognises the child's place in the family, and the community, as a starting point for service development. Community members who have benefitted from the Centre's services frequently progress to become workers.

But there are challenges, not least around the financial viability of the Centre. It is an independent provider and has to secure funding to remain viable. This has become increasingly problematic because of the political drivers to mainstream services. Despite being acknowledged as a centre of excellence, Sheffield Children's Centre is driven by a set of principles and practice which are very different from those of local and national government. Although there is no doubt that the Centre adds value to the community it has operated outside of some of the 'normal' organisational channels, making it vulnerable in the longer term.

(Broadhead, Meleady and Delgado, 2008)

Most of us would probably endorse the general commitment to partnership and more integrated working. As with networks, however, the real challenge is how to make partnerships work, so that genuine improvements in services are achieved for those who use them. Glasby and Dickinson (2008) suggest that it can be difficult to evidence real improvements from partnerships. Why might this be and what do we know about the dynamics of partnership working? To try to answer these questions, the next section of this chapter looks at the evidence emerging from recent research.

What helps partnerships to succeed?

The work of Armistead (2007) and Peck and Dickinson (2008) is particularly helpful in understanding what helps and hinders partnership working. They also explore the particular requirements of leaders working in cross-boundary contexts. Peck and Dickinson note that, in relation to partnership development, there has been an over-emphasis on the roles of senior managers within organisations, rather than on individuals developing relationships between partners.

Earlier work by Kanter (1989) suggested that the bulk of managers' efforts went into partnership creation – less than 10% of their input went on actually managing the resulting partnership. This is worrying, because the real work of partnership building commences once the formal arrangements have been put in place. The lack of a common operating framework, an imbalance in partners' power, value differences, ambiguous lines of authority and communication and different professional discourses can all have a detrimental impact on the way that a partnership functions. These core elements cannot be taken for granted; time needs to be invested in getting to a position of shared understanding and agreement. Even when this has been reached, the thorny issue of power will remain because partners are rarely equals.

ACTIVITY **4.3**

Power sources in partnerships

Power comes from a variety of sources, including:

- *control of financial and other resources;*
- *formal lead responsibility for the initiative;*
- *individual /organisational track-record or status;*
- *professional knowledge;*
- *accountability arrangements.*

Think about the power sources in a local service partnership. How would you categorize the power exerted by its key members? Can you rank the partnership members on the basis of their power? What impact does this have in the way the partnership functions?

A range of different partnerships have been reviewed by Coulson (2005). Whilst acknowledging that generalisations were difficult to make, the following observations were offered.

- Partnerships are dynamic organisations which need time to grow. They should be evaluated over time to judge whether they demonstrate the capacity to learn about their environment, and to learn from what works and what does not.
- In many situations partnerships represent progress but they are not a panacea. Partnership members still have loyalty to other organisations, for which they seek to minimize risk.
- Partnerships may not necessarily have the resources to do a proper job.
- Partnerships are not of equals – each member contributes something different. Some have a more central function than others; they are not all part of the solution and choices have to be made.
- Community representatives can be a source of key ideas and need to be actively involved in decision-making.

- Partnerships are for the long term but there may be conflict and members will come and go. This will have an impact on their ability to deliver on promises made.

Several writers have observed a tendency by partnerships to rely too heavily on very senior leaders. The assumption is that these people will be able to give authority and endorsement to the partnership. However, this can sometimes be a disadvantage in the longer term because of the competing demands on leaders' time. The membership of the partnership may become inconsistent and the focus on shared priorities lost.

More successful partnerships have occurred when genuine communities of practice have developed; local solutions to local problems have been worked out in collaboration with community stakeholders and middle and junior managers have worked to embed change, by working across the boundaries of their professions and organisations. Lead professionals can have a huge impact in this way and there are numerous examples of good practice on the internet. These partnerships may not always have formal legal status but there is perhaps a stronger commitment to achieving change.

Leadership skills and capabilities for partnership working and integrated services

This final section of the chapter reviews current thinking on the skills and capabilities required by leaders tasked with delivering integrated services in complex environments. These new contexts are challenging traditional models of leadership but there is as yet no general consensus on what might replace them.

Table 4.2 provides an overview of traditional and alternative views of leadership. Its author, Tim Simkins, concedes that:

> the alternative view embodies a less coherent set of ideas than does the traditional view. Different variables are emphasised by different writers in different ways and in relation to different contexts

> (Simkins, 2004, p6).

Table 4.2 Traditional and alternative perceptions of leadership

The traditional view	The alternative view
Leadership resides in individuals	Leadership is a property of social systems
Leadership is hierarchically based and linked to office	Leadership can occur anywhere
Leadership occurs when leaders do things to followers	Leadership is a complex process of mutual influence
Leadership is different from and more important than management	The leadership/management distinction is unimportant
Leaders are different	Anyone can be a leader
Leaders make a crucial difference to organisational performance	Leadership is one of many factors that may influence organisational performance
Effective leadership is generalisable	The context of leadership is crucial

Source: Simkins, 2004

Nevertheless you may find it helpful in understanding some of the issues raised in this section and in the review of leadership theory provided in Chapter 1.

Until relatively recently, much of the writing on leadership has tended to focus on single organisations. The growth of networks, collaborations and partnerships therefore raises an obvious question: Are additional or different skills and behaviours required for successful leadership in these contexts?

The dynamics and tensions inherent in this type of work have been the focus of research by Huxham, *et al.* (2000, 2005). They write about the ambiguity and uncertainty which can often characterise collaborations, emphasising the frequent lack of trust and highly political nature of much partnership working. Despite this, they suggest that there is reason to believe that certain models of leadership can make a positive difference. Without necessarily holding 'official' leadership authority, emergent and informal leaders can perform the essential work of binding the partnership together. They do this by creating a positive, open culture and involving and mobilizing others.

Weiss, *et al.* (2002) use the term 'leadership efficiency' in their research on partnerships between healthcare providers in America. They argue that good leadership is essential if the partnership is to work differently and achieve its goals. The efficient leaders' contribution is to stimulate synergy within the partnership. The ways in which they do this are summarised as follows:

- taking responsibility for the partnership;
- inspiring and motivating partners;
- developing a common language in the partnership;
- combining perspectives, resources and skills of partners;
- resolving conflict among partners;
- reframing partnership issues and being creative in finding new solutions;
- enabling differences to be voiced;
- fostering respect and trust.

Here in the UK, Alimo-Metcalfe and Alban-Metcalfe (2005, 2008) have undertaken extensive leadership research in the public sector. Focusing on transformational leadership behaviours and using data generated by their Transformational Leadership Questionnaire (TLQ) ©, they have identified the qualities most frequently associated with successful leadership. Their *Engaging TLQ* model (2008) reflects the new world of distributed and collaborative leadership. It can be applied to a range of complex environments. It does not assume that leaders will be all-powerful or that they will have formal authority over their colleagues. Instead it focuses on the need to develop strong personal and inter-personal behavioural skills in order to *engage* others and secure their commitment and motivation to the change process. For this reason it can be usefully applied to multi-agency working.

We explore issues raised by Alimo-Metcalfe and Alban-Metcalfe and others in Chapters 8 and 9.

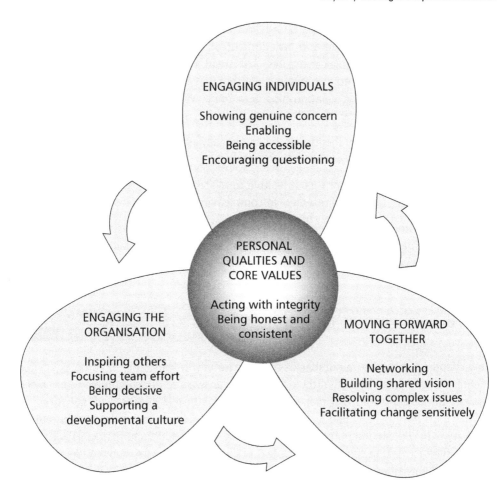

Figure 4.1 The engaging TLQ model

Source: Alimo-Metcalfe, B and Alban-Metcalfe, J (2008) reproduced with the permission of the authors

In situations where the required changes may be very complex, perhaps spanning many organisational systems, it becomes even more important to pay attention to relationships and process. Unfortunately what frequently happens instead is that there is an over-concentration on task and the identification of solutions to perceived problems.

Armistead, Pettigrew and Aves (2007) conducted an action enquiry with managers and leaders involved in partnership work. The range of partnerships represented in the focus groups covered many sectors but the participants had two things in common; all needed to work across organisational boundaries and influence others. For these people, leadership was about making partnerships effective and they identified four potential challenges to effectiveness: differing expectations, consensus building, dealing with conflict and performance.

The authors noted that, *we need to accept that there are multiple perspectives of how leadership manifests itself in multi-sectoral partnerships* (Armistead, Pettigrew and Aves, 2007, p225). Interestingly, although their participants felt that leadership in partnerships was *different*, their discourse was based on *traditional* conceptions of leadership and organisations. There was little acknowledgment of shared or distributed leadership as alternative models for complex structures. Armistead, *et al.* suggest that this points to a need for further research into distributed leadership models, how they work in partnerships and member organisations' relationships with them. What they were able to propose, however, were three guiding principles for leaders working in partnerships.

1 Individuals need to know themselves, be emotionally intelligent in their relationships with others and deploy behaviours that fit the context.

2 Individuals and organisations must be able to relate to other partners/ stakeholders, be vulnerable to influence and receptive to complementary forms of leadership.

3 Uncertainty and unintended consequences often result from interventions into complex systems. Organisations and partnerships therefore need to have faith in self-regulation and acknowledge the limits of policy-led regulation and political leadership.

C H A P T E R   S U M M A R Y

This chapter has covered a number of themes relating to leadership in complex environments. We have established that there are no easy answers to difficult problems or 'wicked issues'. Good leadership can make a difference to the effectiveness of networks and partnerships but it is only one factor. More importantly, the model of leadership required will vary with context and purpose. For this reason, good leaders and managers will always devote time to making sense of the context within which they are working. Being able to understand the issues, communicate them to colleagues and actively shape the response is what sense making is all about. Good leaders do this collaboratively and pay attention to their relationships with others in order to secure engagement and deliver sustainable change and improvement.

FURTHER READING

Broadhead, P, Meleady, C and Delgado, MA (2008) *Children, families and communities: Creating and sustaining integrated services.* Maidenhead: Open University Press and McGraw-Hill International.

Glasby, J and Dickinson, H (2008) *Partnership working in health and social care.* Bristol: Policy Press.

Peck, E and Dickinson, H (2008) *Managing and leading in inter-agency settings.* Bristol: Policy Press.

Chapter 5

From transition to transformation: Leading the management of change

Paul Close

Introduction

What do we know already about the 'management of change' in integrated practice, following the *Every Child Matters* agenda?

In 2006 The University of East Anglia reported on their evaluation of 35 Pathfinder Children's Trusts in the UK. Their findings identified desirable change processes that would take Trusts forward as:

> *. . . well-paced programmes that generate an incremental build up and expansion of change by example and persuasion at diverse levels with a ripple effect leading to a general sense of professional empowerment, motivation and positive momentum. . . . while recognising that change overall might be slow in terms of demonstrating measurable improvements, multiple small initiatives in the meantime provide the quick wins necessary to create the climate of trust and enthusiasm to bring reluctant partners on board. . . . People leading this process need change agent skills of a high order.*
>
> (UEA, 2006, p6)

By 2008 the Local Authorities Research Consortium (LARC), with data from both service users and staff, reported on the impact of this change process on three kinds of services (children with anti-social disorder (ASD), poor key skills 3 (KS3) attenders and looked-after children) in 14 local authorities. Their impact evaluation model took into account resource inputs to services, changes in behaviour and attitudes of staff to new ways of working, outcomes for service users, and embeddedness in how ways of working for these improved outcomes had become systematised. They found that:

> *the process of culture change seems well under way for staff, particularly where leadership and management is viewed in a positive light, and positive improvements are being recorded for individual children. However, increased workload and the need*

> *to develop a language of integration at local level are concerns for staff, and for children, more robust measures of emotional well-being are needed.*
>
> (Kinder, *et al.*, 2008, p4)

Add to this the question raised in Dunn's study (Dunn, 2009) about whether integrated working is really providing the *informal unobtrusive services and genuine one-to-one relationships valued by young people*, and we are beginning to get a complex picture indeed.

But this is all very big picture stuff. Where do we start in trying to understand some of these aspects of managing change in more depth? What *is* culture change, for example, and what are the high order change agent skills that those of us in leadership roles need to develop?

Chapter overview

This chapter presents and develops a conceptual framework for understanding the management of change in integrated services. It then explores the debate around whether new leadership skills and qualities are required for managing change in such complex contexts. Both the framework and subsequent debate reflect the leadership themes and dilemmas of complexity, culture and power examined in Chapters 4, 8 and 9.

Specifically, the chapter will:

- consider and unite professional and organisational perspectives on leading and managing change;

- draw practice examples from both early years and youth service contexts to reflect the *Every Child Matters* agenda;

- provide further opportunities for enquiring into issues of professional and organisational culture in integrated services, an area currently under-conceptualised in this field.

Understanding change in integrated services: A conceptual framework

The framework we will use for understanding and managing change unites professional and organisational perspectives by initially drawing from the work of two key commentators. This is then exemplified with case studies and practice examples from related service and professional contexts.

Bolman and Deal (2003), argue that we can understand change from four perspectives or *organisational frames*, each representing key traditions of organisational thinking. They call these frames:

1 human resource;

2 structural;

3 symbolic;

4 political.

Anning, *et al.* (2006) also see change from four perspectives, this time in terms of professional dilemmas facing staff seeking to develop integrated practice. They call these professional dilemmas:

1 interprofessional;

2 structural;

3 ideological;

4 procedural.

Bolman and Deal provide us with ways of thinking about change in the organisations we work in as professionals. Anning, *et al.* identify the actual professional tasks and issues we need to focus on when leading the management of change in integrated services.

Clearly, there is some overlap between these frames and dilemmas although both take a structural view of change. Their respective human resource frame and interprofessional dilemmas present a psychological view of change, and their symbolic frame and ideological dilemmas, a cultural view of change. Anning's procedural dilemmas, within, for example, developing new protocols in integrated practice, could be placed into a number of frames. Here, I have chosen the political frame because it is often during processes of decision making that issues of status and hierarchy come to the fore and need to be managed.

Thus we have four ways of thinking about change which we will call thinking psychologically; thinking structurally; thinking culturally, and thinking politically. Each of these ways of thinking will focus on a key challenge for managing change in integrated practice.

- *Thinking psychologically:* learning through role change.

- *Thinking structurally:* designing and managing multi-agency teams.

- *Thinking culturally*: questioning assumptions, values and beliefs around professional practice.

- *Thinking politically*: working through influence and negotiation.

Table 5.1 summarises the relationships between these organisational frames and professional dilemmas and the roles and tasks that those in leadership positions are charged with in order to manage change in each of these areas. This framework will form the basis for discussing the analysis and implementation of change in this chapter.

We will now explore what these ways of thinking about change mean in theory and practice.

Table 5:1 Organisational frames and professional dilemmas in integrated practice

Organisational frame (Bolman and Deal, 2003)	Professional dilemma (Anning, et al., 2006)	Leadership role	Change themes/tasks
Human resource *(thinking psychologically)*: support and participation	Interprofessional: learning through role change	Facilitator and coach	Transition and resistance: dealing with anxiety over role change and involving reluctant partners
Structural *(thinking structurally)*: formal role relationships	Structural: lines of accountability	Analyst and architect	Planning and design: designing and managing multi agency teams
Symbolic *(thinking culturally)*: the meaning and significance of work	Ideological: understanding and giving voice to values, beliefs and models of practice	Visionary and storyteller	Values and routines: examining cultural assumptions, 'storying' the service through role-appropriate behaviour
Political *(thinking politically)*: arenas of competing interests	Procedural: concerns about status, confronting disagreements about treatments and interventions in developing new procedures	Advocate and negotiator	Power and influence: influencing agendas, working through negotiation

Thinking psychologically about change

'Thinking psychologically' is about dealing with personal feelings during a change process. In an integrated setting these might be feelings of anxiety when moving into a new and unfamiliar role. Bolman and Deal call thinking psychologically the *human resource frame* because it derives from a tradition of organisational thinking from the 1960s called the Human Relations movement when employee well-being and participation started to receive attention in an organisational literature which had previously seen employees as cogs in a machine. Key to this personal view of change are the notions of *psychological transition* and *understanding resistance*.

Psychological transition

Bridges (1995) argues that we move through three stages of psychological transition in taking on change: *endings, neutral zone* and *new beginnings*. *Endings* mean letting go of something, recognising what's over and what isn't, what we've lost of our old way of life and what has remained the same. The *neutral zone* is the limbo between the old identity and the new, when an *inner sorting process* takes place in which old and no longer appropriate habits are discarded and newly appropriate patterns of thought and action are developed. The *new beginning* is typically an event we can recall that demonstrated to us that, psychologically, we had now made a new beginning as a result of this change. Bridges maintains that no real change can happen in an organisation without the staff who work in it making internal psychological transitions themselves. He also says that organisations are particularly poor at recognising and 'marking' psychological endings their staff have to make in their professional learning journeys.

A second, and well known, model of psychological transition comes from Hayes (2002), drawing from thinking in bereavement counselling (Kubler Ross, 1970). Hayes' model sees psychological transition in seven phases, from shock, to denial, depression, letting go and acceptance of reality, testing, consolidation, and ultimately, internalisation, reflection and learning.

ACTIVITY **5.1**

Think of a change in your personal or professional life that has required some form of psychological transition and that you'd be happy to discuss with a colleague.

Run through the experience in your mind using the Bridges and Hayes models where relevant and make some jottings.

What are the strengths and limitations of the respective models for analysing your experience?

Discuss your findings with a colleague.

The psychological transitions we have to make when moving into new professional roles can cause us to feel needy, incompetent and powerless. Here, the leadership roles to help us deal with these feelings are facilitator and coach, helping us to develop new skills, creating opportunities for involvement and providing psychological support.

Such support might involve discussions at an individual level about threats to professional identity and status, comfort zones and job satisfaction, pay, conditions and career trajectories. At team level these transitions might surface as concerns about supervision and training and development. In fact, the nature and appropriateness of supervision, particularly for professionals who may be seconded into multi-agency teams for fixed periods and then return to their 'parent' organisation, is very important. For example, Robinson, *et al.* (2005) tell the story of the demoralisation of a teacher who learns many new skills in a multi-agency team only to have them ignored and considered irrelevant on his return to his school because of inappropriate supervision and support.

A key aspect of skills development in integrated team working that can generate anxiety is the deployment of specialists and generalists.

Consider this scenario

ACTIVITY 5.2

You are a psychologist working as part of a multi-agency team. One of the good things about your team is the way that everybody learns from everybody else so that you all broaden your skills. However, you are gradually becoming aware that there is a downside to this, which is that your colleagues no longer seem to recognise that you have specialist expertise that they do not have. There has been a discussion of a particular case that you think requires specialist input from a psychologist, but your colleagues disagree and do not seem to feel that your view should have more weight than anybody else's. What do you do?

(Anning, et al., 2006, p21)

These issues are explored further in Chapters 6, 7 and 8.

Understanding and dealing with resistance

The second key concept in thinking psychologically about change is understanding and dealing with resistance. Airport recipe books about leadership and management see 'resistance' as simply something to be 'overcome' and offer endless advice on how to overcome resistance. The psychodynamic literature on change (Nevis, 1989) takes a more nuanced view, seeing resistance as an inevitable and ambivalent part of multi-directional energy in our make-up. The leadership task, therefore, is to understand more about where the resistance comes from in order to deal with it, and to connect with the driving forces in 'resistant people' as well as the restraining forces. Resistant people have values too!

Nevis (1989) identifies four drivers of resistance:

1 a desire not to give up something of value;

2 a misunderstanding of the change and its implications;

3 a belief that change does not make sense for the organisation;

4 a low tolerance of change.

The first three drivers can be talked through. The last is more difficult!

Block (2000) tells us we need to name resistance in order to externalise it. We now recount how a Sure Start multi-professional team created time during its regular meetings to name and tackle resistance amongst its own members.

CASE STUDY

Child and family referral in a Sure Start team

A Sure Start team comprising staff from Health, Social Work, Education and Clinical Psychology were developing a referral and allocation programme for children and families. Over a series of meetings the team sought to develop a whole team inter-agency focus on discussing the needs of families which had been referred, or had referred themselves to, Sure Start and suggesting ways in which support and advice could be offered and accessed to meet requirements. This, it was hoped, would provide an effective holistic system for looking at children's needs by developing innovative collective thinking, staff support and collective responsibility. However, in the first few meetings, considerable overt and covert resistance by team members was encountered, such as lack of attendance, continuing complaints about timing and frequency of meetings and rumours of staff questioning its rationale.

To address these concerns it was agreed that time for 'whole team evaluation and feedback' should be built into each meeting where professional concerns and anxieties could be aired in a 'safe' environment with agreed ground rules.

A number of issues emerged during these feedback sessions that were essential to the team's continued effective functioning. They included, for example, how far individuals felt able to disagree with or challenge other professionals and the opportunity for team members who had little experience of dealing with complex cases to discuss 'personal impact'. The feedback sessions also showed that individuals used the group for different purposes, for supervision, for endorsing referral judgements or as a means of gathering further information. Crucially, these sessions provided the opportunity to address the resistance by overtly recognising and valuing people's feelings about the emotional impact of dealing with complex family cases. As a result, attendance much improved over time and a much wider range of professionals contributed in meetings. As Woodhouse and Pengelly (1991) note an effective sentient group, within which to externalise and understand the anxiety and thus recover personal boundaries in the work, had been created (cited in Morrow, et al., 2005, p99)

Thinking structurally about change

Thinking structurally about change concerns planning, design, and formal role relationships. It draws from a tradition of organisational thinking that emphasises the rational and formal aspects of the change process. We all have to make service plans and there is an enormous variety of approaches to planning for change according to service context, just as there are planned change models in the literature. You have read in Chapters 2, 3 and 4 about the range of organisational and other forms of social systems that underpin integrated practice. It is worth being familiar with a range of planning approaches that different services use and the assumptions about the change process that inform them. The following example of planned change shows how a particular service area adapted a change model from the literature to introduce its own client-focussed planning process to improve the lives of young people with a disability.

CASE STUDY

Planned change in Manchester: Introduction of essential lifestyle planning

The learning disability service in Manchester wanted to introduce a version of person -centred planning called Essential Lifestyle Planning in all its services. It decided to use Kotter's eight steps model (Kotter, 1995) and extended it with further steps to include a greater emphasis on learning and consultation. As the implementation group recognised, the process was cyclical rather than linear as some stages had to be revisited at least once. Kotter's eight steps are asterisked within this adapted model and three examples of action taken at selected stages are described below.

Adapted model incorporating Kotter's eight steps.

- *Establishing a sense of urgency*.*

- *Forming a powerful guiding coalition*.*

- *Keep it on the agenda and build support.*

- *Learn from others.*

- *Learn from your own experience and consult with others.*

- *Create a vision*.*

- *Communicate the vision*.*

- *Empower others to act on the vision*.*

- *Plan for and create short term wins*.*

- *Consolidate improvements and produce still more change*.*

- *Institutionalise new approaches*.*

- *Continue to learn and review.*

A sense of urgency was created at the beginning of the process with an audit of current plans that showed the majority of them had no long-term objectives; too few related to developing relationships and most focussed on areas of self help and independence. This was checked out with focus groups of service users, parents and carers, community team staff and direct support staff and used to convince managers that change was needed.

A powerful guiding coalition was achieved through the formation of a cross functional team called the Planning and Development Group. An advert went out asking people who were interested to make contact and the development officer chose people who represented different parts of the organisation, with an emphasis on 'hands on' workers.

Others were empowered to act after staff on the planning and development group had tried the new planning approach out on themselves and colleagues, Ten team leaders were coached to implement an Essential Lifestyle Plan each with one person with a disability over six months.

(Sanderson, et al., 2002, p174)

Design factors are especially significant when considering the management and membership of multi-agency teams. How teams are designed will have implications for members' work deployment, contract status and impact on shared decision-making as well as lines of accountability. Change alters the clarity and stability of roles and relationships, creating confusion and unpredictability. You saw in Chapter 4 how complex systems thinking can help to explain some of these issues. The change task in thinking structurally is to understand the choices involved in the design of multi-agency service teams so as:

- to be able to plan and design the best team for a population and service;

- to carry out research into which team type is most effective, efficient or associated with certain phenomena such as staff turnover or client complaints;

- to enable teams to clarify how they are organised and the choices open to them for the future;

- to enable managers to understand and review teams for which they are responsible
  (Ovretveit, 1997).

Ovretveit also identifies five ways in which multi-agency teams might be organised to deliver services.

1 *The fully-managed team.* A team manager is accountable for all the management work and the performance of all team members.

2 *The co-ordinated team.* One person takes on most of the management and coordination work but is not accountable for the clinical work of individual team members.

3 *The core and extended team.* The core team members are fully managed by the team leader with extended team members (usually part-time) remaining managed by professional managers in their agency of origin.

4 *The joint accountability team.* Most team tasks, including leadership are undertaken by the team corporately, usually by delegating to individual members. Team members remain accountable to managers in their agencies of origin but in practice may not have strong management links with them.

5 *The network association.* This is not a 'formal team' as such but different professionals working with the same client group who meet together on a need to share common work/clinical interest. Each practitioner remains under the management of their own professional manager but decisions about client care are often formulated collectively at network meetings.

Ovretveit reminds us of eight management tasks essential to team functioning:

1 drafting job descriptions;

2 interviewing and appointing;

3 introducing the person to the job;

4 assigning work;

5 reviewing work (holding accountable);

6 annual performance appraisal and objectives setting;

7 ensuring practice quality, training and professional development;

8 disciplinary action.

Anning notes three lines of accountability that may be problematic in multiprofessional work:

1 line management;

2 coordination;

3 professional support.

ACTIVITY 5.3

With a partner, choose two of the team types described above. What issues could arise around management tasks and lines of accountability in each of these team types? Make some notes and then discuss your ideas.

Thinking culturally about change

'Culture' has variously been defined as *the way we do things round here* (Deal and Kennedy, 1982, p4) and *values, beliefs and taken for granted routines* (Schein, 1985, p1). Discussion of culture has a long history in the anthropological literature (see Bateson, 1999) but only really began to be appreciated in the organisational literature in the 1980s, when a world recession was demanding new ways of thinking about how to motivate (and control) employees in organisations beyond the rational *scientific* and *human relations* approaches of the past.

The problem with culture is that, because it is 'a taken for granted', we are often only made explicitly aware of our own values, beliefs and working routines when they are challenged. Atkinson, *et al.* (2002) for example, describe a social worker moving into education and finding the culture *very status conscious, where information was only shared between people at similar levels*. An early years' team saw themselves *like a butterfly, jumping about all over the place to create things and bring things together*, very different, they thought, *from organisations that look for a culture of routine, focus and agreed aims* (Atkinson, *et al.*, 2002, p130).

Thinking culturally about change means trying to understand the taken for granted values, beliefs and routines of our own and other professional groups and organisations and questioning them, as appropriate, when moving towards integrated working. This takes time. It is not amenable to quick tips and prescriptions, yet is vital to a deeper understanding of the factors that drive people to change or resist and to make decisions in integrated settings. Chapters 6, 7 and 8 explore these ideas further in the context of professional and organisational ways of working, beliefs and work practices.

We can use two ways of understanding culture and culture change in integrated services: through the notions of (a) models of practice and (b) occupational identity.

Models of practice

Anning, *et al.* (2006), in their study of five multiprofessional teams, found that each team operated according to 'dominant' and 'complementary' models of practice in understanding issues affecting children and young people. The Youth Justice team used a dominant *social/structural* model, with a complementary model of *individual impact*. The mental health team used a dominant *family/systemic* model with a complementary model of social deprivation. The nursery team used a dominant *individual needs* model with a complementary *holistic approach* model. The child development team used a *medical model* with a complementary model of *social/psychological support.* While there is not scope here to enter into a detailed discussion of these professional models of understanding (although these are further explored in Chapters 6 and 8), Anning, *et al.* make the point that professional identities don't necessarily give rise to universally fixed or shared explanatory models:

> the essence of internal variations in explanatory models suggest there are dilemmas for teams in achieving cohesion through negotiating shared practice models, while at the same time embracing and celebrating complexity and diversity.
>
> (Anning, *et al.*, 2006, p59)

These dominant and complementary 'models of practice' can remain at the implicit level in multiprofessional settings and creating opportunities to discuss the values and assumptions behind them can encourage both more reflective and more inclusive decision making. For example, in group validation sessions, the Anning study made social workers more aware of how they approached dilemmas through a professional problem solving approach at case level, while health colleagues brought a more systemic organisational emphasis.

And of course, in articulating our values behind models of practice we not only have to resolve differences of values between team members. We also have to take account of the values of service users and what that means for our practice engagement with them.

Consider this scenario.

ACTIVITY 5.4

A front line family worker was aware of the clash of values between members of the multi-agency team for which she worked. In discussions of cases, decisions about what services should be made available to users were hotly debated by those from former Social Services, Health and Education backgrounds. But a further clash of values was apparent when she dealt directly with service users. She was currently worried about a case of a lone parent father of a three year old with complex special needs. She had concerns over discipline techniques and an alleged lack of nurturing warmth. Some team members had previously felt that formal action should be taken with social services. And others had felt that this would destroy the chance of working collaboratively to resolve the problems.

How do you think the family worker can best voice her concerns in dealing with the different values of the team members and of the parent in responding to the rights and needs of the child within a family unit?

(Anning, et al., 2006, p23)

The concept of *models of practice* invites us to think about the 'taken for granteds' of what we have become as a result of our training and socialisation as professionals.

The concept of *occupational identity* poses the questions of 'what we are' and 'what we do' and, as can be seen from the discussion so far, this has the potential for being both clear, contentious and ambiguous, all at the same time! The following research summary offers a framework for thinking culturally about occupational identity.

Occupational identity: 'Thinking culturally' – a research summary

By thinking culturally, according to Martin (2002), we can approach the questions of occupational identity from three perspectives, which she calls *integration, differentiation* and *fragmentation.* This, in turn, is understanding what we share, understanding how we differ from other professional or organisational groups and understanding what is unclear or ambiguous about our cultural experience of the professional organisation in which we work. Martin maintains that at any one time we may experience all three perspectives simultaneously; while their relative importance may be strongly related to our position and vested interests in the organisation/professional group to which we belong.

Souhami (2007) uses these three perspectives to explore the experience of social workers making sense of their new occupational identity in a new Youth Justice team. From an 'integration' perspective, social work members of the Youth Justice team described themselves as part of a tightly cohesive team, bound together by shared aims, practices and values. From a differentiation perspective, they contrasted their work with more punitive orientations of other criminal justice agencies. At the same time from a fragmentation perspective, the 'normal ambiguity' of youth justice social work and difficulties of defining its 'functional territory' made the work of the team difficult to articulate.

If you wish to explore the literature on organisational and professional cultures in more depth, read Chapters 6 and 8 and also have a look at the work of Scott, *et al.* (2004) in a healthcare context. The first chapter gives a useful review of the organisational culture literature, the second, various tools and techniques that have been developed to understand culture.

ACTIVITY **5.5**

Think about any organisation or professional group of which you've been a member. What values, ways of thinking and doing things do you think were shared by the majority of members? Were there any sub cultures within that group or organisation which saw themselves as different from each other?

What was complex, ambiguous or unclear about your experience of the group or organisation?

So what do leaders actually *do* when 'thinking culturally' about their role in the change process? Bolman and Deal call thinking culturally the 'symbolic' frame, because, for leaders, thinking culturally is about the conscious use of symbolic action and behaviour to reinforce meaning and significance in the work. This might involve using personal example to convey values and norms, using ritual to reinforce values, or telling stories to convey culture. During an evaluation project I was struck, while sitting in on a series of Sure Start team meetings, by the regularity with which the team leader found opportunities at some stage or other of every meeting to 'tell the story of Sure Start' in different ways . His way of 'storying progress' and reinforcing cultural assumptions about what was important in the Sure Start ethos, clearly met a particular need of team members for cohesion during a period of extreme flux and transformation.

A key question around culture change and integrated services is whether multiprofessional teams can create new hybrid cultures of their own that inform their ways of working or whether they are destined to follow the culture of one dominant professional group. Atkinson, *et al.* (2002) think that new career paths offering increased mobility across professional groups are creating *hybrid professionals* who understand, and therefore are able to work effectively across, *the cultures, structures, discourses and priorities* of different professional groups (Atkinson, *et al.*, 2002, p225). This is, of course, a matter for debate and is discussed at various points throughout this book. It depends largely on the extent to which such 'hybrid professionals' feel they can *think politically* about change and influence agendas, to which we now turn.

Thinking politically about change

Once we have understood something of the psychology, structure and culture of the professional contexts that make up integrated services, how are we to influence agendas within them? Echoing Machiavelli, a lot of the organisational literature still tends to see politics in rather negative terms, as 'dirty tricks'. A good exception is the work of Buchanan and Badham (2008) who suggest that skilled 'positive' political behaviour is both essential *and* ethical if we are to champion the voiceless and implement change effectively.

In this section I will argue that professionals need to develop political understanding and skills in three interrelated areas in order to become more effective influencers.

- First, it is important to understand *our terms of reference* around political behaviour.

- Second, we need to become *more aware of power relationships within teams and between agencies* in our respective settings and, crucially, feel able to create safe contexts for open discussion of these relationships.

- Third, professionals working individually within the field of integrated services need to develop both tactical and strategic understandings of how they *work through negotiation* with other professional groups and organisations.

Political behaviour: Understanding our terms of reference

As we might have expected, the literature on power, politics and organisational change (e.g. Buchanan and Badham, 2008) tells us that politically skilled change agents have a range of high order skills which our evaluation studies expressed the need for in our chapter introduction.

Politically skilled change agents can read complex situations effectively, such as the shifting politics of various agencies and the changing motives and moves of key stakeholders. They understand their sources and bases of power, both personally and for others in the organisation and appreciate trade-offs that need to be made where necessary to achieve ultimately desirable goals. They are able to construct credible accounts for their actions, and have a behaviour repertoire that includes impression management and other influencing techniques. As Boddy and Buchanan (1992) put it, they are able to work *frontstage* in presenting rationally considered plans of action, while appreciating the *backstage* politics, culture and psychology of the situation that will enable those plans to be successfully implemented. In consequence, they develop the ability to construct and consistently maintain their reputation as skilled political players who act with fairness and integrity.

Developing personal awareness of power bases and influencing tactics

Table 5.2 shows some power bases and influencing tactics that we might use to manage change. The respective lists are in no particular order and are not meant to cross reference in any way.

Table 5.2 Power bases and influencing tactics

Power bases To develop?	Influencing tactics To use . . . or watch out for!
Coercive power	Impression management
Reward Power	Compromise
Legitmate power	Coalition
Expert power	Selective information
Referent power	Rule manipulation
	Scapegoating

Source: French and Raven, 1959 cited in Buchanan and Badham, 2008

Coercive power is the belief of followers that the change driver can administer penalties or sanctions that are unwelcome. Reward power is the belief that the change driver has access to valued rewards which would be dispensed in return for compliance with instructions. Legitimate power is the belief that the change driver has the formal authority to give instructions, and expert power is the belief that the change agent has superior knowledge relevant to the task at hand. Referent power means consciously developing ourselves as desirable role models in the perceptions of others who are then inclined to identify with and follow us. (Notice the word 'belief' used here. That we have a power base can be as much about perception as 'fact'!)

The influencing tactics mentioned are ones we might adopt ourselves or those that we might need to watch out for! Doubtless, as you reflect on your experience you will be able to think of more tactics yourself.

ACTIVITY **5.6**

Try to recall a situation where you saw someone use what you thought was politically skilled behaviour in an organisational setting to achieve a particular goal. What power bases or influencing tactics did they draw on? Would you say their behaviour was ethically sound in that it had a desirable outcome?

Developing awareness of power relationships at interprofessional team level

At multiprofessional team level, it is important to surface implicit assumptions about status and hierarchy early on so team contributions can be maximised. For example, Miller, Freeman and Ross (2001) in their study of six clinical teams, found that individuals from different professional groups brought very different assumptions about *communication* and *learning* when joining integrated teams. Social workers and health visitors felt communication should be *complex and rich* and all contributions to learning were of equal value regardless of status. Medics and mental health professionals felt, respectively, that communication should be managed by the team leader only and that it should be brief. Both medics and mental health professionals believed that they could only learn from those of equal or senior status. We explore such issues further in Chapter 8.

Developing awareness of power relationships at agency level

At inter-agency level, a mechanism for recognising the location of power has been identified by Loxley (1997) who poses some sharp questions for members of stakeholder groups seeking to discuss and clarify their terms of reference and terms of engagement. Barret and Keeping (2005) supplied the examples (see Figure 5.3).

Creating safe arenas where such political questions can be discussed openly can lead to better longer term judgements about whether a specific partnership is destined for 'collaborative advantage' or 'collaborative inertia', (Huxham and Vangen, 2006), a concept examined in more detail in Chapter 3.

Working through negotiation

We saw, when *thinking psychologically* about change, that sharing specialist skills and expertise can be something of a dilemma in integrated working. Professionals working with organisations in the field need to understand more of the processes of working through negotiation, if they are to be more effective at sharing their skills and expertise with other colleagues, Individuals working with organisations are not only purveyors of professional skills. They are also ambassadors for their service, and *organisational consultants* in the sense of needing to read the politics and practice context of the organisations with which

Table 5.3 Thinking politically about partnerships

Question	Example
Who defines the problem?	Does everyone make a contribution to problem identification or is this the province of one professional group?
Whose terms are used?	Is everyone able to communicate through the use of mutually agreed and commonly understood terms or does one professional language predominate?
Who controls the domain or territory?	Is control always mutually negotiated, does it vary in accordance with which professional knowledge and expertise best fits the particular needs of the service user at a given point in time or does control sit predominantly with one professional group?
Who decides on what resources are needed and how they are allocated?	Are resources issues mutually agreed, determined in accordance with varying professional contributions or dictated by one professional group?
Who holds whom accountable?	Is it assumed that one professional group will have overall accountability or is everyone's accountability recognised?
Who prescribes the activity of others?	Is there a joint agreement regarding the activities of those involved or does one professional group prescribe activities?
Who can influence policy makers?	Does one professional group have a stronger influence than others in lobbying policy makers?

Source: Loxley, 1997, cited in Barret and Keeping, 2005, p23

CASE STUDY

Working with Isabel and staff

Isabel, a four year old diagnosed with autistic spectrum disorder, has some behavioural and communication difficulties. She has spent over a year in a private nursery where the staff are experienced and trained in this field. With the support of a key worker, she has been fully included in the life of the nursery, with few adaptations. The visiting SEN teacher suggested that Isabel would benefit from the use of a timeline and the staff were willing to try this strategy. However, on reflection, after a period of time, staff realised that Isabel was not benefiting from the timeline, and it was making her stand out as different to all the other children. The position of the timeline was also seen as exclusive as it highlighted to the other children and the parents that Isabel was a problem and was special. The nursery manager telephoned the visiting SEN teacher and explained that she was going to remove the timeline from the wall. There was a rather heated discussion. When the SEN teacher returned, the situation was again discussed. The manager pointed out that they worked with Isabel every day and knew best, but the SEN teacher felt affronted that her idea had been rejected. After that point, no other children with SEN were referred to that nursery and the nursery manager lost confidence in local SEN support services.

(Jones and Pound, 2008, p147)

What processes of 'working though negotiation' might have avoided this situation developing?

they contract, however informally, while operating in process as well as expert and diagnostic consultant roles (Schein, 1998).

New leaders in learning organisations?

So far, our conceptual framework has helped us explore four key leadership functions in the management of change, with examples from service contexts. These have been *providing support and gaining involvement* (thinking psychologically), *planning and designing change* (thinking structurally), *questioning taken for granted values and assumptions* (thinking culturally) and *influencing and negotiating agendas* (thinking politically). We could argue, though, that any leader within a single organisation needs to operate in all these functions effectively. What then, is different about leading change in integrated practice?

This final section proposes that there are special characteristics of integrated practice that require new emphases within existing leadership roles and skills, and that these new emphases require in turn particular forms of support and development.

What, then, do these 'new leaders', as we shall call them, need to be able to do?

New leaders are bridgers rather than bonders

A recent paper from the National College of School Leadership on *collaborative leadership* for leaders of extended schools coined the phrase *bridging rather than bonding* to describe a key skill required by professionals assuming such roles (Coleman, 2007, p49). In essence, it argued that, while a key leadership role for those in single organisations is bonding or developing cohesive relationships by bringing people together as far as possible towards a single purpose, the role of an extended schools leader is bridging the various professional cultures to find common ground. This, of course, requires a sophisticated understanding of a range of professional cultures and of a *shared* visioning process.

New leaders draw from the principles of 'learning organisations'

In the 1990s two leading commentators, Argyris (1992) and Senge (1994) developed a number of key elements which they felt were essential to what they called *learning organisations*. Two of these elements of particular relevance to new leaders in integrated services are: *double loop learning* and *systems thinking*. Double loop learning was the habit of bringing to the surface and reflecting on tacit assumptions behind ways of doing things, our thinking culturally. Systems thinking brought a no-blame perspective to working in complex environments as we are all part of a single system and no one can stand outside the cause of their problems. This might seem something of a paradox when, for example, finger pointing begins in child abuse cases but new leaders have to understand collective accountability. As Senge predicted, *learning organisations of the future will make key decisions based on shared understandings of interrelationships and patterns of change* (Senge, 1994, p204).

Both Argyris's and Senge's writings have stood the test of time and are worth exploring further. Argyris is particularly strong on breaking through what he calls *defensive routines* in organisations and Senge has much of practical use to contribute on *shared visioning* processes.

New leaders are self–authoring

Paton and Vangen (2004) used the phrase self-authoring when they discussed the needs and characteristics of new leaders of multi-agency teams with the advent of Children's Trusts. They argued that the more complex and fast changing an environment becomes, the more change takes place at the middle of the organisations where professionals are interacting with, and having day to day contact with, children and families, and so the less leaders in the middle can expect to rely on 'strategic direction' from the top, in the traditional sense (see also Chapter 4). New leaders therefore need to be more self-initiating, self-managing and self-evaluating as complexity grows. The paradox here is that the more such leaders have to deal with change the more certain they need to be of their own identity as leaders, independently of changing roles, relationships and commitments. In other words, self- authoring in rapid change requires more internal awareness of self, in addition to the more usually understood external awareness and behavioural repertoires that we expect of leaders. Chapters 6 and 7 explore many aspects of personal development, authenticity and growth in relation to leaders of integrated services.

New leaders have to work with (even more) ambiguity

Recurrent themes running through much of the literature on integrated practice are the need for a common language and clear and unambiguous communication. When are we going to drop the rationalist view that in complex environments there is some ultimate clarity out there and everything can be resolved? This is not a cry for deliberate obscurity, but recognition that new leaders should be gaining deeper understanding of the reasons for the inevitable ambiguity of integrated practice, rather than becoming frustrated by the lack of clarity. A good understanding of the ambiguity and ambivalence of any change process involving complex relationships makes for better judged actions. Language and communication are inherently ambiguous, culturally constructed concepts. All leaders have to work with ambiguity, *new leaders* in integrated practice even more so.

Supporting and developing new leaders will take time

Understanding and working with the cultures, structures, discourses and priorities of various agencies takes time, and needs sophisticated support. Leaders in multi-agency settings have to operate effectively, with limited support in highly complex and unstructured contexts. They need the capabilities to work with many cross-cutting expectations and strong value commitments. Developing shared vision and involving other agencies is more problematic when working in dispersed and locally based teams. This calls for new combinations of ongoing professional development such as:

- mentoring;
- reflective journaling of critical incidents;
- the use of organisational consultants to help multi-agency teams develop complex projects;
- an emphasis on psychological processes of change.

These activities are all being used in the two integrated practice leadership programmes currently being run by the National College for School Leadership: *the National Professional*

Qualification for Integrated Centre Leadership (NPQICL) and *the Multi Agency Team Development programme* (MATD). What is still under-emphasised in such programmes is political skill in influencing the agendas that we discussed above.

The workload involved in integrated practice was seen as problematic in the LARC report (Kinder *et al.*, 2008) that opened this chapter. Effectively dealing with new forms of stress generated by potential role conflict and role ambiguity in multi-professional environments is clearly of utmost importance. What we need here is a pooling of knowledge from the various professional and organisational literatures of how to deal with the demands of stressful complex interagency situations through various forms of supervision and support. From the organisational literature, we might draw ideas from what can be done strategically to raise awareness, remove stressors and develop senses of belonging in organisations (Sutherland and Cooper, 2000). From the professional literature we might learn from what can be done on an individual level in education contexts to build resilience, by, for example, reflecting on thoughts, feelings and actions around critical incidents through the *coping triangle* approach of cognitive behavioural therapy work (Hayes, 2006). Chapters 8 and 9 consider more dilemmas and difficulties involved in integrated practice.

In short, then, leadership in integrated services calls for sophisticated understandings of change. It also requires imagination in how we bring what we already know about effective leadership to such complex contexts, where strong values and subtle influence need to coexist.

C H A P T E R   S U M M A R Y

Building up the underlying psychological capacity for leadership in integrated practice will take time. It involves more than acquiring various analytic frameworks and inter personal polish because what has to be reconfigured is the self that is acquiring these skills.

(Paton and Vangen, 2004, p7)

This chapter has presented and explored four ways of thinking about managing change in integrated practice, which are firmly embedded in traditions of organisational theory and have clear application to practice in *'learning organisations'*. They were: *thinking psychologically, thinking structurally, thinking culturally* and *thinking politically.* It has also made some proposals about the skills and development needs of leaders in these complex environments which are further explored in Chapters 8 and 9.

The title of this chapter *from transition to transformation* describes a change process not a leadership style. Collaborative, rather than transformational leadership, as mentioned here and discussed elsewhere in this book, is needed for integrated practice. And collaborative leadership requires political savvy and an understanding of professional cultures and organisational structure if we are each to make the *psychological transitions* as professionals to transform services for adults, children and families.

Anning, A, Cottrell, D, Frost, N, Green, J and Robinson, M (2006) *Developing multi professional teamwork for integrated children's services.* Maidenhead: Open University Press.

Barrett, G and Keeping, C (2005) The processes required for effective interprofessional working. In Barrett, G, Sellman, D and Thomas, J (eds) *Interprofessional working in Health and Social Care: Professional perspectives.* London: Palgrave.

Bolman, LG and Deal, TE (2003) *Reframing organisations: Artistry, choice and leadership,* 3rd edn. San Francisco: Wiley.

Buchanan, D and Badham, R, (2008) *Power, politics and organisational change,* 2nd edn. London: Sage.

Martin, J (2002) *Organisational culture: Mapping the terrain.* Thousand Oaks, California: Sage.

Raynor, A (2004) *Individual schools: Unique solutions. Tailoring approaches to school leadership.* London: Routledge.

Scott, T, Mannion, R, Davies, H, Marshall, M (2004) *Organisational culture and healthcare performance.* Abingdon: Radcliffe Press.

Anning and Bolman and Deal provide the theoretical base and conceptual framework for this chapter. Martin and Scott provide good analyses of organisational culture and Buchanan and Badham of organisational politics in a managing change context. Raynor's book on school leadership brings an engaging complexity theory perspective (explored in more detail in Chapter 4) to address the leadership issues identified in the second part of this chapter.

Chapter 6

Ethics, vision and values: The challenge of spirituality

Bernard Moss

Introduction

This chapter explores the fundamentally important issues of ethics, vision and values in people-work practice. It recognises the challenging context of contemporary consumerism that can undermine people-work's value-base, and the pressures upon people-workers to become dispirited functionaries. The challenge of Integrated Practice to provide a seamless service requires a level of organisational collaboration that many may find daunting, but the benefits for those who use services are considerable. There is a particular opportunity therefore for leaders and managers to create and sustain the vision of best practice, based on sound ethics and values, in order to make Integrated Practice a reality.

Chapter overview

This chapter:

- discusses some of the tensions and dilemmas facing leaders, managers and people-workers in an intensely consumerist society;

- discusses ways in which people who use services may also be captivated by consumerist values and resist the value-base of those seeking to help and support them;

- suggests ways in which the contemporary understanding of spirituality and Spiritual Intelligence (SQ) provides signposts and ways forward to ensure that the spirit of people-work is maintained and celebrated.

Ethical tension and dilemmas facing people-workers

Without a vision, the people perish

In many ways this ancient apothegm (from the book of Proverbs 29:18) lies at the heart of all leadership, especially in people services. Organisations can get so caught up in the everyday things that a sense of direction and purpose can easily be lost. It then begins to feel, for those 'at the sharp end', that it is rather like going endlessly round the roundabout and never heading off in the right (or for that matter, any) direction. Leadership, as was argued and discussed in Chapter 1, is about having the vision to see where the organisation needs to be heading, and to enthuse and motivate the workforce to share their energies to move together in that direction, in order to achieve the agreed objectives. Leadership therefore is also about helping others 'catch the vision' of what the organisation is all about so that everyone feels they have a role to play.

The famous story of the janitor at the NASA Space Centre illustrates this well. When asked by President JF Kennedy about his job, he replied *I am helping to get men into space, Mr President* (cited in Gilbert, 2005, p14). Here was someone whose work was very mundane, where the temptation must have been to limit the scope of the vision to the area just in front of his rhythmically sweeping broom. But instead he saw his role as part of a greater whole, and took pride in being one cog in a complex machine. Many managers would be deeply envious of an organisation that evoked that depth of loyalty and shared vision in all its employees.

ACTIVITY 6.1

Think for a moment about an organisation you are familiar with, where you had what some felt was a very minor role to play – perhaps a clerical or administrative assistant; or a cleaner; or a shelf-stacker in a supermarket. Did you have any understanding of what the organisation as a whole was trying to achieve? Did anyone explain to you how the role you were playing helped the organisation fulfil its objectives? Or did you see your work as 'just a job' with the pay packet at the end of the week or the month? What difference would it have made to you if someone had explained that to you?

But vision can be a complex phenomenon. The world's dictators have had their dreams and visions of what society might look like, and often the cost of that dream has been the lives and happiness of millions of people whose well-being, and sometimes their very lives, have been sacrificed on the altar of one dictator's ruthless ambition. Vision is not enough: there has to be a complex inter-relationship between ethics, vision and values, where each informs, enriches and critiques the other. This chapter therefore explores some of these complex but fundamental relationships in people-work, and the role of leadership in trying 'to get it right' at both the personal and organisational level.

If this is true at an organisational level it is more so when organisations either wish to, or are compelled to work collaboratively. The Integrated Practice agenda has at its heart the belief that the needs and best interests of people who require various types of help and support to deal with the challenges and complexities of living, will best be served by people-work organisations 'pulling together'. Rather than service users having to navigate provision from agency 'x' to support group 'y' and then on to government department 'z', people should be able to benefit from a seamless service where the controlling interest of everyone should be about how to deliver the most effective and relevant service. The significance and importance of this has already been explored in earlier chapters, but it is worth pausing for a moment to appreciate the significance of this approach.

ACTIVITY 6.2

Think of an example where you have tried to obtain a particular service, or some help, for yourself or for someone close to you. Have you had the experience of feeling you were being 'fobbed off'? Have you ever had to trail round different agencies seeking the help you require? The trailing round could be on foot, or on the telephone or through a range of electronic sources, of course. How did all of this make you feel? Did you reach the point of frustration where you felt that these agency workers were really only interested in maintaining their own position and status, rather than really trying to help you obtain the comprehensive help and support you needed?

It is all too easy perhaps for people who work in various helping agencies to lose sight of what it must feel like to be on the receiving end of this fragmented approach to health and social care provision, especially when people are unwell, vulnerable and bewildered. The drive towards integrated care is a serious attempt to address these important issues. But before such collaborative practice can be achieved, there needs to be a clear understanding on the part of each agency about what is its core purpose, what it can and cannot do, and what are the legal and professional boundaries that both enable and constrain its engagement with others. Integrated practice is not aiming to achieve a mishmash of ill-conceived though well-intentioned 'do-gooding'; on the contrary, it is seeking to clarify how the skills, knowledge and expertise of various organisations can be responsibly and effectively pulled together for the benefit of people in need.

One of the litmus tests of any organisation, therefore, is the extent to which it can articulate the basic values that underpin and drive its work. These values will determine the range of activities and behaviours that the organisation will feel comfortable in pursuing, as well as the activities and behaviours that will be eschewed. Handy (1995) captures this well in his discussion about how important it is in any organisation that managers and workers have a shared sense of meaning and purpose. He addresses the all-too-common phenomenon of 'anomie' and alienation in the work-place: workers and managers feeling undervalued, wandering somewhat purposelessly through the tasks in hand, on the fast road to emotional and professional 'burnout'. He illustrates this with his reaction to an open air sculpture in Minneapolis by Judith Shea called *Without words*. It consists of three shapes, one of which is a bronze raincoat standing upright but empty. He comments:

> *To me that empty raincoat is the symbol of our most pressing paradox. We were not destined to be empty raincoats, nameless numbers on a payroll . . . if that is to be its price, then economic progress is an empty promise. There must be more to life . . .*

> *The challenge must be to prove that the paradox can be managed and that we, each one of us, can fill that empty raincoat.*
>
> (Handy, 1995, p2)

Handy goes on to comment further:

> *Those who talk about vision as essential for the future of an enterprise are right, but it has to be the sort of vision that others can relate to. Not many in the lower realms of the organisation can get excited by the thought of enriching the shareholders. 'Excellence' and 'quality' are the right sort of words, but they have been tarnished by repetition in too many organisations . . . We need to believe in what we are doing*
>
> (Handy, 1995, p265)

In people-work that sentiment, or value-base, may seem self-evident. After all, the Codes of Conduct and values statements of many helping professions set out very clearly the dignity and value of each individual whom the agency is seeking to help and support. The whole thrust of anti-discriminatory practice has a similar value-base. Negative discrimination and oppression need to be recognised and challenged *precisely because* they undermine this basic principle of the dignity and value of each individual. People-work, in all its varied forms, has a vital role to play in counteracting the 'empty raincoat syndrome'. The current drive towards a personalisation agenda is, at one level at least, a clear commitment to the principle that the individual person must be centre-stage in the planning, as well as in the implementation, of care services.

One very powerful way of getting to grips with the values that underpin the work of various helping agencies is to dip into their Codes of Practice, and to look for the similarities and differences of emphasis in their approach. These codes are important not least for the way in which they set out what the public should expect to receive from the agency: they provide a quality benchmark against which service delivery can be measured. (for a more detailed discussion of Codes of Practice, see Beckett and Maynard, 2005; Moss, 2007; Woodbridge and Fulwood, 2004).

For the purposes of our immediate discussion, however, we will dip briefly into three codes to see what it said about working with other colleagues. The professional code for nursing practice requires its members, in caring for patients and clients, *to co-operate with others in the team* (www.mnc-uk.org). The General Medical Council requires its members *to work with colleagues that best service the patient's interest.* (GMC 2004 cited in Woodbridge and Fulwood, 2004). The General Social Care Council's Code of Practice for social workers requires social workers *to ensure that relevant colleagues and agencies are informed about the outcome and implications of risk assessments* (www.gscc.org.uk. Section 4.4).

A cursory reading of these three excerpts may kindle a sense of optimism for integrated practice: they all talk about the importance of *working with* other colleagues. But at this point we need to ask whether they all mean the same thing even when they use similar language, and whether the boundaries drawn in practice by each agency pre-determine who are colleagues and members of the team, and who are not. We need to ask whether in fact we have a number of agencies who are 'divided by a common language'.

Select two codes of practice – one of them should be from an agency you are very familiar with. You may work for it or have had a practice placement in it. The second code should be from an agency with which you are far less familiar. This is an exercise about comparing and contrasting the two codes.

Using two columns, jot down what each agency says in its code about its aims, purpose and values.

What language does it use to talk about the people who come to it for help, support or treatment? (e.g. clients; patients, service users, enquirers, etc.)

What does each of them say about collaborative working?

Having prepared your two lists, what would you identify as the potential for developing collaborative practice?

What would be the dilemmas or obstacles?

Services users and contemporary consumerist values

In our discussion so far we have focussed on the values that an agency sets out as its benchmark for its service delivery. We have touched on the challenges for leadership and management in helping everyone involved to catch the vision of what the agency exists for, and to work to these values. We have highlighted the importance of workers feeling that they are playing a full part in helping the agency to fulfil its aims and objectives.

People-work agencies, however – be they medical or social – do not work in a vacuum. Inevitably they will hear the 'music' of contemporary society, and will be affected by its melodies, dissonances and rhythms. Indeed, both through their individual members, and sometimes as organisations, they all participate in a variety of ways, (through political parties, faith communities, media and creative arts, pressure groups; special interest groups, and as consumers) and contribute to the development and richness of this music. Organisational values and personal values are sometimes in sharp counterpoint; and societal music can sometimes profoundly affect the ways in which helping agencies see themselves and those whom they seek to help. There can be no clearer example of this than the impact of the strident and demanding melodies of consumerism.

Zygmunt Bauman (2007a; 2007b) has coined the phrase *liquid modernity* to capture some of the profound changes to society brought about by the power of the consumerist culture. Here, only those who can and do purchase are valued; those who cannot or do not, are marginalised. Bauman suggests that:

> *The society of consumers devalues durability, equating the 'old' with being 'outdated', unfit for further use and destined for the rubbish tip. It is by the high rate of waste, and by the shortening of the time distance between the sprouting and the fading of*

desire, that subjectivity fetishism is kept alive and credible despite the endless series of disappointments. The society of consumers is unthinkable without a thriving waste-disposal industry. Consumers are not expected to swear loyalty to the objects they obtain with the intention to consume.

(Bauman, 2007a, p21)

The significance of this analysis is that it encompasses each and every one of us, whether we are salaried people-workers, well-paid managers or struggling in the land of '*un*' as *un*employed 'beneficiaries' of the welfare benefits system. Our value is measured by our capacity to consume and the credit culture, for all its current uncertainty and chaos, buys heavily into this scenario, whether we are on benefits or a good salary. Bauman's analysis suggests that the consumer culture is all pervasive: people would rather build up mounting debts than go without some of the goods that continue first to entice, then to disappoint, and then to drive us onwards towards the latest 'better' replacement.

The reason for setting the scene with the help of Bauman's analysis is to highlight the starkness of the contrast between traditional social work/ social care/ people-work values and the value base of the society in which we all now operate. How do we respond to the growing tendency in a range of helping agencies to regard people who come to them as 'customers'? The ethics, vision and values of the various people-work agencies that seek to collaborate and work together jointly for the benefit of those people entrusted to them, or who come to them for help and support, are in stark contrast to the societal values that impregnate the very fabric and DNA of all our daily living. And this presents people-workers with a profound dilemma: to what extent do they collude with the consumerist culture in the work they undertake with people who use their services? How do we respond, for example, to the claim that a pair of designer jeans or trainers are a vitally important call upon the household budget of a family living on state benefits? What happens when, with the personalisation agenda, someone chooses to spend their allocated resources on fulfilling the demands of a consumerist society because it makes them feel good for once, rather than meeting some of what the professional helpers deem to be their real 'needs'? What happens when some people might respond to Handy's 'Empty Raincoat' with a shrug of shoulders, and simply say, *just go and buy another raincoat!*

These important questions have developed an even greater poignancy with the recent almost catastrophic turmoil in worldwide financial markets. Household names in the world of banking and finance have had to be rescued, and the perhaps naïve assumption that consumerism will see us through has been radically challenged. The feared 'R' word – recession – has begun to be uttered by the pundits. Mega-bonuses are now coming under close scrutiny as millions of ordinary people begin to feel the pinch. Yet to people who are accustomed to living on or below the poverty line in the UK, let alone those in other countries whose drop into starvation hangs daily on a thread, all of this must seem unreal when even a fraction of an ordinary person's income in the UK would represent for them and their families untold riches. Poverty – and affluence – may well be relative, but they nevertheless highlight the values of a society, and how individual members of it are regarded. Ironically it may be such straightened times that enable us to reassert the value-base that underpins people-work.

These are profound issues and take us to the heart of the challenge for leaders who are seeking to develop, sustain and operationalise a values-based vision for their organisations. Neimeyer (2002) expresses this powerfully when he argues that:

> We are faced with the onerous task of revising these taken-for-granted meanings (and to ask whether they are) adequate to the changed world we now occupy. Simultaneously we must deal with urgent questions about what this loss signifies, whether something of value might be salvaged from the rubble of the framework that once sheltered us, and who we are now in light of the loss or losses sustained. All of this questioning plays out on levels that are practical, existential and spiritual.
>
> (Neimeyer, 2002, p38)

Neimeyer's principal field of study is in grief and loss, where he has developed a theoretical framework called 'meaning reconstruction' to help people find their ways through into a revised world view following the loss of a significant relationship. His comments nevertheless have a wider relevance and pertinence to our discussion about vision and values. In the 'liquid modernity' of a consumerist society, the challenge to leaders in people-work organisations is to engage creatively in this new meaning-making dialogue that will enable them and their organisations to reinterpret their ethics, vision and values in ways that are relevant to contemporary practice.

ACTIVITY 6.4

What's in a name?

There has been a noticeable trend in recent years to change the name of organisations in order better to reflect their aims, values and role in society. This can be seen in both statutory agencies, (Social Services Departments, for example, have gone through a re-naming process) and in the not-for-profit sector several charitable organisations have chosen new names.

Make a list of some of the organisations that have changed their names. Can you identify the different reasons for these changes? What aspects of 'meaning-making' have been at work? How far are they in response to the challenge of liquid modernity?

The challenge of contemporary spirituality

It is at this point that the contemporary debate around the theme of spirituality has some important things to say. The main strands of this debate have been discussed elsewhere (Moss, 2005), but one theme running through the countless attempts at definition is that of meaning-making. Whether one approaches the topic from a religious or a non-religious direction, the power of the meaning-making paradigm is clear: it helps us to articulate what it means to be human, individually and in relationship to other people. Therefore, having a vision about the direction in which an organisation could or should be heading is in itself an act of meaning-making. In doing so the leader is giving shape and direction to the values and vision for the organisation and for all those who work within it.

It is significant that the concept of spirituality has been adopted by some key players in the field of leadership and management. The leaders of the Institute for Management Excellence, Barbara Taylor and Michael Anthony, have articulated some basic principles of spirituality in the workplace which help to ensure that the organisation has a strong values-based vision and purpose. Some of the themes they cluster together under this heading include: creativity, respect, vision, partnership, energy, flexibility, communication and fun, and the capacity to find and express oneself. These principles, they argue, lie at the heart of what makes an organisation successful – and this success includes profitability.

There are close links here with the concept of Spiritual Intelligence, as expounded by Zohar and Marshall (2000). Building on the earlier concept of IQ and Emotional Intelligence (EQ or EI), which is explored in more detail in Chapter 7, these authors suggest that Spiritual Intelligence (SQ) is the most fundamental and important of the three. They argue that:

> *Unlike IQ which computers have, and EQ which exists in higher mammals, SQ is uniquely human . . . and the most fundamental of all three. It is linked to humanity's need for meaning . . . [and] is what we use to develop our longing and capacity for meaning, vision and value. It allows us to dream, and to strive. It underlies the things we believe in and the role our beliefs and values play in the actions that we take, and the shape we give to our lives.*

(www.dzohar.com)

> *Indeed, it is our SQ that gives us an ultimate security upon which we can base our capacity to be innovative and creative.*

(Moss, 2004, p39)

Here then perhaps is a way forward for our discussion about ethics, vision and values in people-work in general, and in the integrated practice that is being explored in this book as a whole, set as it all is within the complex context of liquid modernity that has been briefly discussed at the outset of this chapter. Spirituality and Spiritual Intelligence linked with the framework suggested by Taylor and Anthony offers leaders and managers, as well as those who work in their organisations, a paradigm for moving forward.

ACTIVITY 6.5

The term 'spirituality' can be somewhat off-putting to some people, perhaps because of its links with religion. But the concept of 'Spiritual Intelligence' we have just introduced takes us into important territory.

Using the brief introduction we have just provided, spend some time reflecting on your own area of work and your organisation (or one that you are familiar with). In what ways does this concept of Spiritual Intelligence help you understand more clearly the values that underpin your work, the role of leadership and management, and how most effectively to respond to those who come to you for help, treatment or support?

It is helpful at this point, however, to remind ourselves about the key aspirations of integrated care. Pierson (2008) captures it well when he says:

Overall, the strategy around integrated care is designed to establish effective joint working between all practitioners involved in delivering care – not just on the health side (trusts and primary care trusts) but also social care agencies and voluntary and community organisations. The intention is to create the 'seamless pathway' through the health and social care system, offering a personalised care-plan for those most at risk . . .

(Pierson, p147)

We might well wish to add to this the clamour of voices arising from various child and adult abuse scandals highlighting the need for interprofessional communication and collaboration (DH, 1999, 2000b for example). As various reports have shown: *Only when there is effective professional partnership working can major tragedies be averted* (Moss, 2007, p38).

There is however a further dimension to this that adds to the richness as well as the complexity of the discussion. Moss continues:

Increasingly we coming to realise that the real experts in these matters are not the professionals but those whose lives and life-stories are centre-stage – namely, the very people who use our services.

(Moss, 2007, p39)

The voice of the people who use the wide range of health and helping services is therefore becoming an ever more important 'driver': it is as much, if not more *their* vision as the professionals' vision that is demanding to be heard. Phrases such as *putting the patient first, patient involvement* and *service user and carer involvement* all underscore this increasingly important emphasis that is also serving as a counterpoint to the increasingly professionalised and territorial activity of the great army of people-workers.

One very clear example of this has been the ways in which the 'survivor' voice of people in recovery from serious mental distress has had a profound impact upon services. The Values Framework of the National Institute of Mental Health in England (NIMHE), for example, states very clearly that such work must be user-centred – it puts respect for the values of the individual users at the centre of policy and practice (Coyte, 2008, p52).

An interesting and fascinating aspect of this has been to listen to the users' voice in the context of holistic care. This has been a dominant facet of professional rhetoric in much health, social work and social care professional discourse: each profession appears to be committed to delivering a holistic package of care. But time and again, users pointed out, it was a partial service that was delivered, with each agency almost having its own limited definition of what 'holistic' meant to them. One major omission has been that of spirituality and religion. Seen by many professionals as being part of the problem (see Powell 2003; Moss 2005 for a discussion), such issues were strongly reclaimed by many users who argued that for very many of them spirituality, and for some of them religious faith, was an important aspect, both of their chosen way of living and also, therefore, of their journey to recovery (Mind, 2008). To have this important dimension being ignored or pathologised by the professionals did them a grave disservice. Spirituality, however defined, whether in a religious or secular framework of reference, provided them with a world view and a set of meanings that enabled them to make sense of who they were, what was happening to them and importantly how to face the future journey into recovery (Moss and Gilbert, 2007).

ACTIVITY 6.6

We have already invited you in Activity 3 to explore the various names that agencies use to describe the people who come to them – service users; customers; patients; clients; users; enquirers, etc. The likelihood is that you have focussed on them as receivers of services. In this activity we invite you to reflect on the preceding paragraphs, which highlight both the centrality of the user experience and also the roles they have to play in helping to train practitioners and in planning and delivering services. This breaking down of barriers between 'helpers' and 'helped' opens new horizons.

How does your agency really understand the term 'holistic'? Is it a realistic aspiration? Can holistic care only be offered through an integrated, collaborative approach, or would this risk losing some of the distinctiveness of your agency's contribution?

In what ways does your agency seek to respond to these developments? Are you able to identify ways in which more progress could be made?

Once more we are brought back to this hauntingly persistent theme of spirituality and spiritual intelligence (SQ), territory into which we began to enter as a result of our discussion of the work of Taylor and Anthony. Speaking from a leadership and management perspective, they highlighted some facets of organisational spirituality that are essential for a successful business to thrive. In its turn, SQ highlights some deeply human aspects of meaning-making, creativity and values-based practice which seem to take us to the heart of what it means to be human. This is both at an individual level and in relationship to others; it involves our capacity to experience awe, and to sense something of the mystery and (in John Barry's powerful phrase) the *beyond-ness of things*. And finally, from the user voice in mental health, there comes the impassioned plea to take spirituality seriously as a core value of humanity and a key component in the journey to recovery.

CASE STUDY

The Somerset Project is a good example of how a collaborative approach to understanding the holistic needs of people experiencing mental distress led to new ways of working. It also illustrates how leadership from the NHS Trust combined vision, values and a deep commitment to enable service users and people on the journey to recovery to lead the project development. User-led research rose to the top of the agenda, and a deeper understanding of spirituality, and how it can inform and influence a range of mental health services was gained. Reports to the Chief Executive of the NHS Trust led to an inclusive policy statement being issued; conferences enabled people to work together more closely, and a heightened awareness was achieved concerning the importance of embracing diversity and ensuring that religious and spiritual needs were not neglected. For a detailed discussion of the project see Foskett and Roberts (2007).

What does this mean for integrated care?

It is important now to articulate what this 'gateway' or 'cluster concept' of spirituality has to say to us in our discussion of ethics, vision and values for integrated care. Pierson (2008) is not alone in reminding us how complex this territory is; how important boundaries are in terms of service delivery, accountability and professional identity, and how easy it is for professionals to regard other professional groups with suspicion and the occasional outburst of hostility. These issues are explored further in Chapter 8. And yet there is no denying the practice imperative and the government drive towards a seamless service. Perhaps what spirituality can offer is less of a common code of practice or an agreed template, but rather a checklist to help people judge whether or not they are heading in the right direction – and by 'people' we specifically include those who use the services, and not just the professionals.

Taylor and Anthony's checklist, mentioned earlier in this chapter, provides useful strands in this tapestry. Their strands included:

Creativity and partnership

It is so very easy for professionals to adopt the 'we know best' approach especially when the people they are seeking to support and help are going through times of crisis that undermine their confidence, and when their capacity for being creative and zestful is impaired. And when several professional and organisations are involved, the risk of this is intensified to the point almost of inevitability. But that temptation has to be resisted. As the user voices in mental health services reminded us, people have an innate creativity and strength, and the task of the professional is not to take over, but rather to recognise the (at times) flickering candle of hope and to fan it into a bright flame (Moss and Gilbert, 2007). The real joy of people-work is not in the form filling, the tedious bureaucracy, but in working with people who are going through difficult times and together finding imaginative and creative ways of moving forward.

Vision and finding yourself

This chapter began with the comment that *without a vision, the people perish*. Spirituality prompts all of us, whether we are helping or being helped, supporting or being supported, to realise that some sense of vision and purpose is important if we are to get the best out of living. Admittedly this is often difficult. Anti-discriminatory practice is important because it reminds us powerfully that society is skewed, and that there are oppressive forces at work that reduce people's life-chances and expectations radically through no fault of their own. Nevertheless, the challenge of creating, developing and sustaining a vision for oneself, one's family, job or career, community or organisation (the list is endless) takes us into the territory as much about what we do *not* want, as into what we *do* hope for.

It is at this point that Bauman's work has an impact because it invites us to consider what it feels like being caught up in the liquidly modern consumer society. Fundamentally, it challenges us to ask how we deal with the structural disappointment that is essential to this analysis: we are being persuaded all the time that we need to replace and renew, but at every turn that process deepens the hunger and emptiness within. At some point we will need to look at the world-view we have chosen and decide whether it is able to sustain us in the really difficult times. It is no surprise that it is in the often frightening and unsettling territory of mental distress, with its existential fear and angst, that the demand to take spirituality seriously has been most strongly heard. To share another person's journey of self-discovery for what they want from life; what they wish to give and to share; what world-view sustains them in the living, their loving and their dying; what impact awe, wonder and mystery has upon them, and how they live their lives accordingly: this is the territory of spirituality and (albeit often fragmentarily) the people-work we are privileged to practise. But it is also a journey that each of us has to make too, and sometimes the people we work with demonstrate far more courage, resilience and determination to follow their vision than we can ever achieve.

Energy, flexibility and communication

The challenge of people-work, and especially the additional challenges that integrated practice brings, make particular demands upon us; practitioners and service users alike. It is all too easy to slip into a functionalist mode of working, whereby everyone goes through the motions but there is no real life or vitality to the encounter. Spirituality, with the word 'spirit' being central to it, encourages us to rise above the temptation to go onto automatic pilot and to communicate something of the opportunity that is being offered in the encounter. Interviews and discussions can then become more of a dance than a route march – there can be a lightness of spirit and a freedom of movement as the best way forward is explored. It will not always be the same person leading the dance; it is unlikely that they will travel in a straight line; but the sense of mutual achievement will be enhanced when the music of the interview sounds its final chord.

Respect

Consider these two statements:

> *There is nothing particularly spiritual about respect.*

> *Respect is the most profound expression of the spiritual that we can offer anyone.*

These apparently contradictory statements remind us that, in any work with people, a profound sense of respect for those with whom we work is an essential component of professional practice. It is written into codes of conduct, and should any worker behave towards someone who has come to the agency for help or support in a deeply disrespectful way, that worker can expect to be disciplined, whether or not a formal complaint has been made against him or her. It is so fundamental to the fabric of professional practice that we do not need a spirituality framework to remind us of its importance.

Yet the very act of treating someone respectfully, especially if there are profound differences between us, remains a deeply human and spiritual encounter. It is a huge privilege to be allowed into someone else's life, especially if that is tinged with sadness, guilt, pain, sorrow or loss. We have to tread carefully so that we do not trample, for the other person is a unique special flowering of the human spirit, even if their behaviour has in some ways denied or despoiled that feature in other people.

Respect also needs to characterise our dealings with other professionals and the work they are seeking to do; it needs to value and cherish the contribution that other organisations can make to the 'seamless service' being offered.

Respect also needs to underpin those occasions where we need to challenge and confront inappropriate behaviour and language: racism and sexism and many other disrespectful attitudes need to be challenged firmly, appropriately and respectfully *precisely because* the core value of respect is being undermined by such behaviour and language.

Fun

The final strand identified in the tapestry of spirituality by Taylor and Anthony seems at one level to be incongruous to people-work and the serious situations we are so often called to deal with. To regard such situations as 'fun' would be the ultimate in disrespectful behaviour, an act of gross trivialisation. So this strand needs to be treated with a degree of care. What spirituality is offering with this suggestion is a counter-balance to the heaviness of spirit and a deadness of approach that can so easily characterise people-workers who become burdened with the problems of others. It is inviting us to look at ourselves 'as people' and to see where the lightness and the joy is in our lives as a whole; where are our moments of celebration and passion, of beauty and wonder and awe: these are important aspects of our living and our loving, and while we must not wear them on our sleeves or flaunt such things with others, they will nevertheless influence us as people in our approach to others. They will counter-act any sense of drabness, and imbue us with a lightness of touch and a warmth of encounter that will enrich our professional lives. We are people first, and professionals second – and the more whole and fulfilled we are as people, the better chance we have to being more effective professionals.

C H A P T E R S U M M A R Y

This chapter has explored the context for Integrated Care, and has outlined some of the tensions inherent in contemporary consumerism for people-workers who struggle at times to maintain their ethics, vision and values. Codes of conduct and statements of values are important indicators about how an organisation sees itself and its role, and how it expects its employees to behave towards others. But something more is needed to help leaders and managers, as well as workers themselves, to sustain the creative vitality of best practice. This chapter has suggested that in the contemporary debate around spirituality we can find some pointers to guide our approach to this often complex territory. What spirituality can offer is a paradigm, or a way of seeing things, that can help us maintain and cherish the deep humanity of everyone we encounter, and to remind ourselves that people-work is above all a privileged responsibility. There is always a risk, individually, collectively and in our integrated practice, that we can lose sight of that essential spirit, and allow ourselves and our work to become mundane, consumer driven, functional and dispirited. But we can also rise to the challenge, and with flair, creativity and mutual respect, stir up the vision of what it means to be fully human, and to celebrate the moment.

FURTHER READING

Coyte, ME Gilbert, P and Nicholls, V (eds) (2008) *Spirituality, values and mental health: Jewels for the journey*. London: Jessica Kingsley.

Moss, B (2007) *Values*. Lyme Regis: Russell House Publishing.

Zohar, D and Marshall, I (2000) *Spiritual intelligence: The ultimate intelligence*. London: Bloomsbury.

Chapter 7

Emotional intelligence, emotion and collaborative leadership

Sam Held

Introduction

The remarkable speed with which *emotional intelligence* (EI), a phrase coined less than twenty years ago, has become common currency is an indicator of its popular success. Many people will have heard of the term and formed a personal interpretation of what it entails, particularly those working in the fields of leadership and management, human resources and personal development coaching. You have explored some aspects of EI already in this book, and also had an opportunity to think about spiritual intelligence in Chapter 6.

EI has secured a highly influential role in the continued development of major multinational companies, government departments, the armed forces and, in Britain, the National Health Service (NHS). The *NHS Leadership Qualities Framework* (LQF) (DH, 2006), developed by the Hay Group, draws heavily on the key concepts of EI. In the context of leading collaboration and integrated practice, EI has frequently been championed as a template for success, and development programmes such as the LQF are fashioned around EI, and in particular around Daniel Goleman's (1995, 1998, 2000) compelling assertions. We also consider the role of emotion in the workplace, specifically the concepts of *emotional labour* and *emotional work*.

In this chapter we will explore the underpinning concepts of EI and consideration of the role of emotion in the workplace, practise relating these concepts to real-life personal experiences, and critically evaluate the strengths and weaknesses of the theoretical approach. Unless specifically noted otherwise, we will take EI to mean the popular construct proposed in the work of Daniel Goleman and colleagues. The reason for this is that this version of EI is almost certainly the one established in the collective consciousness. We will use the terms 'collaborative', 'integrated' and 'interprofessional' interchangeably, and mindful of Barr's (2002, p30) caution, as general terms without *strictly private meanings*. We recognise that integrated working involves many more professional groups than are specifically named in this chapter, and no professional group is implicitly excluded.

Chapter overview

This chapter will discuss the potential benefits for leaders in collaborative contexts of theories of EI, their associated skills and competencies and the role of emotion in workplace settings. We will be looking at the development of EI, its main characteristics and claimed benefits and its relevance to the complexities of leadership in an integrated service environment. This chapter will specifically:

- consider the theoretical basis and key principles of EI and emotion;

- discuss the relevance of EI to integrated working and consider the relationship between EI and emotions in this work based context;

- critically evaluate the main claims and propositions of prominent EI theorists, particularly in terms of the advancement of the practice of leadership in complex collaborative environments.

The evolution of emotional intelligence

Prior to the 1920s, research on human intelligence was restricted to the study of cognitive skills and abilities. Thorndike (1920) is generally credited with signalling a possible other dimension to intelligence, which he labelled social intelligence. He described it as *the ability to understand and manage men and women, boys and girls, to act wisely in human relations*. There is some debate about the first major academic research on emotional intelligence, but it is generally ascribed to John Mayer and Peter Salovey who first used the phrase in 1990. They defined EI as *the ability to perceive emotion, integrate emotion to facilitate thought, understand emotions, and to regulate emotions to promote personal growth* (Salovey and Meyer,1990, p317). Daniel Goleman became popularly linked with the concept with following the remarkable success of *Emotional Intelligence: Why it can matter more than IQ*, in 1995. Goleman, then a journalist, had become interested in EI through Salovey and Mayer's work. He took one of their premises, that a high IQ is not necessarily a prerequisite for a successful life, and expanded on it to write a number of books that far exceeded the expectations of author and publisher alike, with Goleman's books selling in their millions worldwide.

Goleman introduces us to various anecdotes about people who, whilst brilliant academically, were unsuccessful socially or in corporate life. Conversely, he identifies others who were undistinguished in academic terms, but were still highly successful in terms of visible success and business achievements. Goleman went on to correlate business acumen with EI. In *Working with emotional intelligence* (1998), 25 EI competencies or surface behaviours were identified with the fundamental claim being made that a high level of EI can make all the difference between success and failure.

Goleman's key theories

Goleman drew on post-Darwinian neuroscience to suggest the evolution of the brain has implications for our emotions and behavioural responses. He hypothesised on the development of brain function over millennia and how it affects our here-and-now behaviour.

Goleman looked at three key areas of the brain in terms of relevance to emotions and behaviours.

1 The brain stem, situated at the base of the brain at the top of the spinal cord. It is believed to control bodily functions and instinctive survival responses, and is the most primitive part of the brain.

2 The hippocampus, thought to have evolved after the brainstem and situated just above it. It includes the amygdala region, the importance of which was identified by Joseph LeDoux (1985). Here, the brain stores emotional, survival-linked responses to visual and other inputs – often referred to as the fight-or-flight responses. The amygdala is thought to 'hijack' the brain in some circumstances, provoking an instant reaction to a situation rather than a considered response, often referred to as the 'knee-jerk' response.

3 The neo-cortex. The large, well-developed, upper region of the brain which is the centre of our thinking, memory and reasoning functions.

Goleman suggests that emotions and reasoning, the two main brain functions that determine behaviour, are located in differing areas. Our emotional centres receive stimuli before our thinking centres, and thus can override rational responses in some situations. When people confront stimuli such as fear, anger or frustration, their first active response comes from the amygdala. Unless intelligent control is exerted, the brain moves into survival mode, stimulating instinctive/intuitive actions that, while possibly right in an extreme situation, may be very wrong in the majority of modern social interactions.

These fight-or-flight reactions still have a vital role to play, but EI is about recognising and controlling this in oneself, while using our rational and empathic skills to anticipate and deal with it in others.

ACTIVITY 7.1

Think of an occasion in your life when you have responded without conscious thought to a fight-or-flight sensory input. What happened? How did you feel afterwards? If you'd had time to consider the sensory input, would you still have responded in the same way?

Now think of a time, preferably in a workplace environment, when you have had a similar fight-or-flight moment, but not been in a position to do either. How did you feel afterwards? Compare and contrast the two events.

How well do you think you know your amygdala?

Goleman initially proposed a framework of five key elements of EI.

1 Self-awareness: examining how emotions affect your performance; using your values to guide decision-making; looking at your strengths and weaknesses and learning from your experiences; and being self-confident and certain about your competence, values and goals.

2 Self-regulation: controlling your temper; controlling your stress by being more positive and action-centred; retaining the ability to think clearly under pressure; handling impulses well; and nurturing trustworthiness and self-restraint.

3 Motivation: enjoying challenge and stimulation; seeking achievement; commitment; ability to take the initiative; optimism; and being guided by personal preferences in choosing goals.

4 Empathy: the ability to understand other people's realities; behaving openly and honestly; avoiding the tendency to stereotype others; and being culturally aware.

5 Social skills: influencing skills; good communication; listening skills; negotiation; co-operation; dispute resolution; ability to inspire and lead others; capacity to initiate and manage change; and ability to deal with others' emotions – particularly group emotions.

Goleman claims that people who possess these characteristics are more likely to be successful in senior management. Anecdotal case studies illustrate ways in which emotional intelligence can have a positive impact in the workplace, with dramatic and shocking real-life events used to exemplify the alleged effects of an absence of EI. This journalistic style has probably helped to contribute to the popular appeal of these books, but few convincing arguments are presented to support measurable correlations between the acts of violence cited and low levels of EI.

In *Working with emotional intelligence* (1998), Goleman defined emotional intelligence as *a capacity for recognising our own and others' feelings, for motivating ourselves, and for managing our emotions, both within ourselves and in our relationships* (1998, p317).

ACTIVITY 7.2

Reflecting on Goleman's definition above, think about past experiences at work or in education where a manager/tutor has shown EI skills and you felt valued, visible and competent. Why did you feel that way? Note some key words that occur to you.

When you have done this, think of one situation where a manager, etc. has provoked feelings of being undervalued or overlooked. Without pausing for reflection this time quickly jot some words or phrases that come to mind.

Compare your two lists – what conclusions could be drawn about the impact of EI on others and on yourself?

Emotional intelligence, leadership and integrated practice

Dulewicz and Higgs (2003) expanded Goleman's five elements of EI to seven, which they broke down into three main categories.

1 The drivers: motivation and decisiveness; these characteristics energise and drive people towards their goals.

2 The constrainers: conscientiousness and integrity; emotional resilience; acting as controls and curbs to the excesses of the drivers.

3 The enablers: sensitivity, influence and self-awareness; these facilitate performance and help the individual to succeed.

These three categories, coupled with Goleman's 1998 five-part definition (see above), form a useful framework for examining the implications of EI for leaders of integrated practice and collaborative working in health, social services, education and associated professional groups.

In health and social work in the United Kingdom, the concept of EI has gained acceptance at the highest levels. In addition to the NHS's significant support for EI through its Leadership Qualities Framework (ibid.), other public sector bodies are espousing EI as a key element of leading and managing the integrated working agendas. The DfES, for example, states quite clearly in its Guidance on the Early Years Foundation Stage (2007).

What is needed to bring about this change is emotional intelligence: the ability to take into account how different professionals view their own roles and bring them together through a common purpose and shared value base, www.standards.dfes.gov.uk/eyfs/resources/downloads/3_4b_ep.pdf

There has probably never been a period in modern British history in which there has been such a sustained emphasis on collaboration and integration. Clinicians, teachers, youth workers, housing officers, Connexions staff, professionals and volunteers in the third sector: only a few examples of the new relationships leaders across these fields are challenged to develop.

The 'new' demands leaders have to meet in the implementation and management of integrated practice are diverse, and not confined to the complexities of organisational change. Leaders need the skills and competencies to manage and lead a new type of workforce which is multi-disciplinary, multi-agency and has multiple expectations. Burgess describes the tensions clearly: *Requirements such as partnership with potential competitors and collaboration with customers who may not want the service call for paradigm shifts that involve individual and organisational growth* (Burgess, 2005, p110).

Traditional hierarchies are less relevant, but the expectations placed on leaders remain relatively constant. Among the dichotomies they face are:

- a need to communicate a compelling vision and purpose while including stakeholders' input at every stage;
- leaders need to take full responsibility for quality and standards yet their teams are made up of individuals who expect professional independence and autonomy;
- they must promote collaboration, integration and teamwork while ensuring that individuals get appropriate recognition and acknowledgement.

While Goleman's five elements of EI (self awareness; self regulation; motivation; empathy and social skills) are desirable attributes for any leader, they are somewhat generic and of limited use in identifying the specific qualities leaders in integrated working contexts most need. On the other hand the three categories proposed by Dulewicz and Higgs (2003):

drivers, constrainers and enablers, map more closely onto contemporary leadership theory. The original iteration of the NHS Leadership Qualities Framework was based on the concept of transformational leadership, which as you read in Chapter 1 is still a significant paradigm in the public sector in Britain. Bass and Avolio's (1994) archetypal *Four I's* of transformational leadership: *I*dealised influence, *I*nspirational motivation, *I*ndividualised consideration and *I*ntellectual stimulation, resonate with the drivers, constrainers and enablers See Chapters 1 and 5 for further descriptions of transformational leadership and Chapter 8 for a discussion on the impact and influence of leadership frameworks and the theories that underpin them.

It seems reasonable, then, to suggest that EI may correlate with transformational theories of leadership (and the subsequent derivatives: distributed, situational and contingent leadership). It is certainly arguable that EI attributes are numbered among the key characteristics of the authentic transformational leader.

The Emotional Competence Inventory or ECI-360 (Boyatzis, *et al.,* 1999) is a popularly accepted tool for evaluating an individual's EI 'rating'

Previously it was used mainly in the private sector but increasingly it is being adopted in larger public sector organisations. In many cases it is used in appraisal for promotion purposes, being seen as an indicator of leadership potential. The ECI reduces Goleman's original five components of EI to four:

Self-awareness:

1 being aware of your emotions and their significance;

2 having a realistic knowledge of your strengths and weaknesses;

3 having confidence in yourself and your capacities.

Self-management:

1 controlling your emotions;

2 being honest and trustworthy;

3 being flexible and dedicated.

Social competence:

1 being empathic;

2 being aware of a group's dynamics and inter-relationships;

3 focusing on others' needs.

Social skills:

1 helping others to develop themselves;

2 effective leadership;

3 change management skills;

4 ability to resolve arguments;

5 influencing skills;

6 excellent interpersonal communication skills;

7 ability to build good relationships;

8 team-player skills.

A notable absence within these four components, though it figured in the original five, and one that is crucial to integrated working, is *value-guided decision-making.* Goleman also omits *cultural sensitivity*, which is unfortunate since his propositions are firmly rooted in western capitalist notions of individualism and the nature of success and do not lend themselves to collaborative and inclusive interprofessional endeavour. You will see in Chapters 4 and 8, how Alimo-Metcalfe and Alban-Metcalfe's work develops this further around the concept of servant leadership, challenging the notion of transformational leadership in public services.

ACTIVITY **7.3**

Look back at Chapter 1. How do the ECI components relate to the various leadership perspectives. Can you determine any aspect of the ECI qualities that are unique and/or innovative?

In *Primal Leadership* (2002) Goleman, *et al.*, identify a number of what they term *emotionally intelligent domains* in our brains and *associated competencies* which can be observed in the behaviours of authentic transformational leaders. They argue that leaders can develop and use these behaviours as circumstances require, and that the underlying competencies can be learned, enabling leaders to switch in and out of the different styles at will. They categorise these competencies under two headings.

Personal competencies – how we manage ourselves:
- emotional self-awareness;
- emotional self-control;
- keeping disruptive emotions under control;
- displaying honesty and integrity;
- initiative.

Social competencies:
- social awareness;
- empathy;
- organisational awareness;
- relationship management;
- inspirational leadership;

- influence;

- developing others;

- change catalyst;

- building bonds.

A critical observer might conclude that these are merely a synthesis of previous EI 'lists' and many of the desirable characteristics of leadership found in the ever-increasing body of literature. A more specific criticism is that a significant number of the behaviours are not measurable in any way. The argument of the book is that the more of these attributes an individual possesses; the more she or he will tend towards leadership success. In itself this is an incontrovertible argument, though not necessarily one which advances the under-standing of leadership.

Of more serious concern in the context of leading integrated working is the thinking behind *Emotional self-control – keeping disruptive emotions under control*. Understanding and *controlling* (my emphasis) emotions is a persistent theme in Goleman's work, and its appropriacy for practitioners in social work, health and related professions is open to question. At surface level it could be argued that there is little difference between controlling emotions and *regulating* (Salovey and Mayer, 1990) or *managing* them. (Waddington and Copperman, 2005). However Goleman's output is aimed at the private and commercial sector, where control of (especially disruptive) emotions is a desirable attribute, whereas in the fields of social work and health the nature of the work means that people routinely work in an environment of elevated affect, are likely to encounter uncontrolled emotions and need more subtle skills to handle emotion than *control* implies. There may be no more a subtle distinction between the notion of control and regulation of emotions in the wider context, nonetheless a difference between the two can be argued to exist in the so-called caring professions. Social care and health professionals must be able to regulate their emotions according to the context of their immediate environment, however in these professions authenticity (or congruence) are valued personal attributes, and control of emotions may be considered synonymous with suppression (see Chapter 6 for an in-depth exploration of authenticity around professional values and spirituality). In the complexity of collaborative leadership, control (of organisations or emotions) is an ephemeral and ultimately unsatisfactory activity.

Margaret Wheatley, cited in Morrison (2007), writing on leadership and organisational theory, maintains that *in life the issue is not control, but dynamic connectedness* (Wheatley 1999, p25). Morrison goes on to suggest that EI competence *is pivotal to gaining the co-operation of other colleagues and services on which social workers depend to achieve their outcomes* (Morrison, 2007, p259), and from his arguments we can infer that he refers to competence that is not based not on control but on awareness of the emotional dimension and the ability to use emotions positively.

Applying EI in integrated practice settings

Can Emotional Intelligence contribute to a deeper understanding of the leadership and management challenges of integrated practice?

It is unlikely that there can be a definitive answer to this question; however EI is a useful framework around which individuals can build and refine their world view in terms of leading in integrated practice. Applying the four key Goleman constructs of self-awareness, self-management, social awareness and relationship management is likely to result in a greater ability to anticipate, understand and work through the many challenges integrated practice presents to a manager and leader. Goleman, you may recall, suggests that each of these constructs includes a set of emotional competencies which are not innate talents, but rather learned capabilities to be worked on and developed in order to achieve outstanding performance as a leader.

Setting aside the question whether some of the claimed competencies (for example empathy) are learnable in the formal sense or are actually personality traits, is the almost mechanistic nature of Goleman's approach relevant to every professional field? Perhaps Mayer's definition of EI is more appropriate for integrated social work, health, education and related fields:

> *From a scientific (rather than a popular) standpoint, emotional intelligence is the ability to accurately perceive your own and others' emotions; to understand the signals that emotions send about relationships; and to manage your own and others' emotions*
> (Mayer, 2004, p28)

This encapsulates the fundamental difference between Salovey and Mayer's construct and those of the 'Goleman School' in that the definition above virtually defines the boundaries of EI as a form of intelligence with a small number of related competencies. This is in marked contrast to EI being characterised in a much more expansive and inclusive way.

Tony Morrison's (2007) paper in the British Journal of Social Work sheds some light on the potential of EI as an identifiable intelligence and relates it to the role of emotion in the organisation of human behaviour. Morrison considers EI and emotion in relation to five core social-work tasks: user engagement; assessment; decision making; collaboration; and dealing with stress. He also looks at the rapidly changing context of social work as it merges with other organisations in the development of integrated service delivery.

Separating EI from 'emotion work' and 'emotional labour' allows other perspectives on the relevance of EI to leaders in interprofessional environments. Waddington and Copperman's (2006) paper *Emotions and interprofessional practice* contains useful and concise definitions of both. To define emotion work they quote Mirchandani who describes it as the *often invisible work which people do as part of caring for their families or performing their paid job* (Mirchandani, 2003, p.722). 'Emotional labour', as discussed by Hochschild (1983), is similar but relates to paid work which requires a person to express and manipulate emotions as a part of their job. Health workers, social and community workers, educators and many other professional groups are all required to perform both emotion work and emotional labour on a daily basis. She suggests that practitioners have to regulate their emotions routinely. She identifies two types of regulation:

1 antecedent-focused emotion regulation – modifying initial feelings by changing the situation or the cognitions of the situation;

2 response-focused emotion regulation – modifying behaviour once emotions are experienced by suppressing, faking or amplifying an emotional response.

To put these two types of regulation into context we can examine the following case study.

CASE STUDY

A community police officer, visiting a house on a routine call about vandalism in the area, discovers an older man who is unkempt, very frail, and who appears to be barely surviving on tinned fish and tap water. The police officer is shocked as the area is well known and the local community is considered to be friendly and neighbourly. The case is reported appropriately and local integrated community care staff intervene promptly. The older man is found to be malnourished and dehydrated, but deemed capable of remaining at home with appropriate services in place. The local community association, with some 'unofficial' input from the community police officer is angry and pressures their local councillor to demand an investigation into how things reached such a state of affairs. The following information comes to light:

- *prior to the last but one 'reorganisation' the man was known to social services, who tried unsuccessfully to provide (what was then) 'meals on wheels';*

- *he has a son who lives seven miles away but they are estranged;*

- *his neighbours gave up trying to approach him as he was always 'rude and aggressive';*

- *he has £147,000 in savings, and in addition to his old-age pension he has a full army pension;*

- *his wife of 42 years died of cancer seven years ago, and hospice staff were seriously concerned about his well-being after her death. This only comes to light because a home care worker's sister used to work in the hospice.*

ACTIVITY 7.4

Consider this scenario. Reflect on the range of emotions the participants may have experienced. How do you think they may have regulated their emotions? Take the police officer as an example: he/she may have been angry about the predicament in which they found the old man. By taking the proper action to get help they may have addressed some of this anger (antecedent regulation), by a contribution to local disquiet about the situation they may be addressing some sense of frustration (response focussed?), and if he/she becomes aware of the background they may feel less angry (again antecedent regulation).

Select another likely participant – how do you think she/he responds?

Hochschild's two types of regulation have similarities with the practical application of EI behaviours in the workplace, but in the context of what are generally termed the 'caring' professions we can argue that they may be similar but they are not exactly the same. In order to expand on this argument we must examine in more depth exactly what we believe to be different, or even 'special', about the place of emotion and the relationship between emotion, thought and behaviours in the caring professions. David Howe (2008), in his introduction to *The emotionally intelligent social worker* expertly captures that 'special' aspect of the caring professions:

> *The people-oriented professions inevitably find themselves working daily with people whose needs are pressing and whose emotions are disturbingly aroused. Illness, physical decline and poverty increase anxiety. Injustice, deprivation and discrimination provoke anger. Loss and rejection leave people feeling hurt and sad. It is critical that social and health care workers understand the part that emotions play in the lives and behaviour of those who use their services. . .Practitioners need to understand how emotions affect them as they work with users and engage with colleagues.*

> (Howe, 2008, p1)

EI notions of emotional competence and self-awareness should be treated with care in professions which involve higher than average emotional 'loads'. Heron (1992) and MacCulloch (2001) warn of the dangers of promoting emotional competence without ensuring that professionals have addressed their own emotional distress. Another unresolved issue for leaders in these 'caring' collaborative environments is that of competing codes, ethics and values. Though these codes may be outwardly similar in spirit, they can create or conceal divisions. You have read about this in Chapter 5; Chapter 8 also explores the ideas around professional identity and values. In the context of EI, Lewis (2005) cites Saarni's (2000) concerns about the relative lack of *a moral dimension* in current models which could allow manipulation by the emotionally competent to flourish in the integrated environment.

We need, then, to apply these insights and considerations to the specific issues affecting the leadership and management of integrated practice.

From *Partnership in Action* (DH, 1998b) to the *Laming Inquiry* (HMSO, 2003) and its consequent developments, collaborative or integrated working has been a priority for a rapidly expanding range of professionals. In collective efforts to ensure better communication and interprofessional practice, and to prevent past mistakes recurring, the various organisations involved are creating the artifacts of integration, and the infrastructure to support them. Higher education institutions, royal colleges and professional bodies have embraced the idea that we must educate new and existing professionals to work in integrated ways.

Writing specifically about these issues, Olive Stevenson (2007) questions the ability of the current integrated working orthodoxy to address the imbalance between creating systems to support collaboration, and understanding the impact of emotions on involved professionals using that knowledge to improve interprofessional practice. Stevenson writes on working with neglected children and their families, an area which is probably the highest profile example of integrated working in the UK to date, however her work has resonance across the whole spectrum of integrated services. Stevenson poses a fundamental question which is:

> *how can organisations which are necessarily and properly run on principles of order and rationality take into account the underlying emotional dynamics which profoundly affect the behaviour of their staff. . .?*

> (Stevenson, 2007, p100)

Effective collaboration is unlikely without creating space to share and understand the emotions vested in the work. Crucially for our examination of links between emotion and emotional intelligence, Stevenson continues:

> *These emotions should not be viewed in solely negative terms; they are the drivers of positive and negative behaviours and they underpin purposeful behaviour.*

(ibid.)

Here we can see a close correlation with Salovey and Mayer's concept of EI. Goleman's concept sits less comfortably here, with its emphasis on controlling *disruptive* emotions. Goleman is not specific on what disruptive means, but he seems to imply that disruptive emotions cause negative behaviours. Recent thinking on leadership in settings such as integrated practice draw on complex adaptive systems theory (see Chapters 3 and 4), and suggests that collaborative arrangements, however formalised, are peopled by independent agents whose behaviour stems from physical, psychological, or social rules rather than a *system dynamic* (Rouse, 2000). The emotions that drive positive and negative behaviours, then, must be seen as both necessary and desirable drivers and constrainers within dynamic systems. If these are not managed and dealt with through formal and informal channels, then the system itself might tip into unnecessary complexity or even chaos, neither of which promote system changes that may be planned or desirable.

Though somewhat of a generalisation, most professional groups have evolved systems and methodologies to understand and make space for emotion for individual practitioners, but these have remained particular to the occupational groups. For example social workers expect their supervision to allow space for some of the emotional content of their work to be addressed, whereas other professions have evolved other 'coping' structures which may be less formal. These differences have not been translated into interprofessional education and practice. This could be, as Waddington and Copperman suggest, *because management of self and emotion are seen as implicit concepts of professional practice and education, which transfer seamlessly into an interprofessional practice context* (Waddington and Copperman, 2006, p5). To make this assumption at the organisational level, however, denies the complexity of integrated practice and demonstrates a huge underestimation of the role of emotion, and by extension emotional intelligence. At the level of ideology there seems to be an implicit assumption that in integrated practice, all professionals are equal. Desirable though this state of affairs may be, in practice it is most definitely not the case, and the relevance for leadership in integrated practice is that there needs to be an emotionally intelligent approach to managing professional attitudes, expectations and stereotypes. Integrated working exposes workers to their own and others' stereotypes, fears of loss of professional identity and lack of control. The leadership task, then, is to populate the edifices of integrated working with professionals at all level who can perceive emotions, integrate them to facilitate thought, understand them, and regulate their own emotions to promote personal and organisational growth. This type of EI equips professionals to work in an atmosphere of connectedness, tolerate uncertainty, and learn from positive and negative emotional experiences. This is closely aligned with the Salovey and Mayer 'version' of EI, which appears to be the perspective most able to accommodate the vital understanding of both emotion and emotion work.

ACTIVITY **7.5**

One of the largest stakeholders in integrated working in the UK is the NHS.

Look at the NHS Leadership Qualities Framework in Figure 7.1. Using sources other than this chapter, map the NHS Qualities against Goleman's key concepts. In what ways do they differ? How do these differences relate to the future of collaborative working and integrated practice (if at all)?

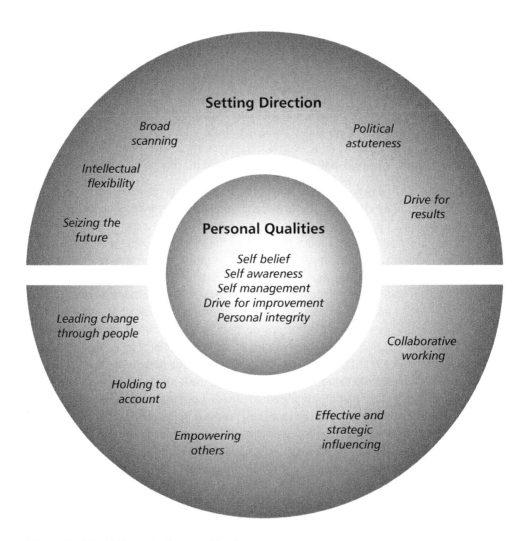

Figure 7.1 The NHS leadership qualities framework

Source: NHS Institute for Innovation and Improvement, (2007). *Leadership Qualities Framework.* NHS Institute for Innovation and Improvement: Warwick.

©Crown Copyright 2007

www.nhsleadershipqualities.nhs.uk/portals/0/the_framework.pdf accessed September 2008

From our examination of the nature of leadership within integrated practice, it would be reasonable to conclude, as would Goleman, that empathy is a key factor. It is interesting to note that the NHS, one of the biggest stakeholders in integrated working does not include empathy in its Leadership Qualities Framework. Could this be an example of managerialism overlooking an EI competence that requires significant and genuine emotional engagement?

Critical concerns about emotional intelligence

The term Emotional Intelligence relates to a whole body of research and knowledge which has evolved into three distinct models: ability-based, mixed and trait models. This means that there can be no single critique, however, the academic and research community have consistently pointed out some of the major weaknesses of EI in general, but in particular Goleman's models.

The suggestion that success depends to a high degree on interpersonal skills is not new, and Goleman has been criticised for taking others' ideas and repackaging them as a 'new' concept. This is particularly notable in the case of Salovey and Mayer's work. Goleman is also criticised for adding to the original concepts many assertions of his own that were undefined and unsupported by research. In his first book he uses the terms 'emotional literacy', 'emotional competence', 'emotional skills' and 'emotional malaise' to support his wider propositions without defining them or explaining their relationship to EI. In the case of emotional literacy, Steiner (1997) writes about his quite distinct concept: *To be emotionally literate is to be able to handle emotions in a way that improves your personal power and improves the quality of life around you* (Steiner and Perry, 1997, p11).

Goleman's appeal to a mass audience is the claim that EI is more important than IQ in the pursuit of success in life. Success in this case refers to success in the workplace, and 'happiness' as a desirable outcome does not appear frequently in Goleman's books.

Woodruffe's (2001) review of Goleman's work pointed out that:

- Goleman claims that emotional intelligence is inherent and biologically based, yet it can be learned and developed;

- the self-report measures of emotional intelligence used by Goleman have considerable limitations in terms of accuracy;

- the EI behaviours or competencies put forward by Goleman, such as self-confidence and leadership, are not at all new, and are factors that are commonly associated with high achievement levels;

- there is considerable blurring of the terms intelligence, competence and behaviours.

One of the weaknesses of Goleman's later work on EI is that the original concept of EI is diluted to the point that it becomes scientifically meaningless. He adds a range of highly subjective qualities such as 'zeal', 'persistence', 'character' and 'maturity' which add little to the concept and practical application as it is difficult to see how these qualities might be learned or developed.

These are general criticisms, but of particular concern for leaders in integrated practice is that most of Goleman's work is applied particularly to individual endeavours, and success is measured (broadly speaking) in profit and loss terms. In his later work Goleman proposes that leaders seek to promote 'EI organisations' in order to lead better, but this is something of a circular argument, and one which carries undertones of stifling that fluid interplay between emotions and intelligence that is a vital element of integrated work in the 'caring' professions. EI and transformational leadership are coming under increasing critique and scrutiny for their emphasis on leaders rather than followers, and aiming for achievement of organisational objectives through transformation rather than empowering others to take forward leadership roles and activities (Stone, *et al.*, 2003).

Whatever the criticisms, Goleman has certainly promoted thinking at the highest levels of management on the subject of EI. He has taken some complex ideas relating to human behaviour and biological evolution, and put them into a simple and comprehensible format that his readership can understand. As a result, many people have found this core proposition, that we can use intelligence to better manage our emotions and draw on our emotional intuition to guide our thinking, to be a helpful approach in both their lives and their work.

CHAPTER SUMMARY

We have examined the origins and rise to prominence of Emotional Intelligence in the western corporate consciousness. The relevance of EI to collaborative leadership has been the key focus of this chapter, and we have considered where EI sits in terms of the importance of working with emotion in interprofessional environments. We have identified that EI in its best known popular form may not be easily applicable to the developing world of collaborative endeavour, as it may suppress the evolution of creative solutions. Some perspectives from the 'scientific wing' of EI, however, may be much more useful. We have suggested that as a tool for personal development for present and future leaders EI may be of significant benefit, and in any event carries little or no risk.

We have considered some criticisms of EI, which seem to have substance, but despite these, the principles of Emotional Intelligence have had a significant impact on thinking about personal, organisational and leadership development in the wider context of the corporate world. The contemporary environment of leading collaborative health and social care organisations in the UK and elsewhere is not isolated from the wider context and can legitimately look outside the boundaries for ways to improve overall outcomes. EI as part of an overall approach to enabling individuals and organisations to work together better has much to commend it, with the caution that it can only ever be part of the solution to better collaborative leadership, and is never the panacea for all the ills of 'joined-up-working'.

FURTHER READING

Burgess, RC (2005) A model for enhancing individual and organisational learning of emotional intelligence: The drama and winner's triangles. *Social Work Education*, 24(1): 97–112

Goleman, D and Cherniss, C (eds) (2001) *The emotionally intelligent workplace*. San Francisco: Jossey-Bass.

Lewis, N, Rees, C, Hudson, J and Bleakley, A (2005) Emotional intelligence in medical education: Measuring the unmeasurable? *Advances in health sciences education* 10: 339–55

Morrison, T (2007) *Emotional intelligence, emotion and social work: context, characteristics, complications and contribution.* British Journal of Social Work 37(2): 245–63

Saarni, C (2000) Emotional competence a development perspective. In Bar-on, Parker and Mayer (eds) *The handbook of emotional intelligence.* San Fancisco: Jossey Bass.

Chapter 8

Professional roles and workforce development

Judy McKimm

Introduction

The success of the integrated service agenda will, in many ways, only be as successful as the workforce that delivers it. The modernisation agenda 'supertanker' is crewed by a huge workforce comprising a wide range of paid and unpaid professionals, managers, support workers, volunteers and service users and carers. Implementing integrated practice that works on the ground for those who need it requires a much broader integration of education and training policies across all elements of the public sector than has ever been managed before. Establishing and maintaining an effective workforce for today's and tomorrow's services poses one of the biggest challenges for leaders and managers of integrated services.

Chapter overview

In this chapter we draw some of the key themes from the book together to consider issues concerned with defining, developing and maintaining an effective workforce for integrated services.

In particular this chapter will:

- consider how different professional groups and bodies interact and define themselves as they participate in the management and leadership of integrated services;

- explore further how vision and values are shaped and modified by service reconfigurations;

- look at how professionals and others work within different models of care and the impact these differences might have on service delivery;

- explore the concept of power;

- review opportunities and challenges for leadership and professional development for integrated services;

- describe the models of communities of practice and activity theory in relation to understanding workforce interactions and professionalisation.

Links are made back into other chapters of the book as appropriate.

Professional roles

A range of different professionals may be involved in the delivery of care to any one individual or family, whether this is for a discrete episode (such as becoming homeless) or ongoing for many years, such as caring for a relative who has a long-term chronic condition. Increasingly, care is being provided by multi-professional teams who may be led and managed by people who are not from their own professional group, or individuals may be required to report to more than one manager. These factors lead to tensions and difficulties, often exacerbated by *bureaucracy and unwieldy systems* (McKimm, Burgess and Rafferty, 2008, p24). In the worst cases this may result in service users receiving poor care, falling through gaps in the system or receiving mixed messages from different professionals. In this section, we consider how the inter-related concepts of 'professions' and 'professionalism' might also contribute towards difficulties in developing and implementing effective integrated services.

ACTIVITY **8.1**

What do you understand by the term 'profession'? List some of the features that define a group of workers as being a professional group and what distinguishes this group from a non-professional group.

Professions are characterised as having the following features.

- They are specialised occupations with a discrete body of knowledge.

- Professionals usually enjoy high status and prestige in society and typically higher reward than non-professionals.

- The occupations and activities that members engage in involve application of the specialised knowledge for which a fee for service is paid by clients.

- Becoming a professional involves participation in education and training that is wholly or partially controlled by the profession itself. This typically involves university education as well as professional training, often in the workplace. Examinations that determine competence at different levels are set by the professional body.

- The profession has a code of conduct and a set of standards to which new entrants and continuing members are required to adhere.

- Those who do not meet the standards and follow approved routes to entry are excluded from the profession (professional closure), they cannot legally practice the range of professional activities.

- Each profession is regulated by statute and has its own professional or regulatory body that awards licences to practice. Regulatory bodies maintain a register of members who meet the defined standard.

- Professionals work autonomously and retain control of their work.

(Freidson, 2000; Foucault, 1975)

Although many of these features still define and regulate professions, the concept is not static. There are many more occupations defined today as 'professional' than the three original professions of divinity, medicine and law. Professions continually define and redefine themselves vis a vis other professions, as well as to the wider society in which the professions operate. Here multiple social factors influence the composition and social power of different professions, including gendering of some professions (for example nursing as predominantly comprising women, Witz, 1990), social class, ethnicity and migration.

Challenges to professional autonomy and control of knowledge and responsibility are made through shifting policies and strategies, and changing public opinion. For example, the self-regulation of the medical profession came under scrutiny following a series of high profile cases involving doctors including the Bristol Inquiry (DH, 2001c), the Shipman Inquiry (2002–2005) and the 'Alder Hey' inquiry (Royal Liverpool Children's Hospital Inquiry, 2001). One of the outcomes of these inquiries was a review of the way that the General Medical Council monitored and regulated doctors' practice in 2004. The GMC responded by carrying out a range of internal reforms, including a strengthening of GMC fitness to practice systems and increased lay representation on review panels for doctors in difficulty (GMC, 2004) and, alongside this, new systems for NHS trusts were established to monitor, identify, report and support doctors about whom there are concerns (DH, 2007b).

Workforce reconfiguration and 'new professionals'

The integrated service agenda poses yet another challenge to some professions through redefining professional roles, reviewing expectations from professionals and non-professionals, establishing new professions and empowering service users. Traditional professions involved in integrated practice include social workers; youth and community workers; health professionals; teachers and lawyers. A large number of 'para-professionals' are also involved, such as housing workers; police; careers and Connexions staff; complementary therapists; service managers and administrators; health-care assistants and community support workers. Many of these groups are engaging in professionalising their activities through setting requirements for a degree as a basic qualification and establishing regulatory bodies and codes of practice.

Changing professional roles and responsibilities have implications for service users, professionals themselves and organisations and services. You have seen throughout this book how easy it is for vulnerable people to fall through the gaps in services: services that should be primarily designed to protect and 'serve' those who use them. Service redesign has prompted shifts in education and training which blur some of the boundaries between traditional professional roles. These include: the development of dual degrees in mental health which graduate professionals who are eligible for registration as social workers and mental health nurses; the introduction of extended roles for some practitioners (including nurse consultants, advanced practitioners or physician's assistant); and developing roles for trained 'generic workers' and practitioners who can provide a range of support services for units or individuals (Anderson, 1997).

These 'new' professionals are being trained to work differently with service users, meeting a wider range of needs and providing more continuous and personalised support. Sector policy shifts such as the NHS Plan and Modernisation Agenda (DH, 2000b) led to a review of the skills of the health workforce which in turn led to widespread reform across organisations. Integrated workforce agendas have the potential for a more radical impact across all public services and systems. This reflects the broad policy direction enshrined in the wider public sector modernisation agenda which emphasises accountability, value for money, local democracy, community engagement, partnership and transparent commissioning and funding arrangements (I&DeA, 2008; Keep, 2002).

Whilst offering new opportunities for change, changing agendas and service reconfiguration also pose new challenges for education and training organisations, professional and statutory bodies and career progression for those working in integrated services. Degeling, W. *et al.* (2003) suggest that the modernisation agenda requires health-care workers and managers to accept loss of clinical autonomy as they move towards sharing power through team-based approaches to dealing with the resource implications of clinical activity. The top-down method of performance management has been challenged by doctors and although the change in work practices is only part of the modernisation agenda, it is fundamental to it. Some job roles will disappear or move under new management structures whilst other, new roles, will emerge. Whatever the shape of the new workforce, it is clear that leaders will require different skills from more traditional service configurations and professional groups and roles. You will read below how some professional groups are responding to these perceived challenges from government.

Maintaining an 'effective workforce'

We have seen how the integrated service and modernisation agendas provide both 'push' and 'pull' factors for the workforce. Co-operation is vital between countries, provider organisations, education and training organisations, and statutory and regulatory bodies to enable the development and retention of an effective, flexible workforce for the new forms of services that are envisaged.

The idea of an 'effective workforce' (Bedford, *et al.*, 2006) provides us with a more flexible and creative way of planning and maintaining a workforce for delivery of services. At any one time, this workforce could include various configurations of paid professionals and other workers, volunteers, service users, carers and students and trainees. By taking a whole system approach and including a range of individuals, groups, agencies and teams as part of the effective workforce, leaders can identify a new shape, structure and skills mix that is required to deliver effective integrated services to the population.

The health workforce is particularly affected by changing migration patterns, with certain ethnic groups more likely to enter some professions than others. A 2008 Organisation for Economic Co-operation and Development (OECD) report noted that fluctuating and unpredictable migration trends for highly skilled health workers mean that other human resource policies need to be set in place including improving recruitment and retention, adapting skill mix or making better use of skilled migrants from overseas (OECD, 2008, p9). On the international scene, the World Health Organisation (WHO) highlight that if health professionals learn together, and learn to collaborate as students, they are more likely to work together effectively in clinical or work-based teams (WHO, 1998). There is an underpinning assumption that teams are the cornerstone of an integrated health and social care workforce.

Economic drivers also support collaboration and partnership working. Faresjo suggests that the need for healthcare professionals to work with others to:

> meet the increasingly complex patients' and clients' needs most effectively is more important today than ever before. This is especially so in rural and remote areas around the world, where available healthcare resources are often quite sparse. In such cases, is it essential that health and social care professionals work together in order to supply sufficient care within available resources.
>
> (Faresjo, 2006, p1)

ACTIVITY 8.2

What have you noticed about the impact on professional roles as a consequence of service reconfiguration?

In particular, think about the way in which an 'effective workforce' is maintained in your workplace and how opportunities for a range of people and teams to be involved are managed.

How do you think disparities in pay and other reward systems might affect workforce design?

New leadership roles

In addition to professional initiatives (such as those relating to allied health professions and psychologists) that emphasise new leadership roles and the need for leadership development (DH, 2008d; BPS, 2007) a number of other initiatives which cut across professional curricula and programmes have been introduced such as the IQF and Common Core of Skills and Knowledge for the children's workforce. The IQF *will support shared values and learning approaches across the whole of the children and young people's workforce* (CWDC, 2008, p3). Integrated practice in children's services has introduced and emphasised the role of 'lead professionals'. These roles need to incorporate management and leadership across organisational, service and professional boundaries: boundaries which span statutory, voluntary and private sector providers. Service users (in this case children and families) will have a named professional, who may be drawn from a range of professional groups, who takes responsibility for assessing and co-ordinating care and is the primary contact and liaison person.

The Hay Group's report on leadership development in the Children's Workforce note three shapes of leadership role that are required to support the ICS agenda.

1 Operational – traditional management accountability for tangible end results; *primarily about 'getting things done', usually through others ... the characteristics which*

differentiate outstanding performers in this type of role are a focus on results, team leadership, confidence, and holding people to account.

2 Co-ordination – project or network type roles with ambiguous accountabilities.

3 Policy or strategic – advisory, planning or staff type roles responsible for the support, policy and innovation. *Roles which focus on policy are 'thinking' roles . . . (people) create ideas, plans and policies, but have to convince others about the value of the thinking . . . the critical characteristics are conceptual thinking, innovation, the ability to understand and influence others, and creating trust.*

The Report goes on to develop this further:

One of the trends in the Children's Workforce is the emergence of co-ordination roles – the essence of integrated working – where accountability for end results is still strong but the role holder does not have direct control over the resources needed to achieve them. This type of leadership role is an essential component of the leadership platform. Furthermore, the differences in the nature of the job, both in the degree of problem-solving (jobsize) and the type of leadership role (shape) imply different characteristics required for success.

The co-ordination roles fit between the operational and policy ones. They are about working with others, collaborating, networking, gaining trust and respect, and building effective relationships. Clearly these characteristics underpin effective integrated working.

(Hartle, *et al.*, 2008, p40).

Co-ordinators or boundary spanners who work across a range of sectors need to believe in collaboration; demonstrate an ability to obtain and distribute information strategically; see problems in new ways; craft solutions and develop and support the skills of others (Bradshaw, 1999, pp42–5). Meyerson suggests that 'tempered radicals' are required who are willing to act on different external agendas and take risks, yet work successfully within organisations (2004). This type of individual often acts as a broker, mediator and negotiator and is increasingly being recognised, recruited and trained for these specific cross-boundary roles (Hartle, *et al.*, 2008; Tennyson and Wilde, 2000).

Translating vision and values into integrated practice

The 2020 Children and Young People's Workforce Strategy sets out the government's vision and values *that everyone who works with children and young people should be:*

- *ambitious for every child and young person;*

- *excellent in their practice;*

- *committed to partnership and integrated working;*

- *respected and valued as professionals.*

(Department for Children Schools and Families (DCSF), 2008, pp6–7)

Whilst these aspirations enshrine values that most professionals and service users would welcome, there are real challenges in embedding these into systems, structures and work practices. These changes are part of whole system change which foregrounds the service user pathway, around which services are allocated in response to need. This requires not only the introduction of common assessment frameworks, but also integrated IT systems, shared records, aligned quality monitoring and assurance systems and defined and robust communication systems to enable sharing of information and flagging up of needs or risk. However even the ways in which such systems are designed and implemented are underpinned by different values and beliefs around the ways (and by whom) that these should be controlled, resourced, structured, managed and led. As you have seen, it is often system failures that have led to a lack of joined up working and subsequently service users falling through gaps in provision.

Increasingly, organisations representing different professionals are working together to define and agree underpinning knowledge, skills and behaviours/values around working collaboratively and interprofessionally. For example, in 2007, the General Social Care Council (GSCC), the General Teaching Council for England (GTC) and the Nursing and Midwifery Council (NMC) produced a joint statement which set out the values and dispositions underpinning effective interprofessional work with children and young people (NMC, 2007).

The statement defines a framework for working which can be taken forward and included into teaching and learning programmes (university and work based) as well as into requirements for practitioners. It is increasingly being incorporated into quality assurance frameworks for programmes, appraisal and professional development and practice. However it is early days, as a CWDC panel member at a 2007 conference to support the Integrated Children's Agenda (ICS) commented: *the ICS agenda is a long and ambitious programme and we need to recognise where we are. This is a first step and we need to build on the relationships we have* (McKimm, Burgess and Rafferty, 2008, p16).

These changes raise issues for those who are expected to lead and manage others, not just in terms of lines of accountability, reporting and systems integration but also much more fundamental ways of working, behaving and even 'being'. As Bernard Moss and Sam Held note in Chapters 6 and 7, we cannot assume that professionals, even those in the health and caring services, share common values, ways of working and management practices.

Figure 8.1 indicates how professional identify is shaped not only by an individual's personal beliefs and values; the concept of 'the other' (i.e. doctors vs nurses); professional codes of practice and ethics, and the legal system in which the professional operates. All these are constantly in flux, influenced by changing organisational cultures and practices, significant events, communities of practice to which the professional belongs or is aspiring towards and the wider society itself. The integrated service agenda will have massive impact on how professional identities are formed, defined, maintained and redefined.

Figure 8.1 A model of professional identity, formation and adaptation

Source: Adapted from McKimm, Preston-Shoot and Tomlinson, (2008)

Language and meaning

We only have to consider the different words policy makers and professions use to define the people with or for whom they are working with to see how meanings are defined and articulated. So in health rhetoric, we typically see the words 'patient' and 'clinical care', and the services described tend to be viewed as predominantly 'health services, not integrated public services (DH, 2008b; British Medical Association (BMA), 2008). In social care, the landscape is changing, but typical words used are 'service user', 'client', 'carer' and 'social care' and in education, we might hear 'pupils', 'students' or 'young people', depending on the organisational context.

ACTIVITY 8.3

Think about your own profession and workplace. What typical words and language are used to define people and practices?

Consider how the following are described (both formally and informally), then compare your descriptions to those of one or two other professions:

- *the service;*

- *the organisation;*

- *the users of the service;*

ACTIVITY 8.3 continued

- those who accompany or are related to the users of the service;

- the care that is provided (systems, structures, how people become involved with and leave the service);

- those who manage the service/care;

- those who lead the service/care;

- Other aspects.

How do you think differences in language reflect the deeper values, beliefs and perceptions that underpin work practices? Observe how this works in practice when people from different professions are working together, whose language is adopted and what are the models that underpin the use of language?

Models of care

Language is underpinned by the models of care that different professions utilise as knowledge and activity frameworks. In health these have predominantly been influenced by biomedical and bio-psycho-social models, reflecting the emphasis on the scientific paradigms that underpin knowledge. Social care (which tends to be associated with the psycho-social model) demonstrated an earlier movement towards the personalisation of care services and systems which begins with and foregrounds the person and their individual circumstances and *not* the services themselves. This contrasts with the way that health services and the role of the professional are often portrayed, particularly in policy documents relating specifically to medicine, dentistry and other health professions.

Collaboration in practice between different professionals highlights a fundamental division between those groups of professionals that assume the condition that needs to be addressed 'belongs' to the individual who has the presenting problem or symptoms, and those who assume it is, at least partly, external to the presenting individual. These two perspectives are not however aligned directly with the bio-medical and psycho-social models and by extension aligning health professionals with the former and social work practitioners with the latter. This would be simplistic and potentially divisive, as the boundaries between them are not at all clear.

Effective leaders need to be able to understand and adopt a range of perspectives to enable communication between different professional and service user groups. Willets, *et al.* (2006, pp101–2) describe five approaches to learning disability services which are underpinned by different models.

1   Medical model – learning disability seen as a medical 'condition' with care delivered by NHS staff (nurses and psychiatrists) often criticised for being paternalistic and viewing disabled people as 'sick', 'ill' or 'abnormal'.

2 Behavioural model – people seen as having maladaptive or inappropriate behaviours, treatment is behavioural psychology to replace problem or abnormal behaviours with more socially acceptable behaviours. This may be inappropriate as not all people with learning disability have challenging behaviours and for others, their challenging behaviour may be due to poor care or experiences.

3 Educational model – sees learning disability as a deficit in learning, social and life skills. Education and training may be the key to help people cope with challenges in life.

4 Social model – society puts social handicaps in place for disabled people. Social change may be needed to promote equity and inclusivity. The rights of the individual are paramount; the professional works in partnership to support individuals and carers.

5 Eclectic model – a balanced model, which combines approaches to care.

Willets, *et al.* also suggest that services need to shift the power from a professional centred model to a service user centred model, coupled with a shift from an ethics and duty model to a 'rights' model where quality support is an entitlement, offered in partnership which acknowledges the equal status and valid perspective of the user of the service. This shift is now being played out in government policy and strategy.

The personalisation agenda

The Putting People First concordat (DH, 2008c) is a major plank in the transformation of adult social care in England supported by a range of government departments and agencies, including health services, social services and local authorities. The concordat marks the start of a major shift in defining policy and integrated service strategies that use shared language and define shared values (such as social justice and empowerment) around personalised social care for adults throughout their lives. A Social Care Institute for Excellence (SCIE) report defines personalisation as:

• *finding new collaborative ways of working and developing local partnerships, which produce a range of services for people to choose from and opportunities for social inclusion;*

• *tailoring support to individual people's needs;*

• *recognising and supporting carers in their role, while enabling them to maintain a life beyond their caring responsibilities;*

• *a total system response so that universal and community services and resources are accessible to everyone;*

• *early intervention and prevention so that people are supported early on and in a way that's right for them.*

(Carr and Dittrich, 2008, p4)

ACTIVITY 8.4

Person centred support is not another thing services have to do; it's what they must do. It's not another job: it's the job (Glynn, et al., 2008, p11).

From your own professional perspective, how do you think your education, training, day to day work and codes of practice reflect this 'new way of working'?

Using Willet, et al.'s models, what are the dominant models that underpin care in your organisation?

Taking another professional group that you work with to support service users: how do you think their views, values and work practices align with yours and how are differences in perspective reconciled?

What implications for service users and the service itself can you identify when views, values and work practices are out of alignment? Can you recall any instances when differences in perspective had a negative impact on care and what were your own views and feelings about this?

The concept of power

Challenges to deeply held values and perceptions around social, health and public sector care can feel threatening and disempowering for individuals and professional groups. We see many power struggles around the ideas of professional identity which are articulated in defining the perceived needs of service users (or patients, or clients) in different ways. For example, the *Putting People First* policy document includes phrases which pose potential challenges to some professions' traditional ways of working, such as:

> the time has come to build on best practice and replace paternalistic, reactive care of variable quality with a mainstream system focussed on prevention, early intervention, enablement and high quality personally tailored services. In the future, we want people to have maximum control, choice and power over the support services they receive.
>
> (DH, 2008c, p2)

Research into the relationship between leaders and followers incorporate the idea of 'power with' or 'power through' rather than 'power over' (Northouse, 2004; Matusak, 1997; Greenleaf, 1977). This links closely with models of collaborative leadership (discussed in Chapter 1) which the Turning Point program defines as:

- leadership shown by a group that is acting collaboratively to solve agreed upon issues;

- uses supportive and inclusive methods to ensure that all people affected by a decision are part of the change process;

- requiring a new notion of power. . .the more power we share, the more power we have to use.

(Turning Point program, 1997)

Effective leaders need to take context, leaders/managers, followers and tasks into account when addressing issues of power and control over activities (Thomas (*after Adair*), 2004). Richards (2004) suggests that power (in the form of control and credit) should be given away strategically to those who *care the most* and who will use it wisely to reach an acceptable solution. This actually empowers the giver, is the mark of a successful change leader and helps to avoid the possible fragmentation of power in complex and multi-professional contexts.

ACTIVITY 8.5

Richards' comment is consistent with policy and reports that suggest that service users and carers should be given power over not only their own care, but also to have input and influence over support systems and structures.

What are the implications of giving power away in this way for all stakeholders concerned?

What checks and balances might need to be in place?

Richards goes on to describe Kouzes and Posner's (1991) citing of Kanter's (1982) *four principles of gaining by giving . . . (which) are: give people important work to do; give people discretion and autonomy; give visibility and recognition; build relationships with others* (Richards, 2004, p4). This can help to overcome issues arising from the fragmentation of power. The diffusion of authority, responsibility and the ability to act can result in no one person or group having power. As Chrislip and Larson suggest, if this continues, power can become fragmented to the point of organisational and individual inertia (1994).

Lukes (1974) identifies three 'dimensions' of power in organisations.

1 Overt power – emphasises the exercise of power through formal decision-making processes (such as committees) and observable behaviour. Power is vested in the ability to define the reality for others so that they internalise the existing order. It often resides in an individual or group having authority through position, rank or status.

2 Agenda-setting power – this is the power of an individual or group to define the agenda and thus prevent others from voicing interests in the decision- making process. Potential issues and conflicts are not brought into the open, to the benefit of those who have power and the detriment of those who do not, the exercise of power can be both overt and covert and creates the illusion of consultation.

3 Hegemonic power – this is the power of an individual or group to define what counts as an issue and to mould perceptions in such a way that the 'other' accepts that there are no significant issues. The power to shape thoughts and desires is the most effective kind of power, since it pre-empts conflict and even an awareness of possible conflicts. This dimension of power is seen in processes of socialisation, control of information and management of meaning.

Hardy (1996) suggests a fourth dimension termed 'system power'. She suggests that here, power is not consciously mobilised by actors but is embodied in *impersonal* and *invisible* forces that produce both advantages and disadvantages for organisational members. Here, power is not susceptible to deliberate manipulation by any one actor, but impersonally embedded within larger systems. It is 'invisible' in that it is often taken for granted and hence unnoticed by those in the organisation. This not only relates to individual organisations, but is magnified when we consider multi-agency and cross-sector working. Becoming aware of the taken-for-granted or assumed power in systems can be a first step towards unlocking conflict, stalemate, barriers to action or inertia.

Leadership and management development

Next we go on to consider how leadership and management development has been reviewed and reconceptualised in the light of broader shifts around workforce redesign.

It can be difficult to retain professional identity in the face of widespread change, training and education of new workers, and new routes to leadership and management. Some initiatives such as *Championing Children* (CWDC, 2008), set out educational frameworks which define the expectation of collaborative leadership in terms of skills, knowledge and behaviours of all those who deliver children's services. The ICS agenda places responsibility on all partners to provide joined-up education and training through collaborative leadership, setting out to bridge traditional divides between professional education and vocational training for both professionals and non-professionals. Many service and education and training providers are working together to develop programmes and strategies to underpin leadership and management development for the children's workforce. However there are barriers to leadership development in integrated services including strategic planning for leadership development; access to coordinated leadership training and development; funding and time (Hartle, *et al.*, 2008, p39).

In Chapter 4, Kay Phillips highlights the importance of identifying different forms of working, including partnership working and networking, and suggests that new forms of working should be developed to meet complex systems needs and that research needs to be carried out to identify 'what works' in integrated practice. A number of projects are under way which start to address some of the issues raised in Chapter 4, such as the need to practice, and research into, distributed or shared leadership. One example of a project which aims to develop, test and research into leadership development and planning through a matrix tool is described in the case study.

CASE STUDY

Leading for Children in Essex, Essex County Council

Essex County Council developed and introduced a new leadership model which summarises and maps out the kind of leadership dispositions, skills and behaviours required of those involved in services for children and young people in Essex. It is intended that these descriptors will be a helpful contribution to developing effective leadership so that children and young people can flourish. It is anticipated that this will be useful in relation both to leadership in integrated settings and to leadership of integrated practice in all settings. The matrix provides rich pictures of what integrated leadership might look like for a variety of participants, ranging from children and young people themselves to leaders of services and whole system leaders.

The matrix has two axes, each of which identifies a number of key areas against which individuals, teams and organisations can be developed, selected for appointment or appraised. Groups, teams, individuals and organisations can complete the cells within the matrix to provide profiles of distributed leadership in integrated settings and practice; as a tool for planning development and change and ensuring leadership participation; for influencing performance management, identifying leadership roles and contributions and developing job descriptions, and as an audit tool to examine strengths and areas for improvement at individual, team and organisational levels.

The horizontal axis defines distinctive features of integrated leadership . . . designed to cover the range of features required in leadership of the integrated system for children and young people in Essex.

Distinctive features of integrated leadership:

- *champion (vision);*
- *chaos management and managing complexity;*
- *guardianship (primary focus on children and young people) and accountability;*
- *emotional intelligence, valuing self and others (respect);*
- *change facilitator;*
- *securing benefits to children and young people.*

The vertical axis describes the different roles of integrated leadership. The wide range of these roles reflects the distributed model of leadership being developed to benefit young people and children.

Everyone is a leader – the range of leadership roles:

- *whole system leadership;*
- *leadership of main professional groupings;*
- *leadership of main strategic areas and settings (including cross-service working);*
- *individual professional;*
- *route maker;*
- *guide (leads the e.g. family and young person through the steps);*
- *leaders in the community;*
- *family leaders;*
- *children and young people as leaders.*

(Essex County Council, 2006)

ACTIVITY 8.6

Compare the Essex Council case study with a leadership development programme with which you are familiar. List the similarities and differences in approach, aims and objectives and those invited to participate.

What is distinctive about frameworks such as the Essex model is that they are inclusive: inclusive of service users, those who manage and lead the service and those who work in specific contexts and settings. The Essex model draws on a range of documents (including *Championing children*, the NHS LQF, Sector Skills Council frameworks and the National College of School Leadership Professional Qualification for Integrated Centre Leadership*)* and uses a 'distributed leadership' model. The model is designed to help provide case examples of how leadership operates in practice in a range of settings and contexts. This reflects Day's (2001) distinction between 'leader' and 'leadership' development. Bolden (writing about distributed leadership) suggests that 'leader development' is an investment in *human capital* to enhance intrapersonal competence for selected individuals whereas leadership development is an investment in *social capital* to develop interpersonal networks and co-operation within organisations and other social systems (Bolden, 2007, p6). Many so-called leadership development programmes actually focus on the former rather than the latter.

Uni-professional leadership development initiatives, such as the Medical Leadership Competency Framework (a joint venture between the Academy of Medical Royal Colleges and the NHS) may serve to run counter to the culture of collaboration in health, social care and public services enshrined in other cross-sector developments and result in mixed messages and unintended consequences for integrated services. The 'Framework' (DH, 2008e) is based on the NHS Leadership Qualities Framework (LQF) you read about in Chapters 1 and 7 (2006). The LQF foregrounds transformational leadership (Bass, 1985; Burns, 1978) and Emotional Intelligence (Goleman, 1998). These leadership theories and approaches have themselves been subject to critique for paying lip service to collaboration, consultancy and democracy (Price, 2003; Allix, 2000).

Although the Medical Leadership Competency Framework describes itself as *based on the concept of shared leadership*, the Framework also notes that *it is a critical fact that doctors have a direct and far reaching impact on patient experience and outcomes . . . (and) legal authority broader than any other health professional and therefore have an intrinsic managerial and leadership role within healthcare services* (DH, 2008e, p6). The leadership Framework identifies many areas where doctors might engage with other health professionals, patients, teams, service users, carers and the public (termed 'others'), The starting point however is around doctors as a professional group and their clinical and service leadership roles, drawing from predominantly health leadership development frameworks rather those in the broader integrated service agenda.

The idea that doctors need different and separately delivered 'medical' leader development from that of other professionals may lead either to a reinforcement of traditional leadership structures and professional stereotypes or (paradoxically) to a rejection of doctors' power and leadership role by 'followers' as doctors become out of step with the huge groundswell of change towards more collaborative and empowerment based leadership models.

For example, in older people's or mental health services, geriatricians, psychiatrists or GPs may assume that doctors should always lead joint care teams whereas in some situations the leadership role may be taken by a social worker, clinical psychologist, generic mental health worker, a health visitor or a trained volunteer. Stone (2003) suggests that:

> the primary difference between transformational leadership and servant leadership, is in the focus of the leader. The transformational leader's focus is directed towards the organisation and his or her behaviour builds follower commitment toward organisational objectives, while the servant leader's focus is on the followers and the achievement of organisational objectives is a subordinate outcome. The extent to which a leader is able to shift the primary focus of leadership from the organisation to the follower is the distinguishing factor in classifying leaders as either transformational or servant leaders

(Stone, 2003, p1).

Professionals operating within different models of leadership which do not stress collaboration, partnership, and moral leadership may actually undermine service shifts towards integrated care. Long-standing power and status differentials between multi-disciplinary team members may lead to the voice of those less powerful not being heard, resulting in the perspectives or input of non-medical, non-professional or service user members being ignored or dismissed, even when the knowledge might be vital for service user care.

Communities of practice and activity theory

A number of writers have identified the need to research into and theorise models of leadership and activity in relation to interprofessional practice and integrated working (Taylor, *et al.*, 2008; Armistead, *et al.*, 2007). We have considered above how the concept of 'professions' is being constantly redefined. Here, we look at two theories which have been influential in offering different explanations of what might be occurring in the workplace.

In integrated services there is a shift towards individuals being identified not simply in terms of their professional status or as linked to one organisation or department, but as members of a *community of practice* (CoP) (Wenger, 1998) such as a children's workforce. A CoP is distinguished from a 'community', although a community also organises itself around shared concepts, values, perceptions and practices (Capra, 1997).

The idea of CoP has informed understanding of how professional groups work and learn together through social interaction, and in particular how learners are 'admitted' to the community through *legitimate peripheral participation* (LPP). A CoP as defined as a model of collaborative, situational, peer-based learning where members work towards a common goal as defined in terms of knowledge rather than task (Wenger, 1998). The process of working together, networking and sharing knowledge and resources can lead to an enriched learning experience as people are exposed to new ways of thinking and problem solving.

Communities of practice can exist at all levels and in many different forms and membership, either formal or informal. They function around peer-to-peer problem solving; sharing best practices; updating and sharing knowledge for daily practice and generating new ideas and innovations. CoPs share a common body of knowledge, a commitment to forming and maintaining a network and are committed to sharing practice, co-creating knowledge, ideas, resources and strategies. Members are self-selected based on expertise or passion for the topic. Boundaries are fuzzy and shifting. Identification with the group, its expertise, purpose and commitment holds the CoP together and they evolve and end organically as long as members feel the need and gain value by engagement.

Professional identity is developed within a CoP as participants play out assigned roles assigned, gain new knowledge, experience and reflection and test their models of practice through experience and reflection (Davis, 2006). Through membership of a CoP, an individual has the opportunity to engage in active participation both professionally and socially, forming networks and building professional identity (Andrew, *et al.*, 2007; McKimm, Millard and Held, 2008). The social learning at all levels which comes through involvement in a CoP is often informal and unacknowledged by the workplace. However, workplaces enable people to use the new knowledge from CoP, they can act as change agents, find new ways of working and feel empowered to challenge and develop practice. This ensures that best practice is incorporated into the workplace on an ongoing basis.

Through *legitimate peripheral participation* (LPP), learners are likely to learn more and become engaged in the CoP by being increasingly involved in work-based activities, learning from a variety of people. The community of practice provides examples of more apprentices at different stages working towards being expert practitioners, masters and role models who embody the behaviours, language and rules within a profession (Davis, 2006; Lave and Wenger, 1991). So how does it work in the real world? In the workplace there are many examples of LPP in action which are often unrecognised as learning experiences. Professional identity is developed by taking on the tasks and responsibilities of that profession, involving experience, identity development, merging with the community and engagement in full professional practice through an inbound trajectory from the periphery to the becoming full participants (Davis, 2006). LPP provides more than an observational *lookout post*: it crucially involves participation as a way of learning – of both absorbing and being absorbed in – *the culture of practice* (Lave and Wenger, 1991).

Recognition of LPP as a valid learning experience and making a conscious effort to establish roles within the boundaries of LPP may enrich learning experiences and provide pathways for establishing professional identity and fully-fledged membership to the CoP. This can also be relevant to leaders and managers. As you begin to move into a CoP which is around leading change or services, participating in professional development programmes, meetings or projects can help new and aspiring leaders develop knowledge and understanding and a new identity as a leader. The concept of a CoP is highly relevant for cross-sector or agency working, enabling the inclusion of a wide range of people, agencies and groupings in activities, including services users, carers and volunteers as well as the paid workforce. For many individual managers and leaders, engaging and identifying with a CoP might be more meaningful in the context of integrated service delivery and planning than working within professional silos. The realignment of policy, services, systems and structures around the agendas we have discussed in this chapter provide fertile ground for leaders and managers to engage with and develop CoPs.

Developing new CoPs (Wenger, 1998; Drath and Palus, 1994) within existing management structures and hierarchies and funding streams geared towards meeting service user needs offers yet another challenge for leaders of integrated services. Ansett (2005) suggests that this leadership approach, grounded in social responsibility and evidencing moral and servant leadership (Gilbert, 2005; Greenleaf, 2002) is highly relevant for the development of strong, transparent relationships. As you read in Chapter 6, new leadership approaches grounded in 'spiritual intelligence' are rapidly establishing their credibility and moderating new managerialism.

Boud and Middleton (2003) argue however that the concept of a community of practice as a framework for workplace learning is too simplistic. They claim that the learning described by Wenger and other researchers is simply means of *doing the job properly* and not able to be articulated as a special form of learning. Although there is value in making learning 'visible' and many workplaces have groups with features of a CoP, such a framework is not sufficient to develop new understanding of how learning happens at work (Boud & Middleton, 2003). Let us now look at Activity Theory which may provide more illumination on work based learning.

Activity theory

Another influential theory that underpins distributed leadership (which, as you have seen, is increasingly influential in integrated services) is Activity Theory (Engestrom, 1999). Engestrom developed the linked concepts of co-configuration, knotworking, expansive learning and boundary crossing to help explain the ways in which actors related to one another within social and workplace systems and how social systems themselves inter-related in the workplace. Activity theory is grounded in a social constructivist perspective which emphasises the active role of participants in constructing and co-constructing meanings in different contexts. Taylor, *et al.* (2008) describe Activity Theory as emphasising *the multiplicity of variables, the relationships between them and the significance of the wider context.* They describe the key concepts in terms of Engestrom's and Warmington *et al.*'s (2004) work in their Knowledge Review of interprofessional and integrated educational practice for the integrated children's agenda.

Co-configuration is a participatory model that emphasises the dynamic, reciprocal relationship between providers and clients. This may include the relationship between young people, their families and education providers.

Knotworking is rapidly changing, distributed and partially improvised collaborations of performance, which take place between otherwise loosely connected actors and their work systems.

Expansive learning is where professionals are learning something that has not been created or constructed before. They are re-thinking goals, activities and relationships and beginning to respond in new and enriched ways, producing new patterns of activity that expand understanding and change practice. Warmington, et al. (2004) found an emphasis placed on consensual models of working, with an ideal work form being conventional team working, and suggest that this may tend to under-acknowledge the importance of internal tensions generated by activity systems as mechanisms for transforming practice.

They emphasise the importance of developing 'tools of disagreement' as expansive learning occurs precisely when existing activity systems generate tensions or contradictions that demand learning 'outside the box to resolve them.

Boundary crossing is where collaboration between workers from different professional backgrounds might generate new professional practices. As (they) share activities they negotiate working practices that cross traditional boundaries. This shifts from the conventional view of barriers between people with different professional roles to identifying space to renegotiate professional practices. This may enable professionals to become more adept at operating within discursive practices of colleagues from other backgrounds, or it may lead to the emergence of hybrid professional types.

(Taylor, *et al.*, 2008, p65)

Taylor, *et al.* go on to note that in the field of interprofessional and integrated working, *complexity is in itself a central characteristic which risks being ignored by policy makers in their haste to implement change and improve services* (2008, p65). Bolden (2007) describes how Gronn (2002) uses Activity Theory as a bridge between agency and structure whereas Spillane (2004) uses it to frame distributed leadership practice in terms of cognition and action. In this way, leadership is seen as an integral part of everyone's daily activities and interactions, *revealed equally within small, incremental, informal and emergent acts as within large-scale transformational change from the top* (Bolden, 2007, p5). These ways of looking at and theorising leadership for integrated services provide us with alternative viewpoints that emphasise the 'spaces' between, spaces that adept leaders can work within to effect service change and transform practices.

C H A P T E R   S U M M A R Y

Developing and maintaining an effective workforce lies at the heart of delivering integrated services. Managers and leaders (as well as policy makers) need to keep sharp focus on how policies, strategies and structures across society affect workforce patterns and the availability of appropriately skilled people to implement the vision. Issues such as how to involve service users, carers and volunteers in the delivery of care need to be addressed alongside professional development activities, education and training. A whole range of challenges underpins achieving an integrated public service agenda relating to values, power, status and control of resources: adding yet more layers of complexity to the integrated service agenda.

FURTHER READING

Andrew, N, Tolson, D and Ferguson, D (2007) Building on Wenger: communities of practice in nursing. *Nurse Education Today*, 28, 246–52

Gabriel, Y, Fineman, S and Sims, D (2000) *Organising and organisations*, 2nd edn. London: Sage Publications Ltd.

Weinstein, J, Whittington, C and Leiba, T (eds) (2003) *Collaboration in social work practice*. London: Jessica Kingsley Publishers.

Chapter 9

Leadership in practice: Difficulties and dilemmas

Judy McKimm and Kay Phillips

Introduction

In this chapter we pull together some of the key themes from the book to consider a range of difficulties and dilemmas relating to the development and delivery of integrated services. Ensuring a more joined up approach is not easy and, despite very considerable investment in recent years, progress can be slow and fragmented. Recent examples have been selected to illustrate the challenges inherent in leading and managing change at every level. This chapter encompasses policy development and implementation, strategic and operational leadership at local level and professional/personal leadership at the front-line of service delivery. We hope that, as you work through the chapter, you will see how important it is to be aware of the policy and strategic contexts whatever your current role.

Chapter overview

We have organised the chapter into three sections to make it easier to focus on specific difficulties and dilemmas within three different contexts which relate to varying levels at which individuals operate.

1　The policy context – considering the challenges associated with the implementation of complex change and how policies define and shape service agendas.

2　The organisational context – reviewing the impact of systems and the importance of collaboration within and between organisations.

3　The personal context – focusing on some of the personal and interpersonal issues that people face when working in integrated services.

Links are made back into other chapters of the book as appropriate, and specifically to Chapter 8 which considers professional roles and workforce development within integrated services.

The policy context

In Chapter 2, Michael Preston-Shoot provided a clear and comprehensive analysis of developments over the last decade in law and policy for integrated practice. We learned that the key driver for policy change was the need to improve the quality of service delivery for service users and carers, particularly society's most vulnerable children and adults and others with complex and multiple needs. From the outset, one of the principal ways of achieving improvement was to tackle service fragmentation, caused by health, education, social care staff and others working in professional 'silos'.

Ten years on, however, hard evidence that more integrated working delivers better outcomes is still quite difficult to find. In 2006, for example, the Scottish Government report, *Exploring the Evidence Base for Integrated Children's Services (ICS)*, noted that the initial expectations of ICS were high. They included:

- higher achievement in school;

- better health;

- less anti-social behaviour;

- better support for vulnerable families;

- possible cost savings via more efficient working between agencies.

But its authors commented that there was still insufficient reliable evidence on ICS outcomes to assess whether children were any less vulnerable to serious neglect or death as a result of the policy changes. Sadly this is brought home by developments taking place as this chapter is being written. Eight years on from the tragic death of Victoria Climbié, the same local authority, Haringey, is facing an independent enquiry into the death of another child, Baby P. Despite 60 contacts with his mother during his short life, professionals failed to prevent the repeated abuse and murder of this 'at risk' child.

CASE STUDY

Haringey Social Services and the case of Baby P

Baby P died in August 2007, following a long period of sustained neglect and violent abuse by his mother and the two men who shared her home. The baby's death occurred seven years after another child, Victoria Climbié, had also died violently at the hands of her guardians in the same borough of Haringey. The Climbié Inquiry which followed Victoria's murder identified many failings in child protection systems and the recommendations of its Chairman, Lord Laming, were enacted in the Children Act 2004. Children's trusts, local safeguarding boards and a new system of serious case reviews were introduced to try to prevent such terrible suffering from ever happening again.

In the case of Baby P it appeared at first that social workers and other professionals had done all they could to protect the child, who had been identified as being 'at risk'. The social workers had made over 60 visits and police and hospital workers had also had contact with the baby and his family. Three months after his death Ofsted inspectors had also given Haringey Council's child protection services a 'good' rating. So what went wrong?

A review of the Council's practice and management was undertaken by Ofsted, the Healthcare Commission and the Inspectorate of Constabulary. This was released in Autumn 2008, following the end of the criminal trial of the three adults directly responsible for Baby Ps death. The review identified a catalogue of failings on the part of Haringey Social Services.

1 *Failure to ensure that the recommendations of the Climbié Inquiry were met.*

2 *Over-dependence on inaccurate performance data; reports were not based on reliable evidence.*

3 *Insufficient management oversight of the Assistant Director by the Director of Children's Services and Chief Executive.*

4 *Failure to identify children at immediate risk and act on evidence.*

5 *Poor gathering, recording and sharing of information – inadequate case files.*

6 *Social workers, health professionals and police did not communicate well; poor handling of referrals between agencies resulted. Some professionals (GPs and hospital staff) were unaware of the child protection referral systems.*

7 *Poor child protection plans.*

8 *Inadequate serious case review into Baby P's death.*

9 *Inconsistent frontline practice and supervision by senior management.*

10 *High turnover of social workers; over-reliance on agency staff.*

11 *Heavy workloads for social workers.*

12 *Failure to speak directly to children at risk.*

This list graphically illustrates a number of themes. The first three points demonstrate poor leadership and weak strategic management systems at the highest level. Points 4 to 8 reveal operational inadequacies in communication and information systems within and across the agencies involved in child protection. Pressures and weaknesses in the professional workforce are evidenced by points 9 to 11. In many ways the final criticism is the most serious; the frequent failure on the part of the professionals to give a voice to the vulnerable child.

Source: The Guardian (2008) Thursday, 2 December, pp4, 5 and 32.

The full 14 page Ofsted Report, written by its Chief Inspector, Christine Gilbert, was not released to the public.

Haringey is not alone in facing criticism for its failure to protect its most vulnerable children. This is extremely complex and challenging work and strategic change is notoriously difficult to achieve. Perhaps by looking at recent policy developments in England we can gain some insight into the task facing the government and those agencies striving to develop the children and young people's workforce. These policy developments have been based on the belief that a more integrated workforce will deliver better integrated, client-centred services, safeguarding the interests of the most vulnerable.

The new *Children's Plan*, published in December 2007, reiterated the need for integrated working and for a set of shared interprofessional values. In April 2008, *Building Brighter Futures; next steps for the Children's Workforce*, made it clear that additional work was needed to bring about the required cultural change across service delivery agencies. The Children's Workforce Network (CWN) is tasked with delivering the required change and its members have therefore had to agree how the policy recommendations can be implemented.

The policy documents re-emphasise the importance of integrated working, graduate leadership, the development of new roles and further professionalisation within the workforce. In response, the CWN is addressing the strategic priorities by concentrating on specific work streams including leadership and management development, integrated working and the remodelling of the workforce and an integrated qualifications framework (IQF)

If we take the last of these, the development of an Integrated Qualifications Framework to develop the skills of the children and young people's workforce, we can see the difficulties and dilemmas that have to be addressed in order to make this a reality. Let's look at it from two different perspectives – the universities and the service delivery agencies.

The universities are being urged to play their part by developing professional capabilities through new programmes and interprofessional learning opportunities for students. Some excellent examples are already in evidence but there are numerous logistical and financial barriers to be surmounted and, at the time of writing, there is no common set of undergraduate professional standards for integrated working.

The *Integrated Children's Services in Higher Education Conference Report* (2008) acknowledged some of the practical challenges of aligning educational change with emerging roles in children's services. These include:

- developing integrated qualifications, awards and career pathways between further and higher education;

- reducing the barriers inherent in university subject and departmental structures. For example education/early years, health and social work programmes are often located, funded and managed separately;

- meeting the requirements of professional and regulatory bodies;

- clarifying funding streams and progression routes to enable staff to move between professions;

- securing appropriate placements for interprofessional learning.

The practical challenges for service deliverers are rather different. At a CWN conference held in 2008, (www.childrensworkforce.org.uk) delegates discussed professional development issues, including the IQF. These are just a few of the points they raised.

- There is a need to work towards a common baseline of skills across the workforce, giving the current and future workforce the competencies and skills they will need. IQF qualifications need to 'guarantee' competence.

- There is confusion amongst sections of the workforce about what is out there in terms of qualifications and training.

- IQF is not the only way to assure quality, especially for dealing with vulnerable children or non school provision. IQF should not be developed in a way that precludes involvement of a wide range of people.

- There is disparity of standards and their usefulness; there needs to be coherence between standards and training.

This example serves to illustrate one of the important messages of Chapter 2. Policy recommendations may appear to be clear and straightforward but there can be very complex issues to address in implementing them. Creating a more integrated workforce requires a huge number of existing systems and sub-systems to change in a wide range of sectors, organisations, professional and regulatory bodies and staff groups. And ideally this needs to happen across the whole country, not in a piecemeal fashion.

You may remember that we discussed the challenges of this type of change in Chapter 4, when we introduced you to complex adaptive systems theory. Because of the complexity, some delivery agencies are asking for a simplification of systems, institutions and decision-making processes to help them make sense of policy developments. There are also calls for more joined up strategy so that, for example, the objectives of Every Child Matters and the National Service Framework for Children might be more explicitly aligned.

Perhaps more importantly, what is envisaged for the new, integrated workforce is a major *culture* change, perceived by some as challenging the professional identities, work practices and values of individual professions. This can be even harder to achieve because it requires genuine engagement by the workforce itself. Despite the challenge that this presents there are examples of excellent innovative practice which demonstrate that good leadership *can* deliver cultural change at local level. See for example the ICS-HE website, which also contains a useful CYP 'policy map' (ICSHE, 2008).

We have seen in Chapters 2, 3 and 4 how different pieces of legislation have sent different messages to agencies, ranging from voluntary co-operation to more formal collaboration or a statutory duty to work together. Organisational partnerships and financial transfer arrangements have been put in place to support more radical change, delivered via integrated working. Good progress has been made in some areas, such as better integration of older people's health and social care services, but there is still plenty of evidence that, at service delivery level, major challenges remain. These include:

- integrated assessment of, and support for, people with mental health needs;

- meeting the individual needs of disabled people;

- implementing the single assessment process for older people;

- supporting carers appropriately;

- sharing information across professions to safeguard vulnerable children.

Trish Hafford-Letchfield wrote in Chapter 3 of the importance of government policy in informing the strategic direction for agencies involved in creating and maintaining sustainable communities. A number of very encouraging developments are emerging in this area. Some district councils in deprived areas, for example, are working with their local primary care trusts to develop and deliver integrated health and wellbeing strategies for their communities. In line with the government public health policy, the focus of these strategies is on maintaining people's physical and mental health (as opposed to treating illness) and on generating a sense of community ownership by engaging local people in leading the change process.

The challenges of making such partnerships work were clearly outlined in Chapters 3 and 4. It is worth reiterating that these strategies will not necessarily be implemented simply by reshaping local organisations and professional responsibilities. Their success depends on local communities and third sector organisations being given more power and control.

Some services are benefitting from legal measures which facilitate the creation of better organisational arrangements. Children's Trusts, established under the Children Act (2004) are managed by local authorities with considerable powers to ensure that multi-agency working takes place to deliver integrated services to children and families.

As the policy and guidance has proliferated, the central messages of collaboration, co-operation and integration have grown stronger and the duties and responsibilities of different service provider agencies have become more explicitly defined. But difficulties and dilemmas remain in relation to policy. These include:

- the number of bodies involved in policy implementation and guidance. The Every Child Matters website serves to illustrate this (www.everychildmatters.gov.uk);

- parallel initiatives which create paradoxes; for example, plans for a workforce strategy for an integrated children's workforce are being pursued alongside unilateral NHS and social care workforce development strategies;

- the sheer amount of policy that agencies have to deal with. There is some evidence that this has created confusion around roles, responsibilities and formal statutory account-abilities. This can be illustrated by looking at the progress of children's trusts.

CASE STUDY

Every Child Matters – are we nearly there yet?

The Audit Commission's report on children's trusts, October 2008
Five years after the green paper, Every Child Matters, the Audit Commission reported that, there is little evidence of better outcomes for children and young people. Although they found that on the ground professionals were working together, often through informal arrangements, the new children's trusts were actually hindering progress. A third of

directors of children's services said trusts' purposes were unclear and centrally-directed approaches were unhelpful. Too much time was being spent on structures and processes, at the expense of improving services for children and families. Different government departments had offered different, sometimes conflicting guidance in their communications to local authorities and there was little evidence children's trusts had offered value for money improvements.

The key findings of the Commission's report were:

- *children's trusts have little if any oversight of budgets and money for children's services;*

- *the relationship between trusts and other local partnerships is unclear;*

- *children's trusts are unsure whether they are strategic planning bodies or concerned with the detail of service delivery;*

- *in going ahead with trusts, the government seemed to have ignored the results of its own pilot study;*

- *there is little evidence that mainstream money has been redirected by children's trusts.*

The Commission recommended:

- *Whitehall should remove barriers to local schemes of cooperation;*

- *children and young people themselves should have more say in how children's services are designed;*

- *'missing partners' should be brought in, notably GPs and agencies concerned with jobs and skills;*

- *children's trusts should do more to involve schools and GPs, Connexions and other agencies;*

- *better integration of children's trusts with other local partnerships.*

The organisational context

Following on from the case study above, Whittington's work is helpful in clarifying how effective partnership working might be developed at organisational level:

Partnerships must be developed and joined up at multiple levels within and between organisations and held together by multiple acts of collaboration (Whittington, 2003, p24)

Three levels at which partnership and collaboration should occur *between* organisations are identified.

1 Strategic level – including planning and agreement of service goals, the resources needed to achieve these and workforce and systems capable of reviewing across and within service and professional boundaries.

2 Intermediate level – here there are two sets of joint activity. One involves joint or lead commissioning of services and the management of pooled budgets etc. The other is joint work to ensure quality assurance and review, participation of all stakeholders and development of effective services with good information and communication systems.

3 Operational level – here work takes place within multi-disciplinary service teams and settings, broad inter-agency groupings and projects or integrated services. Front line service teams in particular have a lot to offer regarding review and development of the service because of their direct interactions with service users and staff from a range of agencies.

In 2005 the Department for Education and Schools defined 'integration' as:

> a set of processes and actions by which partners ensure outcome-focused frontline delivery. It means a holistic approach within which needs can be identified and priorities – national and local – can be addressed.
>
> (DfES, 2005b, p11).

What challenges does this present at organisational level and what are some of the common difficulties and dilemmas?

Integrated client-centred services require effective cross-boundary working by key agencies and individuals. Depending on the particular service issue this boundary-spanning might involve working across sectors, organisations, departments, professions or teams. In all cases there will be some requirement to share information and knowledge and perhaps to modify systems and practice to effect improvement.

Table 9.1 Lists of the areas alongside the levels of activity within the organisation.

Level	Areas of partnership and collaboration
Strategic	Planning and management of: • service goals • acquisition/deployment of resources including the workforce • 'whole system review', learning and development
Intermediate	• joint and lead commissioning • management of pooled budgets • management of integrated services • quality assurance, governance, regulation and standards and participation of service users and carers • focused review, research and service development • planning and delivery of workforce learning and development • development of information and communication systems
Operational	• service delivery in multi inter-disciplinary contexts and settings • service delivery working across departmental and agency boundaries by staff and teams of non-integrate services/multi-agency networks • in both scenarios, contribution to service review, organisational learning and development

Source: Whittington, C. (2003, p25)

It might be imagined that working across different organisations poses the greatest challenge but systems and structures within single organisations can just as easily conspire to prevent integrated assessment of need and service delivery. Consider this simple example, based on a real service user experience.

CASE STUDY

What is an urgent priority?

A local authority Occupational Therapist assessed an 80 year old woman with a neurological condition which was impairing her mobility and balance. The woman's GP had identified the need for a walk-in shower for her sheltered housing bungalow as she could no longer get in and out of her bath safely. The OT assessed her case as an 'urgent priority' because of the risk of falling, and a letter was received shortly after the home visit, confirming that her needs had been communicated in writing to the Housing Department's Adaptations Manager, whose team would fit the shower. They would be in touch in a few weeks.

Ten months later there had been no further communication from either the OT service or the Adaptations Manager. After repeated telephone calls from the family, it transpired that the 'urgent priority' identified by the OT became just another job on a numbered list in the adaptations department. OT staff were unaware of this. All jobs, big and small, urgent and non-urgent were on the same very long list and had to work their way to the top. No target date could be given by either team for the job to be completed. Furthermore if the year's financial allocation ran out there would be no shower.

The family felt their only option was to make a formal complaint to the local authority. Four weeks later the shower was fitted.

ACTIVITY 9.1

How might both of these teams change their systems and ways of working to improve this situation, communicate more effectively with service users and deliver a more user-centred service?

What this example illustrates is the importance of really scrutinising existing systems as part of any process of culture change. Systems are part of an organisation's culture; they are *the way things are done around here*. They may meet the needs of the individuals maintaining them but systems can be used to block change at every level. We don't know, for example, whether the Adaptations Manager in our case study has changed his system for managing his list of jobs, or whether the OT team continue to send 'urgent priority' referrals to him in the same way.

Sometimes the systems issues are far more complex. Systems for recording and sharing service user/patient information are often scrutinised as part of formal enquiries when things go wrong. They are a crucial part of professional working but a continuing concern for cross-agency working is the inconsistency of professional case notes, the incompatibility of IT systems across different agencies and the extent to which different professionals use electronic records. In Chapter 2 we heard, for example, how all of this can mitigate against information sharing, financial tracking and the implementation of common assessment processes.

These difficulties and dilemmas can be compounded by poor awareness of the specific areas of work which require close collaboration. Policy guidance stipulates when there is a legal requirement for organisations to work together to deliver integrated services. But there are many other areas where closer collaboration, whilst not mandatory, would benefit service users. Collaboration can also help all stakeholders to develop a better understanding of specific roles and responsibilities.

Figure 9.1 is adapted from the work of Bill Critchley and David Casey (1984). Although their original ideas were applied to effective team-working, we have found that their model has relevance for integrated service delivery. Casey and Critchley suggest that most of our work tasks can be divided into three broad types, puzzles, complex puzzles and problems.

1 Puzzles have a solution and therefore we can usually work on these with a reasonable degree of autonomy and find a solution.

2 Complex puzzles often require an input from others, so there is a need for some co-operation and knowledge sharing to enable us to reach agreement on a preferred solution.

3 Finally, there are the really challenging problems, which we may not be able to fully resolve but might work on together to achieve some incremental progress and improvement.

It is these challenging problems which require us to engage in genuine collaboration, using high level inter-personal skills. Note too that the difficult problems also require us to be more open with others, possibly revealing what we *don't* know as well as what we know. For interprofessional working, within or between organisations, this can feel quite risky. The authors argue that, at the very time when information needs to be shared most openly, there may be a tendency to withhold information or conceal our lack of understanding.

ACTIVITY 9.2

Think of a challenging problem or issue that you are dealing with and try to engage in some critical thinking, using the model and these questions as a prompt.

- *What makes your issue challenging?*
- *Who do you need to collaborate with and why?*
- *What interpersonal skills will you need?*
- *What information can you share with others?*
- *What do you hope they might be able to share with you?*
- *What are the risks involved?*
- *What progress would you like to make?*

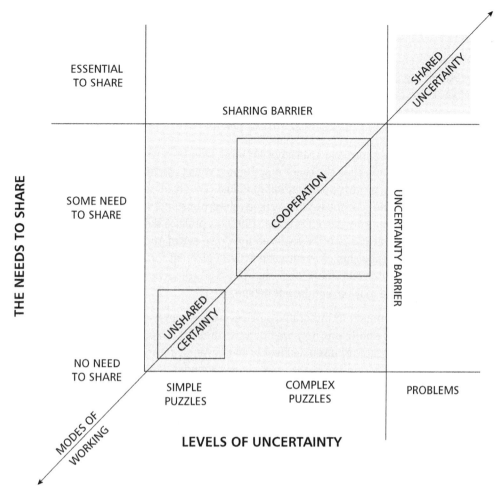

Figure 9.1. Working effectively on complex problems

Source: Adapted from Critchley and Casey (1984). Reproduced with the permission of the author, Bill Critchley

Good leadership and management at different levels throughout organisations can help to address these dilemmas. Chapter 4 identified the need for *engaging leadership*; leaders with specific highly-developed interpersonal skills, capable of engaging colleagues in the development and delivery of integrated services. Other models, for example Heifetz's ethical Adaptive Leadership model (1994) or Greenleaf's concept of Servant Leadership (1977), place a similar emphasis on values, personal integrity and the ability to motivate others to contribute to the change process. You might wish to revisit Chapters 2, 3 and 6 to remind yourself of the skills that these leaders demonstrate. Chapter 7 may also be helpful in encouraging you to reflect on your own personal leadership style and development needs.

The personal context

We have seen that a range of issues have to be addressed if you are leading or managing multi-professional or inter-disciplinary teams. It is often at the inter-personal level that these are played out and next we consider some of the personal aspects of integrated and collaborative working.

In any system change, people move through psychological transitions in order to adapt to and take on the change. Paul Close reminds us in Chapter 5 that Hayes suggests that this may feel similar to the loss or bereavement cycle so that people move from shock, to denial; depression; letting go and acceptance of reality; testing; consolidation, and ultimately internalisation, reflection and learning (Hayes, 2002).

There can be real dilemmas and challenges for those who (as a result of service redesign) are unable to maintain an active clinical or practice role whilst working as a leader or manager. There is a risk that professional credibility is lost. Ovretveit suggests that this 'double jeopardy' is heightened for those who work in interprofessional settings as skills are diluted and individuals become deskilled (Ovretveit, 1993). As practice skills and knowledge become outdated this skill set needs to be replaced by a new set of knowledge and skills around management and leadership. This must be actively planned for and managed in terms of seizing professional development opportunities and acknowledging and accepting that professional practice may have to be left behind.

In the context of working in integrated services, the responses to change by individuals, professional groups and teams may well be very different. There may be tensions around loss (or perceived loss) of professional identity and power as service configurations, language and meaning shift to enshrine the new policy agendas. Responses to such changes (particularly with increasing accountability and rationed services) might include protectionism, tribalism redefining of professional boundaries and corralling of resources and 'territories' (Stepney and Callwood, 2006; Becher, 2001). These issues play out at policy, organisational and professional levels as well as in teams and one-to-one interactions. Understanding what might be going on, not only for yourself, but also for various groups and individuals with whom you are working, will help you to work more sensitively and collaboratively across boundaries with the aim of reaching consensus and defining shared values and practice.

Working as a boundary spanner means being able to gatekeep innovation and take risks, and being able to translate, mediate, and negotiate complex new ways of working, training and education between multiple partners. Leaders at all levels need to develop a range of 'soft' and 'hard' skills to enable them to deliver and manage provision, whilst at the same time collaborating to seek innovative solutions to underpin new service configurations and demands. These skills may be acquired through proactively learning about the 'tribes and territories' (Becher, 2001); cultures, systems, practices and processes; gaining supported and mentored leadership experience and undertaking targeted personal and professional development in education, management and leadership.

The Hay Group report suggests that for a given task, the type or degree of participation can be defined in four roles which they call RACI.

1 Responsible – the 'doer' of the activity.

2 Accountable – who is ultimately accountable, the 'buck stops here'.

3 Consulted – who must be 'kept in the loop'.

4 Informed – who must be informed (FYI).

Although this is a useful checklist, the report acknowledges that accountability needs to be identified at all levels, particularly in a *multi-agency, integrated working model where it is critical to identify who is accountable for the outcomes* (Hay Group Report 2008, p39).

In thinking about how to relate to others who may see and understand the world in very different ways, the SIFT model (Changing Minds, 2008) can help you to understand people's perspective and also to influence their thinking and negotiate shared care or service outcomes. The model suggests that individuals understand and respond to the world through complex cognitive processes which can be summarised as follows.

- Sensing – directing our attention to areas of specific interest.

- Inferring meaning – we infer personal meaning through a range of filters.

- Formulating intent – making a decision on what to do involves choosing between quick intuitive reactions (rapid cognition) and slower, more thoughtful considerations.

- Translating into action – this involves using the physical and verbal means at our disposal.

Underpinning these activities are many complex systems that regulate and moderate our thought processes including deep needs, values and beliefs, mental models, and personal goals. As we have seen, these can be related to professional and organisational context as well as individual factors. Using the SIFT model in practice involves the following.

- Appealing to people's primary senses of seeing and hearing by ensuring we gain their attention, that they understand what we are saying or doing through providing a pro-portionate amount of information and that what they sense from us is consistent with how they perceive the world (this might involve providing information in a range of media or changing the physical environment).

- Ensuring that the meaning we are trying to convey is received and understood. This might involve linking the specific experiences or conversations in which we are involving people with their internal world through examples, illustrations, reference to previous discussions, checking out of key points and providing consistent information. In persuading people to change views or actions, it is helpful to try to set up a situation where people cannot create a valid meaning or false meaning other than that which you are trying to persuade them is the right way. Here we might use formal documents or strategies or involve credible others to provide evidence to the person of the value and 'truth' of what we are saying.

- Observing how people make decisions and learning how to determine when short-cut decisions are helpful (such as a quick reaction to danger) or when they are based on unconscious or learned scripts and behaviours and thus may be undermining. We can also learn how to help people make the decisions we would like them to, by circumventing short-cuts and limiting alternative courses of action. This may involve avoiding potential conflict and setting an environment in which creativity can flow and solutions can be generated.

- Finally, the intent must be translated into actions and words. Here it is helpful to consider both verbal and non-verbal cues and behaviours (such as tone of voice, timing, the language being used, gestures, proximity, dress and posture) and how these might influence your leadership and management style. If you can become more aware of how you appear to others (through mindful reflection, feedback, video or taping) then you can start to change. Remember that actions and communications are a reflection of the deeper workings of your mind and sometimes bias can creep in and influence what we say and do.

Another factor to consider when we think about leading and managing interprofessional teams within integrated services is that of managing diverse groups, teams and organisations within an increasingly multi-cultural society. Developing an awareness of differences in communication styles, values, beliefs and expectations linked with culture and ethnicity will enable you to be a more effective communicator with both colleagues and service users. Chapters 5 and 7 identify other models and explanations which emphasise the role of emotion, values, ethics and spirituality in developing effective integrated, collaborative and partnership working. We have briefly considered some of the cultural issues concerned with professions in Chapter 8 and although there is little research into ethnicity and race in terms of leadership (particularly in the UK health and social care context) some writers have focused specifically on a consideration of gender and leadership.

For example, Alimo-Metcalfe and Alban-Metcalfe have carried out a number of large-scale studies in many public sector organisations, including education, local government and health. One output was the *Transformational leadership questionnaire* (TLQ) which Kay Phillips describes in Chapter 4. A 2005 study of 'nearby' leaders (Shamir, 1995), included 2013 NHS managers and professionals, 50% of whom were female and 10% of whom described themselves as from BME (black and minority ethnic) backgrounds. The study indicated that there were very little differences between the responses from leaders and managers from different ethnic or gender groups. A later report, in 2006, which included findings from other research, 360 feedback and a deeper analysis of the data from the 2005 NHS study, suggested that women are more likely to adopt (and to be perceived to adopt) a transformational style, whereas men are more likely to adopt (and to be perceived to adopt) a transactional style of leadership (Alimo-Metcalfe and Alban-Metcalfe, 2006, pp296–7). Writers identify that further research is needed to tease out issues relating to gender and ethnicity and leadership, particularly around the 'new paradigms' of leadership which emphasise servant leadership and partnership working.

Consideration of your role and career development in the light of your individual and personal needs, drivers, qualities, strengths and areas for development (which includes defining your personal values, beliefs and principles) will help you make a more lasting difference as well as provide more personal fulfilment. As you read in Chapter 8, developing a greater awareness and understanding of others in terms of their professional identity, cultural background and work role in the light of the impact of change on their work practices (as well as evaluating their personal qualities and values) will enable you to work more effectively with others in a range of settings. In this chapter we have also stressed the importance of developing a greater understanding of different organisations' systems, structures, cultures and work practices. This is particularly relevant when you are working as a *boundary spanner* in a cross-agency or cross-sector role, and we have seen that leadership skills such as co-ordinating, networking and brokering are highly desirable when working in the complex and crowded stage in which integrated services are located.

The DH project *Creating an effective interprofessional workforce* (CIPW) developed 'effective leadership' grids that identified four key elements of leaders of an interprofessional workforce.

1   Leaders are fully aware of the big picture.

2   Leaders have a vision for change.

3   Leaders have the ability to build a shared vision whilst fostering creativity and innovation.

4   Leaders work with partners to develop strategies for collaborative working.

(DH 2007b)

This idea of the 'big picture' leader fits well with Antrobus's description of political leaders (2003). In her analysis of nurses as leaders, Sue Antrobus suggests that nurses (in common with many other professionals) have traditionally been poor at leading and influencing change and policy. She notes that *in complex decision-making arenas, where competing values create competing factions, effective political leadership is crucial to negotiate resolution* (Antrobus 2003, p43). She provides a framework for nurses as political leaders which is equally relevant for leaders and managers of integrated services. This begins by being aware of the political landscape and goes on to list the following skills and knowledge as being essential for political leadership.

- Identifying the right issue for policy change – whole systems thinker.

- Mapping a constituency and developing a collective voice – facilitator and enabler.

- Moving the issue from the tactical to the strategic and developing strategic objectives – strategic thinker.

- Identifying stakeholders and mapping their positions in relation to your issue – political operator.

- Constructing different messages for different stakeholders using evidence and experience – articulate speaker.

- Building and using networks for influence – influential operator.

- Negotiating coalitions and aligning common goals – collaborative worker.

- Reviewing learning and evaluating strategic objectives – reflective thinker.

(Antrobus, 2003, p43)

CHAPTER SUMMARY

You have seen in this chapter that leadership and management are both closely linked and uniquely different. A well-rounded leader can do both, but will always know which of the two to employ in any given set of circumstances

Leading teams and organisations through change is never easy but leadership skills and understanding make it less difficult and leaders who can draw on a wide range of leadership approaches tend to have a longer 'shelf-life' than those who major in one or two styles.

You have seen also how developing an understanding and awareness of policy agendas helps you to situate what is happening at professional, community, organisational or department level. Horizon-scanning and understanding the wider context is a vital leadership and management activity which is particularly important as you move into more senior posts. It also helps you to plan your career development as you will be more prepared for and aware of forthcoming workforce and system changes as well as opportunities for professional development and possible role change. The leadership journey is a long and sometimes thankless one, however there is a wealth of opportunities for developing services based on collaboration, trust and partnership which can provide service users with the care they deserve and want.

We leave you with two questions to consider. Alford and Naughton (writing about the role of faith-based principles in contemporary organisations) pose these questions which are relevant to all leaders and managers and which enshrine many of the issues we have discussed throughout this book:

What kind of person should I as a manager or employee strive to become? What kind of organisational community should I as a manager or employee strive to maintain? (Antrobus 2001, p8).

FURTHER READING

Atkinson, M, Jones, M and Lamont, E (2007) *Multi-agency working and its implications for practice: A review of the literature.* Reading: CfBT

www.nfer.ac.uk/research-areas/pims-data/summaries/multi-agency-working-and-its-implications-for-practice-a-review-of-the-literature.cfm

Lord, P, Kinder, K, Wilkin, A, Atkinson, M, and Harland, J (2008) *Evaluating the early impact of integrated children's services.* Slough: NFER.

www.communitycare.co.uk/Articles/2008/05/29/108270/improving-outcomes-for-children.html

Quinney, A (2006) *Collaborative social work practice.* Exeter: Learning Matters.

Robinson, M and Cottrell, D (2005). Health professionals in multi-disciplinary and multi-agency teams: Changing professional practice. *Journal of interprofessional care*, 19 (6) 547–60.

Concluding comments: Service user perspectives

Judy McKimm and Kay Phillips

The chapters in this book have presented a number of different perspectives on the leadership and management of integrated services. We have examined different theoretical models and related these to practice, encouraging you throughout to apply your learning to your personal, professional and organisational contexts.

We reviewed a range of leadership theories in Chapter 1, identifying those currently deemed most appropriate for the development of integrated services. Chapters 2, 3, 8 and 9 focussed on developing a better understanding of the 'big picture'. This big picture includes the policies and drivers shaping integrated service development and some of the enablers and constraints that can influence leaders' ability to deliver and improve service quality. Additionally we reviewed contemporary workforce developments, including the emergence of new roles designed to aid integration by straddling traditional professional boundaries.

But this book also tackles leadership approaches at a more personal level. It is about *how* managers and leaders might work more effectively as well as *what* they need to understand about their context to lead and manage in an informed way. To help you to consider your personal approach to leading and managing, Chapters 4, 5, 6 and 7 have emphasised the importance of working in different ways; being clear about your own and others' values; understanding and working in an emotionally intelligent way and employing an empathetic and engaging approach. Behaving consistently and authentically is emphasised as one of the hallmarks of the sort of leader people say they want, and as you have seen, it is not necessarily the most senior leaders that effect the most lasting and influential change. If enough leaders work and practice collaboratively and attend actively to service users and colleagues, positive change will be effected through the 'ripple effect' of lots of 'little leaders'. Zander and Zander (2002) remind us of the art of possibility of changing people and cultures through relationships and shared frames of meaning.

Throughout the book, and particularly in Chapter 5, there has been an underlying theme that *quality* services are those that truly aspire to meet the needs and interests of those who use them. Perhaps, therefore, it is a fitting way to conclude by making service user perspectives of integrated and user-centred services more explicit.

Service user involvement has become a more formalised part of service development in the last decade. As a result there is a growing body of knowledge emerging from practice and commissioned research. In addition, organisations like the Joseph Rowntree Foundation have supported a variety of research initiatives in recent years, in which service providers, voluntary/charitable organisations and service users have been involved in collaborative research. The reports from these studies and other work (a full list of projects may be accessed at www.jfr.org.uk) enable us to draw out some common themes in relation to service user views and needs.

The social care sector has led the way, developing effective approaches to service user and carer involvement in the fields of mental health, learning disability, older people's services and support for vulnerable children and young people. In the health sector, networks of service users have contributed to the development of national service frameworks and the improvement of services for patients with cancer and a range of long-term conditions. At local level health service users are formally represented on the boards and governing councils of hospitals and mental health trusts.

It is fair to say that there has been a degree of scepticism regarding the value of this increased involvement. Both researchers and service providers have questioned whether there is real evidence that user participation improves services. A 2006 study, *Making user involvement work: Supporting service user networking and knowledge* (Branfield, Beresford, et al.) found that users recognised the need to work through networks, communicate more effectively and share information in order to increase their impact and develop a stronger national voice. They felt that the strong, closed cultures of health and social care, together with their own limited resources, reduced their capacity to develop and share their knowledge. More worryingly, the service users also felt that their knowledge wasn't taken seriously or valued by the professionals. This may, however, be about to change.

As services become more personalised and as service users gain more discretion over the spending of their financial allocation for care and support, their power and influence is increasing. Government is committed to 'personalisation', 'self-directed support' and 'individual budgets' in health and social care, aiming for increased choice and control for the people who use services. Leaders and managers as well as frontline staff therefore need to find ways of working with users and carers to value their knowledge and ensure that the services they provide are in line with user requirements. As one service user explained:

> *People think the only thing we know is how to moan. But they are not listening. We know what needs changing, what works and what doesn't work. We know this because we live it 24/7, 52 weeks a year with no days off.*
>
> (Branfield and Beresford 2006, page 2 of report summary)

As trained professionals working in health, education, social care and other services it is tempting to assume the mantle of 'expert' but this statement reminds us that the real expert is the person who lives with the medical condition(s), the complex social problems and/or the related social and economic challenges which may accompany them. Unless the knowledge of service users is genuinely respected their involvement is likely to be tokenistic and their ability to influence service quality minimal.

What are the common themes emerging from research with service users? A recent study, *Person-centred support: what service users and practitioners say* (Glynn, Beresford, et al., 2008) provides some extremely helpful insights. This research brought together for the first time the views, ideas and experiences of service users, face to face practitioners and managers. Together they explored people's understanding of person-centred support, the current barriers to developing this type of service model and ways of overcoming them. The report incorporated new evidence from the national *Standards We Expect* project, bringing together direct experience in 20 areas of the UK, different service sectors and a wide range of service user groups. The full report can be accessed online at; www.jrf.org.uk/bookshop/eBooks/2173-person-centred-support.pdf.

A brief summary of some of its key findings is presented in Table 10.1, together with some quotations from participants in the study. They serve to remind us all of the importance of putting the person, rather than the service, at the centre of the process.

Table 10.1 Person-centred support: What service users and practitioners say

Choice and control *Being able to decide for yourself what you want to do and not letting anyone decide for you. Other people may have good intentions for what you need but you might know better how to achieve it.* (service user)	Users want to be able to make choices and to change things if they change their mind or things aren't working out. Choice and control contrast with more paternalistic approaches to service provision, where service users might be passive recipients of services and there are assumptions that the 'service knows best'.
Setting goals *It is about saying what your dream is. So that everyone can have a dream.* (worker)	The setting of goals does not merely establish an end point or target to work towards. Person-centred planning, a well-established approach to person-centred support, has a focus on the process of taking steps toward overall goals.
The importance of relationships *Then the greatest thing that happens is you get this empathy and when that happens there just seems to be a natural progression . . .* (worker)	Service users and face-to-face workers in particular identified the importance of the relationship between an individual service user and their key worker. There was a widely held feeling that time and effort must be invested in forming a relationship before person-centred support can be made real.
Listening *I feel if someone was to come around and see us and talk and ask exactly what we need, even if they couldn't provide it, at least it would show us that someone is caring and listening to us.* (service user)	Participants emphasised the importance of listening. Many service users highlighted this, contrasting bad experiences of services where their views had not been listened to or they were dominated by people who thought they knew better. Service users made it clear that they should be asked their opinions and listened to.
A positive approach *(Highlight) positive abilities, not the negatives. . . Giving the person the opportunity to achieve.*(service users)	Some participants felt very strongly that a person-centred approach must value people and focus on the positive.
Information *You need the right information to help you choose. It must be informed choice.* (service user)	There was agreement about the central role played by accessible, relevant and reliable information for service users. Many people spoke of personal experiences of not knowing what services were available to them and the difficulties this created. Meaningful choice is not possible without high quality, up to date, accurate information.

| Learning | Service users should be supported to try new experiences and learn through these. This learning can be viewed in the context of life experience and towards the development of independent living skills. |
| *When it doesn't work for you, try something else.* (service user) | |

| Flexibility | Flexibility implies the service's ability to adapt as people's needs change or they decide to pursue different goals. |
| *Remembering everyone is different and has different needs.* (service user) | |

The authors of the report emphasise that person-centred services are based on these core values and principles identified by the project participants. This is not about changing the *technical* ways in which services are delivered. Instead, it as a *value-driven* approach to service development and delivery:

> *This may require transformational change in an organisation, 'not tinkering' with what already exists . . . Person-centred support is about core values, not hints or tips. There are no easy short-cuts. You have to adopt the correct core values*
>
> (Glynn, Beresford, *et al.*, 2008, p111).

The study acknowledges that there may be professional, political, financial and organisational challenges to face in achieving this culture shift (these are detailed in other sections of the report) but service users are keen to participate in the change. Real progress can be achieved by working together and building relationships based on trust and honesty. We want to leave the last word to one of the service user contributors. It's an important message for all service leaders and managers:

> *Believe in people: It works.*

Bibliography

Alford and Naughton (2001) *Managing as if faith mattered: Christian social principles in the modern organisation*. Indiana: University of Notre Dame Press.

Alimo-Metcalfe, B (1998). *Effective leadership*. Local Government Management Board.

Alimo-Metcalfe, B and Alban-Metcalfe, J (2005) Leadership: Time for a new direction? *Leadership*, 1(1): 51–71.

Alimo-Metcalfe, B and Alban-Metcalfe, J (April-June 2005) The crucial role of leadership in meeting the challenges of change. *Vision: the Journal of Business Perspectives*, 9(2): 27–39.

Alimo-Metcalfe, B and Alban-Metcalfe, J (2006) More (good) leaders for the public sector. *International Journal of Public Sector Management*, 19(4): 293–315.

Alimo-Metcalfe, B and Alban-Metcalfe, J (2008) Creating organisations that maximise the potential of their people. *Research Insight*. The Chartered Institute of Personnel and Development (CIPD).

Allix, NM (2000) Transformational leadership: democratic or despotic? *Educational management and administration*, 28(1): 7–20.

Alvesson M, Wilmott, H (1996) Strategic management as domination and emancipation from planning and process to communication and praxis. In Stubbart, C, and Shrivastava, P (eds) *Advances in Strategic Management*, 12(A): 85–112. Greenwich CT: JAI Press.

Anderson, L (1997) The introduction of generic workers into the ward team: An exploratory study. *Journal of Nursing Management*, 5: 69–75.

Andrew, N, Tolson, D and Ferguson, D (2007) Building on Wenger: Communities of practice in nursing. *Nurse Education Today*, 28: 246–52.

Anning, A, Cottrell, D, Frost, N, Green, J and Robinson, M (2006) *Developing multi professional teamwork for integrated children's services*. Maidenhead: Open University Press.

Anning, A and Edwards, A (2006) *Promoting children's learning from birth to five*. 2nd edn. London: McGraw Hill International

Ansett, S (2005) Boundary spanner: The gatekeeper of innovation in partnerships. *Accountability Forum* (April 2005) 6, 37–44, www.greenleaf-publishing.com (accessed 16 December 2008).

Antrobus, S (2003) What is political leadership? *Nursing Standard*, 17(43), 40–44.

Argyris, C (1964) *Integrating the individual and the organisation*. New York: Wiley.

Argyris, C (1992) *On Organisational Learning*. 2nd edn. Oxford: Blackwell.

Armistead, C, Pettigrew, P and Aves, S (2007) Exploring leadership in multi-sectoral partnerships. *Leadership*, 3: 211–230.

Atkinson, M, Jones, M and Lamont, E (2007). *Multi-agency working and its implications for practice: A review of the literature*. Reading: CfBT, **www.nfer.ac.uk/research-areas/pims-data/summaries/multi-agency-working-and-its-implications-for-practice-a-review-of-the-literature.cfm**.

Atkinson, M, Wilkin, A, Stott, A, Doherty, P and Kinder, K (2002) *Multi-agency working: A detailed study*. National Foundation for Educational Research (NFER).

Audit Commission (2008) *Every Child Matters: Are we nearly there yet?* Report on Children's Trust. London: Audit Commission.

Bainbridge, I and Ricketts, A (2003) *Improving older people's services: An overview of performance.* London: Department of Health.

Balloch, S and Taylor, M (eds) (2001) *Partnership working: Policy and practice.* Bristol: The Policy Press.

Barr, H (2002) *Interprofessional education: Today, yesterday and tomorrow.* A Review commissioned by the LTSN for Health Sciences and Practice from the UK Centre for the Advancement of Interprofessional Education (CAIPE).

Barrett, G and Keeping, C (2005) The processes required for effective interprofessional working. In Barrett, G, Sellman, D and Thomas, J (eds) *Interprofessional working in Health and Social Care: Professional perspectives.* London: Palgrave.

Bass, B (1985) *Leadership and performance beyond expectations.* New York: Free Press

Bass, B and Avolio, B (1994) *Improving organisational effectiveness through transformational leadership.* Thousand Oaks, CA: Sage.

Bate, SP (2000) Leading the NHS from a different place. *Health Services Management Newsletter,* 6(2): University of Birmingham.

Bateson, G (1999) *Steps to ecology of mind.* Chichester: University of Chicago Press.

Bauman, Z (2007a) *Liquid times: Living in an age of uncertainty.* Cambridge: Polity Press.

Bauman, Z (2007b) *Consuming life.* Cambridge: Polity Press.

Becher, T (2001) *Academic tribes and territories: Intellectual enquiry and the cultures of disciplines.* Milton Keynes: Open University Press.

Beckett, C and Maynard, A (2005) *Values and ethics in social work: An introduction.* London: Sage.

Bedford, RD, Poot, J and Ryan, T (2006) Niue: *Population policy scoping study.* Report for the New Zealand Agency for International Development (NZAID). University of Waikato: Population Studies Centre.

Begum, N (2006) Doing it for themselves: Participation and black and minority ethnic service users. *Participation Report 14.* Race Equality Unit and Social Care Institute for Excellence. Bristol: Policy Press.

Bell, M, Shaw, I, Sinclair, I, Sloper, P and Rafferty, J (2007) *An evaluation of the practice, process and consequences of the integrated children's system in councils with social services responsibilities.* London: Department for Education and Skills.

Bennis, W and Nanus, N (1985) *Leaders: The strategies for taking charge.* New York: Harper and Row.

Beresford, P (2006) Developing inclusive partnerships: User-defined outcomes, networking and knowledge – a case study. *Health and Social Care in the Community,* 14(5), 436–44.

Beresford, P, Croft, S (2001) Service users' knowledge and the social construction of social work reform. *British Journal of Social Work,* 34, 53–68.

Bernard, LL (1926) *An introduction to social psychology.* New York: Holt.

Bichard, M (2004) *The Bichard inquiry report.* London: The Stationery Office.

Blagg, D and Young, S (2001) What makes a good leader? *Harvard Business School Bulletin.* April, www.hbswk.hbs.edu (accessed 16 December 2008).

Blake, R and Mouton, J (1964) *The managerial grid.* Houston, Texas: Gulf.

Block, P (2001) *Flawless consulting.* 2nd edn. San Francisco: Jossey Bass.

Boddy, R and Buchanan, D (1992) *The expertise of the change agent.* London: Heinemann.

Bolden, R (2007) *Distributed leadership.* University of Exeter Discussion papers in Management, Paper number 07/02. Exeter: University of Exeter.

Bolman, L.G and Deal, T.E (2003) *Reframing organisations. Artistry, choice and leadership*. 3rd edn. San Francisco: Wiley.

Bose, P (2003) *Alexander the Great's art of strategy*. London: Profile Books.

Boud, D and Middleton, H (2003) Learning from others at work: Communities of practice and informal learning. *Journal of Workplace Learning*, 15(5), 194–202.

Boyatzis, RE, Goleman, D, and Rhee, K (1999) Clustering competence in emotional intelligence: Insights from the Emotional Competence Inventory (ECI), in Bar-On, R and Parker JD (eds) *Handbook of emotional intelligence*. San Francisco: Jossey-Bass.

Bradshaw, L (1999) Principals as boundary spanners: Working collaboratively to solve problems. *NASSP Bulletin*, 83(38).

Brandon, M, Howe, A, Dagley, V, Salter, C, Warren, C and Black, J (2006) *Evaluating the common assessment framework and lead professional guidance and implementation in 2005–6*. London: Department for Education and Skills.

Branfield, F and Beresford, P (2006) *Making user involvement work: Supporting service user networking and knowledge*. York: Joseph Rowntree Foundation.

Braye, S and Preston-Shoot, M (2009) *Practising social work law*, 3rd edn. Basingstoke: Palgrave Macmillan.

Braye, S, Preston-Shoot, M and Thorpe, A (2007) Beyond the classroom: Learning social work law in practice. *Journal of Social Work*, 7(3), 322–40.

Bridges, W (1995) *Managing transitions*. London: Nicholas Brealey.

British Medical Association (2008) *Role of the patient in medical education*, **www.bma.org.uk** (accessed 16 December 2008).

British Psychological Society (2007) *Leading psychological services*. Leicester: British Psychological Society.

Broadhead, P, Meleady, C and Delgado, M.A (2008) *Children, families and communities: Creating and sustaining integrated services*. Maidenhead: Open University Press and McGraw-Hill International.

Bryman, A (1996) Leadership in organisations, in: Clegg, SR, Harvey, C and Nord, WR (eds) *Handbook of organisational studies*. London: Sage.

Buchanan, D and Badham, R (2008) *Power, politics and organizational change*. 2nd edn. London: Sage.

Burgess, RC (2005) A model for enhancing individual and organisational learning of emotional intelligence: The drama and winner's triangles. *Social Work Education*, 24(1), 97–112.

Burns, J.M (1978) *Leadership*. Harper and Row: New York.

Bush, T (2003) *Theories of educational leadership and management*. London: Sage.

Bush, T (2007) Educational leadership and management: Theory, policy, and practice. *South African Journal of Education*, 27(93): 391–406.

Bush, T and Glover, D (2002) *School leadership: Concepts and evidence*. Nottingham: National College for Schools' Leadership.

Callaghan, G, Wistow, G (2008) Can the community construct knowledge to shape services in the local state? A case example. *Critical Social Policy*, 28(2): 165–86.

Capra, F (1997) *The web of life: A new synthesis of mind and matter*. London: Flamingo.

Carnwell, R, Carson, A (2005) Understanding partnerships and collaboration. In Carnwell, R and Buchanan, J (eds) *Effective practice in health and social care: A partnership approach*. Berkshire, New York: Open University Press.

Carpenter, J, Barnes, D, Dickinson, C and Wooff, D (2006) Outcomes of interprofessional education for community mental health services in England: The longitudinal evaluation of a postgraduate programme. *Journal of Interprofessional Care*, 20: 1–17.

Carr, S and Dittrich, R (2008) SCIE *adult services report 20: Personalisatio – a rough guide*. London: SCIE, **www.scie.org.uk** (accessed 11 December 2008).

Cestari, L, Munroe, M, Evans, S, Smith, A and Huxley, P (2006) Fair access to care services (FACS): implementation in the mental health context of the UK. *Health and Social Care in the Community*, 14(6): 474–481.

Changing Minds (2008) *The SIFT model*, **www.changingminds.org** (accessed 3 January 2009).

Charities Evaluation Services (2006) *Using an outcomes approach in the voluntary and community sector: A briefing for funders, commissioners and policy makers on the National Outcomes Programme*, **www.ces-vol.org.uk/index.cfm?format=126**.

Child, J and Faulkner, D (1998) *Strategies of cooperation: Managing alliances, networks and joint ventures*. Oxford: OUP.

Children's Workforce Development Council (CWDC) (2007) *Common assessment framework for children and young people: Managers' guide*. London: Department for Education and Skills, **www.cwdcouncil.org.uk** (accessed 16 October 2008).

Children's Workforce Development Council (CWDC) (2008) *Championing Children*, **www.cwdcouncil.org.uk** (accessed 10 December 2008).

Children's Workforce Development Council (CWDC) (2008) *Clear Progression 2008: the next steps towards building an integrated qualifications framework for the children and young people's workforce*, **www.iqf.org.uk** (accessed 12 December 2008).

Children's Workforce Development Council (CWDC) (2008) *Multi-agency working online resource for managers and practitioners in Children's Services*, **www.cwdcouncil.org.uk/projects/multiagency.htm** (accessed 12 August 2008).

Chrislip, DD and Larson, C (1994) *Collaborative leadership*. San Francisco: Jossey-Bass.

Clarkson, P and Challis, D (2004) The assessment gap. *Community Care,* (July): 15–21, 38–9.

Cleaver, H, Barnes, J, Bliss, D and Cleaver, D (2004) *Developing information sharing and assessment systems*. London: Department for Education and Skills.

Cole, GA (1997) *Strategic management*. 2nd edn. London: Letts.

Coleman, A (2007) *Collaborative Leadership in extended schools: Leading in muiti-agency environment*. Nottingham: National College for School Leadership.

Cooperider, D and Whitney, D (2003) *The power of appreciative inquiry: A practical guide to positive change*. San Francisco: Berrett-Koehler.

Coulson, A (2005) A plague on all your partnerships: Theory and practice in regeneration. *International Journal of Public Sector Management*, 18: 151–63.

Covey, SR (1992) *Principle-centred leadership*. London: Simon and Schuster.

Covey, SR, Merrill, AR and Merrill, RR (1994) First things first. New York: Simon and Schuster.

Coyte, ME, Gilbert, P and Nicholls, V (eds) (2008) *Spirituality, values and mental health: Jewels for the journey*. London: Jessica Kingsley.

Critchley, B and Casey, D (1984) Second thoughts on teambuilding. *Management Education and Development*.15(2): 163–75.

Cropper, S (1996) Collaborative working and the issue of sustainability, in Huxham, C (ed.) *Creating collaborative advantage*. London: Sage.

Dame Denise Platt DBE (2007) *Leadership in social care*. Speech made at the Social Care Leaders Programme Celebration Event in London on 29 June 2007. Commission for Social Care Inspection, **www.csci.org.uk** (accessed 1 December 2008).

Davis, J (2006) The importance of the community of practice in identity development. Internet *Journal of Allied Health Sciences and Practice*, 4(3): 1–8.

Day, D (2001) Leadership development: A review in context. *Leadership Quarterly*, 11(4): 581–613.

Deal, TE and Kennedy, AA (1982) *The rites and rituals of corporate life*. Cambridge, Mass: Perseus.

Degeling P, Maxwell S, Kennedy J, Coyle B (2003) Medicine, management, and modernisation: a 'danse macabre'? *British Medical Journal*, 326: 649–52.

Department for Children, Schools and Families (2007) *The children's plan: building brighter futures*. Norwich: The Stationery Office, **www.dcsf.gov.uk/childrensplan/downloads/The_Childrens_Plan.pdf** (accessed 13 March 2009).

Department for Children, Schools and Families (2008) *Building brighter futures: Next steps for the children's workforce*. Nottingam: DCSF, **www.teachernet.gov.uk**.

Department for Children, Schools and Families (2008) 2020 *Children and young people's workforce strategy*. Nottingham: DCSF, **www.teachernet.gov.uk** (accessed 3 January 2009).

Department for Communities and Local Government (2007) *Third sector strategy for communities and local government*. London: DCLG.

Department for Education and Skills (2005a) *Integrated children's system: A statement of business requirements*. London: The Stationery Office.

Department for Education and Skills (2005b) *Statutory guidance on inter-agency co-operation to improve the wellbeing of children: Children's trusts*. London: The Stationery Office.

Department for Education and Skills (2006) *Working together to safeguard children: A guide to inter-agency working to safeguard and promote the welfare of children*. London: The Stationery Office.

Department for Education and Skills (2007) *The early years foundation stage: Effective practice – guidance for multi-agency working*. London: The Stationery Office, **www.standards.dfes.gov.uk/eyfs/resources/downloads/3_4b_ep.pdf**.

Department of Health (1998a) *Modernising social services*. London: The Stationery Office.

Department of Health (1998b) *Partnership in action (new opportunities for joint working between health and social services) a discussion document*. London: The Stationery Office.

Department of Health (1999) *Working together: a guide to inter-agency working to safeguard and promote the welfare of children*. London: The Stationery Office.

Department of Health (2000a) *Framework for the assessment of children in need and their families*. London: The Stationery Office.

Department of Health (2000b) *No secrets: Guidance on developing and implementing multi-agency policies and procedures to protect vulnerable adults from abuse*. London: The Stationery Office.

Department of Health (2000c) *Data Protection Act 1998: Guidance to social services*. London: The Stationery Office.

Department of Health (2000d) *The NHS Plan: A plan for investment, a plan for reform*. London: The Stationery Office.

Department of Health (2001a) *National service framework for older people (LAC (2001) 12)*. London: The Stationery Office.

Department of Health (2001b) *Continuing care: NHS and local councils' responsibilities (LAC (2001) 18)*. London: The Stationery Office.

Department of Health (2001c) *Learning from Bristol: The report of the Public Inquiry into Children's heart Surgery at the Bristol Royal Infirmary 1984–1995*. London: The Stationery Office.

Department of Health (2002) *Guidance on the single assessment process for older people (LAC (2002) 1)*. London: The Stationery Office.

Department of Health (2003) *The Community Care (Delayed Discharges etc.) Act 2003: Guidance for implementation (LAC (2003) 21*. London: The Stationery Office.

Department of Health (2006) *Leadership qualities framework*. London: The Stationery Office, www.nhsleadership qualities.nhs.uk (accessed 12 September 2008).

Department of Health (2006b) *The Business Planning Sourcebook*. London: The Stationery Office.

Department of Health (2007a) *Better outcomes for children's services through joint funding: A best practice guide*. London: The Stationery Office, **www.everychildmatters.gov.uk** (accessed 24 August 2008).

Department of Health (2007b) *Trust Assurance and Safety: The Regulation of Healthcare Professionals in the 21st Century*. London: The Stationery Office, **www.official-documents.gov.uk** (accessed 2 January 2009).

Department of Health (2007c) *Creating an Interprofessional workforce (CIPW) for health and social care in England, Executive summary*. London: The Stationery Office, **www.cipel.ac.uk** (accessed 23 December 2008).

Department of Health (2008a) Transforming social care LAC (2008) 1). London: The Stationery Office.

Department of Health (2008b) *High quality care for all: The NHS next stage review final report*. London: The Stationery Office.

Department of Health (2008c) *Putting people first: A shared vision and commitment to the transformation of Adult Social Care*. London: The Stationery Office.

Department of Health (2008d) *Framing the contributions of allied health professionals: Delivering high quality healthcare*. London: The Stationery Office.

Department of Health (2008e) *Medical leadership competency framework: Enhancing engagement in medical leadership*. Coventry: NHS Institute for Innovation and Improvement, **www.institute.nhs.uk** (accessed 20 October 2008).

Department for Schools, Children and Families: *Ten Year Strategy for Childcare* (2005).

Doveston, M, Keenaghan, M (2006) Growing Talent for Inclusion: Using an appreciative inquiry approach into investigating classroom dynamics. *Journal of Research in Special Educational Needs*, 6(3): 153–65.

Drath, W.H and Palus, C.J (1994) *Making common sense: Leadership as meaning making in a community of practice*. Greensboro, North Carolina: Center for Creative Leadership.

Drucker, P (1967) *Managing for results*. London: Heinemann.

Dulewicz, V, Higgs, M, and Slaski, M (2003) Measuring emotional intelligence: Content, construct and criterion-related validity. *Journal of Managerial Psychology*, 18(5).

Dunn, K, (forthcoming, 2009) Joined up service or surveillance culture? *International Journal of Children and Society*. (Special Issue) Professional practice with children and young people: What do we know about the outcomes of integrated working?

Edwards, R and Townsend, H (1965) *Business Enterprise: Its growth and organisation*. London: Macmillan-Palgrave.

Engestrom, Y (1999) Activity theory and individual and social transformation. In Engestrom, Y, Miettinen, M and Punamaki, RL (eds) *Perspectives on activity theory*. Cambridge: Cambridge University Press.

Essex County Council (2006) *Leading for children in Essex. Explanatory document and matrix*, (August 2006), www.cwdcouncil.org.uk (accessed 12 December 2008).

Farnham, D (2005) *Managing in a strategic business context*. London: Chartered Institute of Personnel Development.

Faresjo, T (2006) Interprofessional education – to break boundaries and build bridges. *Rural and Remote Health*, 6: 602, **www.rrh.org.au/publishedarticles/article_print_602.pdf**.

Fayol, H (1949) *General and Industrial Management*. London: Pitman Publishing.

Ferlie, E and Pettigrew, A (1996) Managing through networks: some issues and implications for the NHS. *British Journal of Management*, 7(S): 81–99.

Fisher, JL and Koch, JV (1996) *Presidential leadership: Making a difference*. Phoenix Arizona: Oryx Press.

Freeman, T and Peck, E (2007) *Adult care joint-ventures: Aspirations, challenges and options*. Birmingham: University of Birmingham with Integrated Care Network and Care Services Integrated Partnership (CSIP).

Foskett, J and Roberts, A (2007) Researching the Soul: The Somerset Spirituality Project, in Coyte, ME, Gilbert, P and Nicholls, V (eds) *Spirituality, values and mental health: Jewels for the journey*. London: Jessica Kingsley.

Foucault, M. (1975). *The birth of the clinic*. New York: AM Sheridan Smith.

Freeman, T and Peck, E (2007) *Adult care joint-ventures: Aspirations, challenges and options*. Birmingham: University of Birmingham with Integrated Care Network and Care Services Integrated Partnership (CSIP).

Freidson, E (2000*) Professional dominance: The social structure of medical care*. London: Transaction Publishers.

Frost, N, Robinson, M and Anning, A (2005) Social workers in multidisciplinary teams: Issues and dilemmas for professional practice. *Child and Family Social Work*, 10: 187–96.

Fullan, M (2004) *Leading in a culture of change: Personal action guide and workbook*. San Francisco: Jossey Bass.

Fulop, N, Protopsaltis, G, Hitchings, A, King, A, Allen, P, Normand, C, Walters, R (2002) Process and impact of mergers of NHS trusts: Multi-centre case study and management cost analysis. *British Medical Journal*, 325: 246–52.

Gabriel, Y, Fineman, S and Sims, D (2000) *Organising and organisations*, 2nd edn. London: Sage Publications Ltd.

General Medical Council (2004) *Fitness to practice (concerns about doctors) legislation*. London: GMC, **www.gmc-uk. org/about/legislation/ftp_legislation.asp** (accessed 2 January 2009).

General Teaching Council (2006) *The statement of professional values and practice for teachers*. London: GTC.

General Teaching Council, General Social Care Council and Nursing and Midwifery Council (2007) *Values for integrated working with children and young people*. London: GTC.

Gilbert, P (2005) *Leadership: Being effective and remaining human*. Lyme Regis: Russell House Publishing.

Gillies, J. (2000) *Adaptable networks: Perspectives from a business context*. Unpublished essay: Cranfield School of Management.

Glasby, J and Peck, E (2006) *We have to stop meeting like this: The governance of inter-agency partnerships – a discussion paper*. Integrated Care Network, **www.icn.csip.org.uk** (accessed 24 August 2008).

Glasby, J and Dickinson, H (2008) *Partnership working in health and social care*. Bristol: Policy Press.

Glatter, R (1997) Context and capability in educational management. *Educational Management and Administration*, 25(2): 181–92.

Glynn, M, Beresford *et al.* (2008) *Person-centred support: What service users and others say*. York: Joseph Rowntree Foundation.

Goleman, D (1995) *Emotional intelligence: Why it can matter more than IQ*. London: Bloomsbury.

Goleman, D (1998) *Working with emotional intelligence*. London: Bloomsbury Publishing.

Goleman, D (2000) Leadership that gets results. *Harvard Business Review*, 7(2): 78–90.

Goleman, D, Boyatzis, R and McKee, A (2002) *The new leaders: Transforming the art of leadership into the science of results* (first published as *Primal leadership*). London: Little and Brown.

Goleman, D and Cherniss, C (eds) (2001) *The emotionally intelligent workplace*. San Francisco: Jossey-Bass.

Goodinge, S (2000) *A jigsaw of services: Inspection of services to support disabled adults in their parenting role*. London: Department of Health.

Grandy G and Mills, AJ (2004) Strategy as simulacra? A radical reflexive look at the discipline and practice of strategy. *Journal of Management Studies*, 41(7): 1153–1169.

Greenleaf, RK (1977) *Servant Leadership: A Journey into the Nature of Legitimate Power and Greatness*. New Jersey: Paulist Press.

Grint, K (1999) *The arts of leadership*. Oxford: Oxford University Press.

Gronn, P (2002) Distributed leadership as a unit of analysis. *Leadership Quarterly*, 13: 423–51.

GSCC (2002) *Codes of Practice for Social Care Workers and Employers*. London: General Social Care Council.

Handy, C (1995) *The empty raincoat: Making sense of the future*. London: Arrow Books, Hutchinson.

Hardy, C (1996) Understanding power: Bringing about strategic change. *British Journal of Management*, 7(1): 3–16.

Harlow, E (2004) Protecting children: Why don't core groups work? Lessons from the literature. *Practice*, 16(1): 31–42.

Harris, J and Broad, B (2005) *In my own time: Achieving positive outcomes for young people leaving care*. Leicester: de Montfort University, Children and Families Research Unit.

Hartle, F, Snook, P, Apsey, H and Browton, R (2008).*The training and development of middle managers in the children's workforce*. Report by the Hay Group to the Children's Workforce Development Council (CWDC), www.cwdcouncil.org.uk (accessed August 2008).

Hayes, C (2006) *Stress relief for teachers: The coping triangle*. London: Routledge.

Hayes, J (2002) *The theory and practice of change management*. London: Palgrave.

Heifetz, R.A (1994) *The work of leadership*. Cambridge, Massachusetts: Harvard University Press.

Heron, J (1992) *Feeling and personhood psychology in another key*. London: Bloomsbury.

Hiscock, J and Pearson, M (1999) Looking inwards, looking outwards: dismantling the 'Berlin Wall' between health and social services? *Social Policy and Administration*, 33(2): 150–63.

H.M Government (1997) *National Health Service (Primary Care) Act 1997*. London: The Stationery Office.

H.M Government (1999) *The Health Act 1999*. London: The Stationery Office.

H.M Government (2004) *Children Act 2004*, London, The Stationery Office.

Hochschild, A (1983) *The managed heart: Commercialization of human feeling*. Berkeley: University of California Press.

Hopkins, D (2001) *Think tank report to Governing Council*, National College of Schools Leadership. Nottingham: NCSL, **www.ncsl.org.uk** (accessed 3 April 2008).

House of Commons (2001) *The Report of The Royal Liverpool Children's Inquiry: Summary and Recommendations*. London: The Stationery Office, **www.rlcinquiry.org.uk** (accessed 4 December 2008).

Howe, D (2008) *The Emotionally intelligent social worker*. Basingstoke: Palgrave MacMillan.

Hudson, B and Henwood, M (2002) The NHS and social care: The final countdown? *Policy and Politics*, 30(2): 153–66.

Hussey, D (1984) *Corporate planning: Theory and practice*, 2nd edn. London: Pergamon Press.

Huxham, C and Vangen, S (2005) *Managing to collaborate: The theory and practice of collaborative advantage*. London: Routledge.

Huxham, C (2000) The challenge of collaborative governance. *Public Management*, 2(3): 337–57.

I & DeA (2008) Community engagement, **www.idea.gov.uk** (accessed 17 October 2008).

Integrated Children's Services in Higher Education (ICS-HE) project (2008), **www.icshe.escalate.ac.uk** (accessed 28 November 2008).

Jackson, V (2008) Individual budgets and transformational change. *Journal of Care Services Management*, 2(4): 322–33.

Jarillo, J C (1993) *Strategic networks: Creating the borderless organisation*. Oxford: Butterworth–Heinemann.

Jenness, V and Grattet, R (2005) The law-in-between: The effects of organisational perviousness on the policing of hate crime. *Social Problems*, 52(3): 337–59.

Johnson G and Scholes K (1993) *Exploring corporate strategy: Text and cases*, 6th edn. New York: Prentice Hall.

Johnson G and Scholes K (2002) *Exploring corporate strategy: Text and cases*, 3rd edn. New York: Prentice Hall.

Jones, C and Pound, L (2008) Leadership in a multi- agency context. In Jones, C and Pound, L (eds) *Leadership and management in the early years*. Maidenhead: Open University Press.

Kanter, R.M (1982) *The middle manager as innovator*. Cambridge: Harvard Business Review.

Kanter, R.M (1983) *The change masters: Corporate entrepreneurs at work*. London: George Allen and Unwin.

Kanter, R.M (1989) *When giants learn to dance*. New York: Simon and Schuster.

Keep, E (2002) The English vocational education and training policy debate: Fragile 'technologies' or opening the 'black box' – two competing visions of where we go next. *Journal of Education and Work*, 15(4): 457–79.

Keough T and Tobin B (May 2001) *Postmodern leadership and the policy lexicon*. Agenda Symposium, Quebec.

Kinder, K, Lord, P and Wilkin, A (2008) *Evaluating the early impact of integrated children's services*. Local Authorities Research Consortium. Slough: National Foundation for Educational Research.

Kotter, J (1990) *A force for change: How leadership differs from management*. New York: Free Press.

Kotter, J, (1995) Leading Change: Why transformation efforts fail. *Harvard Business Review*, March-April: 1–20.

Kotter, J (2001) What leaders really do. *Harvard Business Review*, December, 85–96

Kouzes JM and Posner BZ (1989*) Leadership is in the Eye of the Follower. The 1989 Annual*: Developing Human Resources. University Associates: 233–39.

Kouzes, JM and Posner, BZ (1991) *The leadership challenge*. San Francisco: Jossey-Bass.

Kouzes, JM and Posner, BZ (1998) *Encouraging the heart: A leader's guide to rewarding and recognizing others*. San Francisco: Jossey Bass.

Kouzes, JM and Posner, BZ (2002) *The Leadership Challenge*, 3rd edn. San Francisco: Jossey Bass.

Kubler-Ross, E (1970) *On Death and Dying*. London: Tavistock.

Laming, H (2003) *The Victoria Climbié inquiry: Report of an inquiry by Lord Laming. Cm5730*. London: The Stationery Office, **www.victoria-climbie-inquiry.org.uk** (accessed 12 September 2008).

Lave, J and Wenger, E (1991) *Situated learning: Legitimate peripheral participation*. Cambridge: University of Cambridge Press.

Lawler J (2007) Leadership in social work: A case of caveat emptor? *British Journal of Social Work*, 37(1): 123–41.

LeDoux, J (1996) *The emotional brain*. New York: Simon and Schuster.

Lewis, N, Rees, C, Hudson, J and Bleakley, A (2005) Emotional intelligence in medical education: Measuring the unmeasurable? *Advances in health sciences education,* 10: 339–55.

Lord, P, Kinder, K, Wilkin, A, Atkinson, M, and Harland, J (2008) *Evaluating the early impact of integrated children's services*. Slough: NFER, **www.communitycare.co.uk/Articles/2008/05/29/108270/improving-outcomes-for-children.html** (accessed August 2008).

Loxley,V (1997) *Collaboration in health and welfare: Working with difference.* London: Jessica Kingsley.

Lukes, S (1974) *Power: A radical view.* London: Macmillan.

Lussier, RN and Achua, CF (2004) *Leadership: Theory, application, skill development*, 2nd edn. Cincinnati Ohio: South Western College Publishing.

Lymbery, M (2006) United we stand? Partnership working in health and social care and the role of social work in services for older people. *British Journal of Social Work,* 36(7): 1119–34.

Lymbery, M (2007) Social work in its organisational context. In Lymbery, M and Postle, K (eds) *Social work: A companion to learning.* London: Sage.

Lyons M. (2006) *National prosperity, local choice and civic engagement: A new partnership between central and local government for the 21st century* London: The Stationery Office.

MacCulloch, T (2001) *Emotional competence: Teaching and assessment issues in health professional education.* ANZAME Conference presentation.

Martin, J (2002) *Organisational Culture: Mapping the terrain.* San Francisco: California Sage.

Martin, V (2003) *Leading change in health and social care.* London and New York: Routledge.

Matland, R (1995) Synthesizing the implementation literature. *Journal of Public Administration Research and Theory*, 5(2): 145–75.

Matusak, LR (1997) *Finding your voice.* San Francisco: Jossey-Bass.

Mayer, J and Salovey, P (1997) What is emotional intelligence? In Salovey, P and Sluyter, D (eds) *Emotional development and emotional intelligence: Educational applications.* New York: Basic Books.

Mayer, J (2004) Be realistic. *Harvard Business Review*, 82(1): 28.

McKimm, J (2004) *Case studies in leadership in medical and health care education. Special Report 5.* Newcastle-upon-Tyne: Higher Education Academy Subject Centre for Medicine, Dentistry and Veterinary Medicine.

McKimm, J and Swanwick, T (2006) *Educational Leadership, Understanding Medical Education.* Edinburgh: Association for the Study of Medical Education.

McKimm, J, Burgess, H and Rafferty, J (2008) *Integrated children's services in higher education project*: Conference report. Southampton: Higher Education Academy Subject Centre for Social Policy and Social Work.

McKimm, J, Millard, L and Held, S (2008) Leadership, Education and Partnership: Project LEAP – developing regional educational leadership capacity in Higher Education and health services through collaboration and partnership working. *International Journal of Public Services Leadership*, 4(4).

McKimm, J, Preston-Shoot, M and Tomlinson, S (2008) *Learning the law: An exploration of how undergraduate medical students acquire understanding of law in relation to professional medical practice.* Paper presented at the Quality Counts conference, Cardiff, 18 November 2008.

Mennin, S.P and Richter, D.M (2003) *The nature of curriculum change: Complicated and complex.* AMEE Conference Presentation: Berne.

Meyerson, D (2004) The tempered radicals. *Stanford Social Innovation Review*, 2(2): 14–23.

Miles, R and Snow, C (1986) Organisations: New concepts and new forms. *California Management Review*, 28(3) 62–73.

Miller, C Freeman, M and Ross, N (2001) *Interprofessional practice in health and social care.* London: Arnold.

Mind (Croydon) (2008) DVD*: Hard to believe.* London: Croydon.

Mintzberg, H (1994) *The rise and fall of strategic planning*. Hemel Hempstead: Prentice Hall.

Mirchandani, K (2003) Challenging racial silences in studies of emotion work: contributions from antiracist feminist theory. *Organisation Studies*, 24(5): 721–42.

Morris, K (2005) From 'children in need' to 'children at risk' – the changing policy context for prevention and participation. *Practice*, 17(2): 67–77.

Morrison, T (2007) Emotional intelligence, emotion and social work: context, characteristics, complications and contribution. *British Journal of Social Work*, 37(2): 245–63.

Morrow, G . Malin, N and Jennings T (2005) Interprofessional Team Working for Child and Family Referral in a Sure Start Local Programme. *Journal of Interprofessional Care*. 2: 93–101.

Moss, B and Gilbert, P (2007) Flickering Candles of hope: spirituality, mental health and the search for meaning. *Illness Crisis and Loss*, 15(2): 179–90.

Moss, B (2004) TGIM: Thank God it's Monday. *British Journal of Occupational Learning* 2(2): 33–43.

Moss, B (2005) *Religion and spirituality*. Lyme Regis: Russell House Publishing.

Moss, B (2007) *Values*. Lyme Regis: Russell House Publishing.

National College of School Leadership (2007) Collaborative leadership. Nottingham: NCSL, **www.ncsl.org.uk** (accessed 9 January 2009).

National Council for Voluntary Organisations (undated) *A little bit of give and take: Voluntary sector accountability within cross-sectoral partnerships.* London: NCCVO. **www.ncvo-vol.org.uk** (accessed 11 August 2008).

National Institute for Health and Clinical Excellence and Social Care Institute for Excellence (2006) *Dementia: Supporting people with dementia and their carers in health and social care*. London: National Institute for Clinical Excellence and Social Care Institute for Excellence.

National strategic partnership forum (2007*) Making partnership work: Examples of good practice*. Leeds: Department of Health, **www.networks.csip.org.uk** (accessed 9 January 2009).

Neighbourhood Renewal Unit (2002) *Collaboration and Co-ordination in Area-Based Initiatives-Research Summary No.1*. London: Neighbourhood Renewal Unit. **www.neighbourhood.gov.uk** (accessed 24 August 2008).

Neimeyer, R and Anderson, A (2002) Meaning Reconstruction. In Thompson, N (2002) *Loss and grief: A guide for human service practitioners*. Basingstoke: Palgrave Macmillan, Chapter 3.

Nevis, E (1989) *Organisational consulting: A Gestalt approach*. Cleveland: Gardner Press.

NHS Institute for Innovation and Improvement. (2006). *Leadership qualities framework*, **www.nhsleadershipqualities. nhs.uk** (accessed 30 March 2008)

Nohria, N and Eccles, R.G (eds) (1992) *Networks and organisations: Structure, form and action*. Massachusetts: Harvard Business School Press.

Northouse, PG (2004) *Leadership: Theory and practice*, 3rd edn. London: Sage.

Nursing and Midwifery Council, General Social Care Council and General Teaching Council for England *Joint Statement Values for integrated working with young people*, **www.nmc-uk.org.uk** (accessed 13 September 2008).

ODPM (2005) *Evaluation of Local Strategic Partnerships: Interim report*. London: Office of Department of Prime Minister.

Office for Public Sector Information. *Children's Act* (2004).

Organisation for Economic Co-operation and Development, OECD (2008) *The looming crisis in the health workforce: How can OECD countries respond?* Paris: OECD, **www.oecd.org** (accessed 15 December 2008).

Ovretveit, J (1993) *Co-ordinating community care: Multidisciplinary teams and care management*. Milton Keynes: Open University Press.

Overeveit, J (1997) How to describe interprofessional working. In Ovretrveit, Mathias and Thompson (eds) *Interprofessional working for Heath and Social Care. Community Health Series*. Basingstoke: Macmillan.

Pascale, RT Millemann, M and Gioja, L (2000) *Surfing the edge of chaos: the laws of nature and the laws of business*. New York: Crown Business.

Paton, R and Vangen, S (2004) *Understanding and Developing leadership in multi agency children and family teams*. London: Department for Education and Skills.

Payne, M (2000) *Teamwork in multiprofessional care*. Basingstoke: Macmillan.

Peck, E, Gulliver, P, Towell, D (2002) Governance of partnership between health and social services: the experience in Somerset. *Health & Social Care in the Community*, 10(5): 331–8.

Peck E and Dickinson H (2008) *Managing and leading in inter-agency settings. Bristol*: The Policy Press in association with Community Care.

Pettigrew, A and Fenton, E (2000) *The innovating organisation*. London: Sage.

Pierson, J (2008) *Going Local: Working in communities and neighbourhoods.* London: Routledge.

Plsek, P.E (2003) *Complexity and the adoption of innovation in health care*. Conference paper for Accelerating quality improvement in healthcare: Strategies to speed the diffusion of evidence-based innovations. Washington: National Institute for Health Care Management and National Committee for Quality Health Care.

Plsek, P.E and Greenhalgh, T (2001) Complexity science: The challenge of complexity in health care. *British Medical Journal*, 323: 625–8.

Pollard, K, Miers, M and Gilchrist, M (2004) Collaborative learning for collaborative working? Initial findings from a longitudinal study of health and social care students. *Health and Social Care in the Community*, 12(4): 346–58.

Powell, A (2003) *Psychiatry and Spirituality – the forgotten dimension*. Brighton: Pavilion/ National Institute for Health Care Management.

Price, T.L (2003) The ethics of authentic transformational leadership. *Leadership quarterly*, 14: 67–81.

QAA (2002*) Subject benchmark statement: Medicine*. Gloucester: Quality Assurance Agency for Higher Education.

QAA (2004) *A statement of common purpose for subject benchmarks for the health and social care professions*. Gloucester: Quality Assurance Agency for Higher Education.

QAA (2008) *Subject benchmark statement: Social work*, 2nd edn. Gloucester: Quality Assurance Agency for Higher Education.

Quinney, A (2006) *Collaborative Social Work Practice*. Exeter: Learning Matters.

Raynor, A (2004) *Individual schools: Unique solutions. Tailoring approaches to school leadership.* London: Routledge.

Reder, P and Duncan, S (2003) Understanding communication in child protection networks. *Child Abuse Review*, 12: 82–100.

Reder, P and Duncan, S (2004) Making the most of the Victoria Climbié inquiry report. *Child Abuse Review*, 13: 95–114.

Richards, R (2004) Power and change. *Education for Health*, 17(1): 3–5.

Robinson, C and Williams, V (2002) Carers of people with learning disabilities and their experience of the 1995 Carers Act. *British Journal of Social Work,* 32(2): 169–183.

Robinson, M and Cottrell, D (2005). Health professionals in multi-disciplinary and multi-agency teams: changing professional practice. *Journal of interprofessional care*, 19(6): 547–60.

Robinson, M, Anning, A and Frost, N (2005) When is a teacher not a teacher? Knowledge creation and the professional identity of teachers within multi professional teams. *Studies in Continuing Education*, 27(2): 175–91.

Rogers, A. and Reynolds, J. (2003) Leadership and vision. In Seden, J and Reynolds, J (eds) *Managing care in practice*. London: Routledge.

Rose, W and Seden, J (eds) *Enhancing social work management*. London: Jessica Kingsley with the Open University.

Rouse, W.B (2000) Managing Complexity: Disease control as a complex adaptive system. *Information Knowledge Systems Management*, 2(2): 143–65.

Saarni, C (2000) Emotional competence: a development perspective. In Bar-On, R and Parker, JDR (eds) *The handbook of emotional intelligence*. San Fancisco: Jossey Bass.

Sackney, L and Mitchell, C (2001) Postmodern expressions of educational leadership, in Leithwood, K and Hallinger, P (eds) *The Second International Handbook of Educational Leadership and Administration*. Dordrecht: Kluwer.

Salovey, P and Mayer, J (1990) Emotional intelligence. Amityville, New York: Baywood Publishing.

Sanderson, P, Kennedy, J Richie, P and Goodwin, G (2002) *People, Plans and possibilities: Exploring person-centred planning*. Edinburgh: Scottish Household Survey Trust.

Schein, E (1985) *Organisational culture and Leadership*. San Francisco: Jossey Bass.

Schein, E (1998) *Process consultation revisited: Building the helping relationship*. Harlow: Jossey Bass.

Scott, T, Mannion, R, Davies, H, Marshall, M (2004) *Healthcare performance and organisational culture*. Abingdon: Radcliffe Press.

Scottish Government Report, *Exploring the evidence base for integrated children's services* (2006) Scottish Executive; Education Department: Edinburgh.

Senge, P (1994) *The fifth discipline: The art and practice of the learning organisation*. New York: Doubleday.

Shamir, B (1995) Social distance and charisma: theoretical notes and an exploratory study. *Leadership Quarterly*, 6: 19–47.

Sheppard, D (1996) *Learning the lessons*, 2nd edn. London: The Zito Trust.

Shipman Inquiry reports (2002–2005). London: The Stationery Office, **www.the-shipman-inquiry.org.uk/reports.asp** (accessed 14 August 2008).

Simkins, T (2004) *Leadership in education: 'What works' or makes sense?* Professorial lecture given at Sheffield Hallam University.

Sinclair, I and Corden, J (2005) *A management solution to keeping children safe: Can agencies on their own achieve what Lord Laming wants?* York: Joseph Rowntree Foundation.

Sinclair, R and Bullock, R (2002) *Learning from past experience – a review of serious case reviews*. London: Department of Health.

Skills for Care and Children's Workforce Development Council (2008) *Leadership and management strategy update, 2008*. Leeds, **www.skillsforcare.org.uk** (accessed 1 December 2008).

Souhami, A. (2007) *Transforming Youth Justice: Occupational identity and cultural change*. Cullompton: Willan.

Spillane, J.P (2001) *Distributed leadership*. San Francisco: Jossey-Bass.

Spouse, J (1998) Learning to nurse through legitimate peripheral participation. *Nurse Education Today*, 18: 345–51.

Stanley, N and Manthorpe, J (eds) (2004) *The age of the inquiry*. London: Routledge.

Star, J (2001) *Tao Te Ching: The definitive edition*. New York: Penguin Books.

Steiner, C and Perry, P (1997) *Achieving emotional literacy*. New York: Avon Books.

Stepney, P and Callwood, I (2006) *Collaborative working in health and social care: A review of the literature*. Wolverhampton: The University of Wolverhampton, **www.wlv.openrepository.com** (Accessed August 2008).

Stevenson, O (2007) *Neglected children and their families: Issues and dilemmas*. London: Blackwell.

Stone, A.G, Russell, R.F and Patterson, K (2003) *Transformational versus servant leadership: A difference in leader focus*. Paper from the servant Leadership Roundtable, October 2003, **www.regent.edu** (accessed 5 January 2009).

Storey, J and Mangham, I (2004) Bringing the strands together. In Storey, J (ed.) *Leadership in Organisations*. London: Routledge.

Sutherland, V.L and Cooper, C.L (2000) *Strategic Stress Management: An organisational approach*. Basingstoke: Macmillan.

Taylor, B and Anthony, M (undated) *Basic Principles of Spirituality in the workplace*, **www.itstime.com/rainbow.htm** (accessed 28 May 2008).

Taylor, I, Whiting, R and Sharland, E (2008) *Integrated Children's Services in Higher Education Project (ICS-HE): Knowledge review*. Southampton: The Higher Education Academy Subject Centre for Social Policy and Social Work (SWAP), **www.icshe.escalate.ac.uk** (accessed 23 August 2008).

Tennyson, R and Wilde, I (2000) *The guiding hand: Brokering partnerships for sustainable development. Report to UN Department of Public Information theory, proxy to practice*. Paper for the Pan-Canadian Education Research Forum.

Thomas, N (ed.) (2004) *The John Adair handbook of management and leadership*. London: Thorogood Publishing Ltd.

Thompson, G, Frances, J, Levacic, R and Mitchell, J (1991) *Markets, hierarchies and networks: The co-ordination of social life*. London: Sage.

Thorndike, R.L (1920) Intelligence and its use. *Harper's Magazine* 140: 227–235.

Thorndike, RL, and Stein, S (1937) An evaluation of the attempts to measure social intelligence. *Psychological Bulletin*, 34: 275–84.

Turning Point Leadership Development National Excellence Collaborative. (2003). *Academics and practitioners on Collaborative Leadership*, **www.collaborativeleadership.org** (accessed 22 May 2008).

Turning Point Leadership Development National Excellence Collaborative (2006) *Collaborative leadership: Fundamental concepts facilitators' guide*, **www.collaborativeleadership.org** (accessed 22 May 2008).

University of East Anglia in association with the National Children's Bureau (April 2006) *Managing Change for children through Children's Trusts*.

van Zwanenberg, Z (2003) *Modern leadership for Modern Services*. Alloa: Scottish Leadership Foundation.

Waddington K and Copperman J (2005) *Emotions and Interprofessional Practice*. Poster Presentation at First Annual International Conference on Working with Emotions, London, September 2005, **www.city.ac.uk/communityandhealth/ispp/staff/copperman.html**.

Walker, A (2005) From research to action. In Walker, A (ed.) *Understanding quality of life in old age*. Berkshire: Open University Press.

Wanless, D (2006) *Securing good care for older people: Taking a long-term view*. London: King's Fund.

Warmington, P, Daniels, H, Edwards, A, Brown, S, Leadbetter, J, Martin, D and Middleton, D (2004) *Inter-agency collaboration: A review of the literature*. ESRC Teaching and Learning Programme III.

Weber, M (1947) *The Theory of Social and Economic organisation*. New York: Free Press.

Weiner, M.E and Petronella, P (2007) The impact of new technology: Implications for social work and social care managers. In Aldgate J, Healy L, Malcolm B, Pine B, Rose W and Seden J (eds) *Enhancing social work management:*

Theory and best practice from the UK and USA. London: Jessica Kingsley in association with the Open University and the University of Connecticut, London.

Weinstein, J, Whittington, C and Leiba, T (eds) (2003) *Collaboration in Social Work Practice*. London: Jessica Kingsley Publishers.

Weiss, E.S, Anderson, R.M and Lasker, R.D (2002) Making the most of collaboration: Exploring the relationship between partnership synergy and partnership functioning. *Health Education and Behaviour*, 29(6): 683–98.

Wenger, E (1998) *Communities of practice: Learning, meaning and identity*, Cambridge: Cambridge University Press.

Wheatley, M (1999) *Leadership and the new science: Discovering order in a chaotic world*. San Francisco: Berrett–Koehler.

Whittington, C. 2003. Collaboration and partnership in context. In Weinstein, J, Whittington, C and Leiba, T. (eds) *Collaboration in Social Work Practice*. London: Jessica Kingsley.

Willets, C, Essex, M, Philpott, A, Zsigo, S and Assey, J (2006) Eclectic models in working with learning disabled people: An overview of some key issues concerning health and wellness. In Brown, K (ed.) *Vulnerable adults and community care*. Exeter: Learning Matters.

Wistow, G (2005) *Developing social care: The past, the present and the future*. London: Social Care Institute for Excellence.

Witz, A (1990) Patriarchy and professions: the gendered politics of occupational closure. *Sociology*, 24: 675–90.

Woodbridge, K and Fulford, K.W.M (2004) *Whose values? A workbook for values-based practice in mental health care*. London: The Sainsbury Centre for Mental Health.

Woodhouse, D and Pengelly, P (1991) *Anxiety and the dynamics of collaboration*. Aberdeen: Aberdeen University Press.

Woodruffe, C (2001) Promotional intelligence. *People Management*, 7(1): 26–9.

World Health Organisation (1988) *Learning together to work together for health*. Geneva: WHO.

Yukl, G (2002) *Leadership in Organisations*, 5th edn. New Jersey: Prentice Hall.

Zander, R and Zander, B (2002) *The art of possibility*. London: Penguin.

Zeidner, M, Matthews, G and Roberts, R.D (2004) Emotional intelligence in the workplace: A critical review. *Applied Psychology: An international review*, 53(3): 371–99.

Zohar, D and Marshall, I (2000) *Spiritual Intelligence: The ultimate intelligence*. London: Bloomsbury.

Index

Lightning Source UK Ltd.
Milton Keynes UK
UKOW05f2345191015

260942UK00001B/42/P